Fifteenth Edition

Rugg's

Recommendations

on the

Colleges

Compiled and Edited by the College Staff of
Rugg's Recommendations

by Frederick E. Rugg

Rugg's Recommendations • Atascadero, California

To
Barbara, Betsie, and Sue

TABLE OF CONTENTS

SOME NOTES FROM THE AUTHOR

WHY THIS BOOK?

As a secondary school college counselor, I heard the following question from a student or parent almost daily: "Can you please give us a list of quality colleges where one can major in psychology (or engineering or business or whatever)?"

For many years I pulled out the college handbooks and came up with a list of hundreds of colleges for each category and spent too much time with the student sifting through the multitude of schools, trying to narrow down the huge list.

I thought about a way out of this dilemma for a long time. People from Harvard would find an easy solution. They might tell the parents and student not to worry about a college major—just go to a fine liberal arts college (like Harvard) and everything will fall into place. After all, it's not the major and professors that count, it's the wonderful student body that makes a great college great. Right?

Well...over the years, I had trouble convincing parents of the merits of that argument. I guess they realize that all good universities are not good in every field.

Today, there's just so much pressure on young people to line up their careers and pick their occupations in life early. Career education seems to start in kindergarten these days. I've noticed that many parents pick right up on it and give Johnny the business if he hasn't chosen his career by the sophomore year of high school or earlier. No matter what I told Johnny and his parents, they still wanted a list of "the quality colleges with a good psychology (or whatever) department."

This book lists the quality departments at quality colleges and it will make the school counselor's job easier. For example, a public school counselor can use it constantly in January when juniors (and sometimes sophomores) line up outside his/her office, asking for a list of colleges to "go with" their PSAT scores. Probably a prep school counselor, a junior and community college transfer counselor, or a librarian might even find more use of this guide for college majors. Since this book is for the aid of the counselor, it is, then, also a guide for students and their parents in the college admissions process.

WHY THESE 780 COLLEGES?

From our experience in the college admissions process, we have chosen 780 quality four-year colleges (out of over 2000 that offer bachelor degrees) to study. We began with the 260 colleges that have survived the careful screening process involved in the granting of a Phi Beta Kappa chapter. The Phi Beta Kappa schools are listed in Appendix A. These colleges received chapters for superior undergraduate performance in the liberal arts and sciences.

To this list were added almost 600 colleges—schools that our staff felt are as good (or better) as several of the Phi Beta Kappa colleges or have excellent specialized programs. We should also note that, in general, the more well-respected the college, the more departments and majors were included. Berkeley is listed under 24 departments while some others only under one. The typical school in the study was noted with 5.0 departments. A departmental page averages 106 recommended colleges.

WHY MOSTLY STUDENT INPUT?

After selecting the colleges to be placed in the study, I had to find a fair way of evaluating each college and its departments. I've always felt that students are usually very fair and objective in evaluating their courses. An article in the *Journal of Educational Psychology* caught my eye (*Journal of Educational Psychology*, 1979, Vol, 71, No. 2, pp. 149-160). Marsh, Overell, and Kesler did an exhaustive study at the University of Southern California in the spring of 1976. Students were allowed to evaluate their professors in 207 undergraduate courses taught by the social studies faculty. The findings were:

1. The correlations between student and faculty ratings on the same factors were quite high and statistically significant.

2. The results reaffirmed the validity of student evaluations of college courses and professors. Many other recent studies have also concluded that student evaluations are reliable tools in judging teachers.

Another interesting article on this subject appeared in the *Chronicle of Higher Education:* "Fair and Useful Evaluation of Professors by Students: Experts Say It Can Be Done," by Suzanne Perry, Dec. 1, 1982, pg. 19. This theme is also noted in Henry Rosovsky's *The University: An Owner's Manual* (W.W. Norton & Co., 1990). On July 21, 1993 the *Chronicle's* Book Page by Peter Seldin goes like this: "...student's appraisals of courses and professors can be invaluable when the questions asked are appropriate."

Thus, our staff decided that we would poll *students* at the 780 colleges and universities for our study. I've always found if you want a straight answer, the young folks seldom waver. So we began a campaign asking college students, "What departments at your college would you recommend most to high school seniors?" Our research staff of 20 made phone calls to random college dormitories, visited college campuses, always questioning students. We found students very willing to provide candid information about their college departments. Ten thousand students were contacted with a minimum of 12 students queried per college. This student input represents 70.0% of our recommendations with 20.0% divided between secondary school counselor input and college personnel participation. The remaining 10.0% comes from unsolicited "tips" from many individuals, frequently parents, some who have spent a hundred hours studying and visiting one department, trying to decide where (and if) to place their $100,000. Some of this latter information is excellent. This past year, we made a special effort to obtain college lists from school counselors who, during the past year, had an extra client—their own offspring. Most of their contributions we feel are outstanding. A counselor doing research for a student usually does a fine job, and comes up with a good list. A counselor doing research for their own son/daughter does the best of jobs. And a final note; finally we reached a critical point two years ago. The input coming to us, much of it voluntary, is better than the old method. For example, last year a counselor from Maine called, tipping us off on the greatness of Western Maryland. We knew it was good. We knew it was very good, but her call led us to investigate more closely. Also, an Ohio Dean of Admissions kept us honest with some input. And a nice lady parent from San Francisco called saying, "Are you sure there's Studio Art at Harvard?" (Yes, there is, but hidden under another department.)

HOW DO YOU USE THIS BOOK?

If you know what you want to major in at college—great!—just look it up. In most cases, you will find each departmental section organized into three groups of colleges:

Group I—Most Selective Colleges
Colleges here are among the 100 most selective colleges in America. They accept very few students with high school averages below 80 (top prep schools can, of course, lower this figure significantly) and College Board scores below (recentered)1200 (SAT-1 combined) and 27 (on the American College Test).

Group II—Very Selective Colleges
Many of the students at these colleges have "B" averages (80-90), and College Board scores between 1100 and 1200 (SAT-1 total) and ACTs between 24 and 26.

Group III—Selective Colleges
Although these colleges are, in general, easier to get into than Group I and II colleges, please keep in mind that they are, in our opinion at least, among the top 735 colleges in the country. Many students at these colleges have College Board scores just under 1100 (SAT-1 total), or just under 24 on the ACTs.

Now that we have an idea of the group breakdown, a student may need help deciding from which group(s) to select his/her colleges. The guidance counselor can help here—having knowledge of colleges and a student's grade point average, class rank, board scores, etc. Most students will want to start with a group of 8 to 10 colleges from the departmental major page. This "major page" is a starting point. Schools can be added to the student's list by his/her counselor—from the counselor's own knowledge of the student, and knowledge of other colleges that might "fit" the student. Schools can be eliminated from a student's list after reviewing the college catalogs (see Appendix F—The Get Going Form), checking out undesirable features (city vs. rural setting, etc.), visiting the colleges, and other personal preferences. If the student does *not* have a major in mind, he or she should go to a typical liberal arts (e.g., English or Math) page to get started. I've also included a letter code system for the college's enrollment figure. The enrollment letter appears beside each college name with the following code:

XL = Extra Large Enrollment (over 20,000 students)
L = Large Enrollment (from 8,000 to 20,000 students)
M = Medium Enrollment (from 3,000 to 8,000 students)
R = Moderate Enrollment (from 1,000 to 3,000 students)
S = Small Enrollment (under 1,000 students)

SOME PARTING SHOTS

I don't care to go into the argument of "Picking a college because it has a great Mathematics Department" vs. "Picking a school because the school overall is great (Yeah Harvard!) and you'll probably change your major anyway." The fact of the matter is that parents, career educators, and other educators are telling 16-year-olds (and younger) to have a career and a major all mapped out and I bet will continue to do so. I'm sure high school counselors will continue to be asked to help Suzy find a list of quality schools with "excellent majors in mathematics." Personally, I see nothing wrong with a high school senior, who loves mathematics, trying to pick a quality school where the math department at that institution is ranked by its students as one of the top majors at that school and is generally recognized as being top notch by college counselors. If Suzy changes her mind after a year or two, she's at least given it a good shot with a premier math department. And chances are excellent that if she changes her major, it was because another outstanding department at that school helped her grow and reassess her career goals. She'll probably stay with that department for her new major. No harm done.

A few other comments on this book and some random thoughts...

1. Some state universities, like Penn State, are very competitive for out-of-staters. A university such as this may be in Group II for in-staters, but, in reality, is a Group I school for "outsiders."

2. In general, a college that is competitive is that way for all majors—but there are some departments that are exceptions. For example, engineering is a tough major and must be considered "Group II" at a "Group III" school.

3. A knowledgeable observer of the college scene will note that some competitive "alternative" colleges do not appear in this work, e.g., Hampshire College (MA), St. John's (MD). The jury is not unanimous on these progressive schools, and they are not included in this book except under "Miscellaneous Majors Pages."

4. A few majors in this book, such as engineering, have *not* been broken down into subdivisions (Civil, Electrical, Mechanical, etc.). Students will have to research these majors more fully. Foreign Languages, however, is broken down.

5. Every year a few more colleges close their doors. Today, colleges are under pressure to compete and "Be Hot." We need a college guide to weed things out a bit, a consumer-oriented handbook. We hope this helps.

6. Don't overlook the *good* small liberal arts college. Too many large universities are too impersonal.

7. Keep in mind that weak departments at Harvard, Yale, Stanford, Princeton, etc. might be equal to or better than the strongest departments at many colleges and universities.

8. This book is an aid for counselors, parents, and kids—nothing more. It is not a guide for the colleges to compare themselves one with the other.

9. Do not be surprised if you discover that the best of the more expensive schools are actually least expensive—because they have financial aid, the part-time jobs, etc. They're able to meet a student's financial need in many cases.

10.   Students should discuss with their counselors the socioeconomic factors of the colleges they are considering. Will the college of your choice have several students enrolled with your socioeconomic background?

11.   When you visit a college, seek out the students who attend and ask them the following question: "When you sign up for classes, do you get 100% of your choices, or only 4 out of 10 courses, or...?"

12.   Most states have a "flagship" university, the leader of the system (e.g., The University of North Carolina at Chapel Hill). In this book it is listed as just "No. Carolina." The other members of the University system are listed as follows: No. Carolina (Asheville), No. Carolina (Charlotte), No. Carolina (Greensboro), No. Carolina (Wilmington).

13.   Some colleges do a great job with private school youngsters, others do a fantastic job with public school youngsters. Some colleges are outstanding with *both* groups. A very fine college with an outstanding record with public school youngsters is Virginia's Roanoke College.

14.   A tip for the high school senior: Don't ease up in your senior year. Take a tough course load with courses such as Physics. College admissions people aren't stupid. The first thing they look at when they review your high school record is the quality of your high school courses.

15.   To parents and counselors: Hang tough. The pieces will finally fit.

16.   If you review only one page in this book, make it the page near the front called "Fred Rugg's One Hundred Colleges...Just Darn Good Schools." This is probably the most used and Xeroxed page in the U.S.A. on the colleges.

17.   This book is not perfect. It has never claimed to be perfect. But it is a good place to start and represents tens of thousands of contacts. We've even moved to many parts of the country to try to put together "the big picture." We do our best.

Frederick E. Rugg

Easthampton, Massachusetts
March, 1980 (1st Edition)

San Luis Obispo, California
January, 1998 (15th Edition)

SOME NOTES ON THE FIFTEENTH EDITION

The fifteenth edition contains over 1000 entry changes since the fourteenth edition. All 80 majors have been revised and changed.

The "Average SAT-1 Total/ACT Total/Recommended majors" pages are included mainly because of counselors' requests. School counselors wanted average score comparisons and an index of colleges showing recommended majors. In all cases, SAT-1 Total Scores are noted and the equivalent ACT score is now provided. These scores are the best estimate by our staff for the entering fall class of 1998. Especially young counselors tell us this section is a quick ready reference—a marker for them.

The fifteenth edition still includes "The Counselors' Choice"—a star (★) indicating the top college for each major. Over the years, many school counselors across the country have helped us with these choices. Lately, however, the choices tend to repeat. In fact, this past year, for the first time, no majors have changed at the top position, and we were led in that direction from input coming to us—volunteered to us.

The fifteenth edition still contains "One Hundred Just Darn Good Schools"—found on the following page. I hear more nice things about these schools than any others. All but five of the colleges return from last year. As in the past, when a state university is noted like Wisconsin, we mean the flagship at Madison, if no other city follows in parenthesis.

Frederick E. Rugg

San Luis Obispo, California
January, 1998 (15th Edition)

ACKNOWLEDGMENTS

I would like to thank the following for their help in the preparation of this guidebook: Phi Beta Kappa Office, Bureau of Educational Statistics, our Research Aides, and especially the great number of secondary counselors who've filled out questionnaires and tip me off on quality departments to look at. I am independent of the colleges and these people are, too.

A "Thank You" also goes to the counselors and students I've worked with who have contributed each in their own way. At last count, I've worked 25,000 hours in five secondary school guidance cubicles with 30 counselors, and conducted over 250 workshops with over 3500 counselors. Of course I've learned from them. Together we've probably done the college admissions process a million times. Also I thank the counselors and students and university officials in the United States and abroad for their help, suggestions, and, yes, their complaints. I appreciate, too, those departments who have sent us vitae on their professors. College PR officers who write always get a reading. And the same goes for anyone who e-mails me.

I am also grateful to George Gibbs, Reg Alexander, Arvin R. Anderson, Howard Ahlskog, Hy Kleinman, Michele M. Charles, Gary Metras, Edward Field, Betty Rossie, Horacio Rodriguez, A.P. Stevens, Madeline Field, Cyrus Benson, John Barker, Fred Ames, Matthew Jagielski, Gilbert Field, Jeff Sheehan, Charles Doebler, Joan Girard, Mrs. Fran Fisher, Ralph Strycharz, Dennis Gurn, John DeBonnville, Kevin L. Miller, Hoover Sutton, Francona, J.R., Rebecca Lou, and Jim Maxey.

And finally, a special thanks to my wife, Barbara, for her patience and industry.

Inquiries and comments about this guide should be addressed to:

Rugg's Recommendations
7120 Serena Court
Atascadero, CA 93422

xii

FRED RUGG'S ONE HUNDRED COLLEGES...
Just Darn Good Schools
"I Hear More Nice Things About These Schools Than Any Others"
The most valuable list in this book. Places where students maximize their education.

Alfred (NY)	Humboldt State (CA)	Regis (CO)
Allegheny (PA)	Idaho, U. of	Rhodes (TN)
Auburn (AL)	Illinois, U. of	Roanoke (VA)
Austin (TX)	Illinois Wesleyan	Rochester Institute of Tech. (NY)
Barnard (NY)	Indiana University	Rockhurst (MO)
Bates (ME)	Juniata (PA)	St. Andrews (NC)
Beloit (WI)	Kansas, U. of	St. Anselm (NH)
Bemidji State (MN)	Kansas State	St. Joseph's (ME)
Berry (GA)	Keene State (NH)	St. Mary's (IN)
Bethany (WV)	Kentucky, U. of	St. Norbert (WI)
Biola (CA)	Knox (IL)	St. Olaf (MN)
Bryn Mawr (PA)	Lawrence (WI)	Santa Clara (CA)
Buffalo (SUNY)	LeMoyne (NY)	Southwestern (TX)
Butler (IN)	Lesley (MA)	Spring Hill (AL)
California, U. of (Davis)	Macalester (MN)	Stanford (CA)
California, U. of (Riverside)	Maine, U. of (Farmington)	Susquehanna (PA)
Colorado Mines	Marquette (WI)	Texas A&M
Creighton (NB)	Mary Washington (VA)	Virginia Wesleyan
Dayton (OH)	Michigan State	Wabash (IN)
Delaware Valley (PA)	Michigan Tech	Washington & Jefferson (PA)
Denison (OH)	Minnesota (Morris)	Washington Col. (MD)
DePaul (IL)	Minnesota, U.of	Washington, U. of
Drake (IA)	Montana State	Wesley (DE)
Earlham (IN)	Montana, U. of	Western Maryland
Edinboro (PA)	Moravian (PA)	Westminster (MO)
Evansville (IN)	Muskingum (OH)	West Virginia Wesleyan
Georgia Institute of Technology	North Carolina State	Wheaton (MA)
Grinnell (IA)	Northern Arizona	Williams (MA)
Guilford (NC)	Northern Michigan	Wingate (NC)
Hanover (IN)	Ohio University	Winona State (MN)
Harvard (MA)	Ohio Wesleyan	Wisconsin, U. of
Haverford (PA)	Pennsylvania, U. of	Wittenberg (OH)
Heidelberg (OH)	Pittsburgh, U. of	Wofford (SC)
Hendrix (AR)	Portland, U. of (OR)	Wooster (OH)
Hiram (OH)	Purdue (IN)	Wyoming, U. of
Hollins (VA)	Radford (VA)	

Over 900 Secondary School Counselors responded to the question, "What colleges do you believe offer students the best opportunity to maximize their education?" The list is above. Please don't count the colleges in this list. There's actually a little over 100. I just couldn't get it down to the magic number.

Rugg's Recommendations • Atascadero, California • 805/462-2503

SECTION ONE

RECOMMENDED
UNDERGRADUATE PROGRAMS

AGRICULTURE

Author's Note: *Students in the schools of Agriculture, in general, tend to have median college test scores below the University's overall median.*

GROUP I
Most Selective

★ CORNELL (NY)	L	Iowa State	XL
Florida, U. of	XL	Pennsylvania State	XL
Illinois, U. of (Urbana-Champaign)	XL	Rutgers (NJ)	L

GROUP II
Very Selective

Auburn (AL)	L	Michigan Tech	M
California, U. of (Davis)	L	Minnesota, U. of	XL
California, U. of (Riverside)	M	Missouri, U. of	XL
Cal. Poly. State U. (San Luis Obispo)	L	New Hampshire, U. of	L
Clemson (SC)	L	North Carolina State	L
Connecticut, U. of	L	Purdue (IN)	XL
Hawaii, U. of	L	Texas A&M	XL
Kansas State	L	Vermont, U. of	M
Maine, U. of	M	Virginia Poly. Inst.	L
Maryland, U. of	XL	Wisconsin, U. of	XL
Michigan State	XL		

GROUP III
Selective

Arizona, U. of	XL	New Mexico State U.	L
Arkansas, U. of	L	North Dakota State	L
Berea (KY)	R	Ohio State	XL
Colorado State	L	Oklahoma State	L
Delaware Valley (PA)	R	Oregon State	L
Dordt (IA)	S	Tennessee, U. of	XL
Georgia, U. of	XL	Texas Tech U.	L
Idaho, U. of	M	Tuskegee University (AL)	M
Kentucky, U. of	L	Utah State	L
Louisiana State	XL	Washington State	L
Mississippi State	L	Western Michigan	L
Montana State	L	Wilmington (OH)	S
Nebraska, U. of	L	Wisconsin, U. of (Platteville)	M
Nevada, U. of (Reno)	M	Wyoming, U. of	L

Enrollment Code

S = Small (less than 1000 students) **M** = Medium (3000-8000 students) **XL** = Extra Large (over 20,000 students)
R = Moderate (1000-3000 students) **L** = Large (8000-20,000 students)

★ THE COUNSELORS' CHOICE ■ Men Only ▲ Women Only

AMERICAN STUDIES

GROUP I
Most Selective

American U. (DC) ....M	Pomona (CA) .... R
Amherst (MA) .... R	Sarah Lawrence (NY) .... S
Buffalo (SUNY) (NY) L	▲ Smith (MA) .... R
California, U. of (San Diego) L	St. Olaf (MN) .... R
Franklin & Marshall (PA) .... R	Stanford (CA) ....M
George Washington (DC) ....M	Tulane (LA) ....M
Georgetown (DC)............................M	Virginia, U. of L
Harvard (MA) ....M	Wesleyan (CT) .... R
Kalamazoo (MI) .... R	William & Mary (VA) .... R
Michigan, U. of XL	Williams (MA) .... R
North Carolina, U. of L	Yale (CT) ....M
★ PENNSYLVANIA, U. OF L	

GROUP II
Very Selective

Arizona, U. of XL	Skidmore (NY)..................................... R
California, U. of (Santa Cruz) ....M	South Florida, U. of L
George Mason (VA) L	Texas, U. of.......................................XL
Hobart & Wm. Smith (NY) .... R	Washington College (MD) ....S
▲ Hollins (VA) ....S	▲ Wells (NY) ....S
Mary Washington (VA) .... R	▲ Wesleyan College (GA) ....S
Minnesota, U. of XL	Wyoming, U. of L

ANTHROPOLOGY

GROUP I
Most Selective

▲Barnard (NY) .... R
  Brandeis (MA) .... R
▲ Bryn Mawr (PA) .... S
  Buffalo (SUNY) (NY) L
  California, U. of (Berkeley) XL
  California, U. of (Los Angeles) XL
  Case Western Reserve (OH) .... R
★ CHICAGO, U. OF (IL) .... R
  Colorado College .... R
  Columbia (NY) ....M
  Dartmouth (NH) ....M
  Duke (NC) ....M
  Florida, U. of XL
  Grinnell (IA) .... R
  Lafayette (PA) .... R
  Harvard (MA) ....M

  Illinois, U. of (Urbana-Champaign) XL
  Macalester (MN) .... R
  Michigan, U. of XL
  New College (FL) .... S
  Northwestern (IL) ....M
  Pennsylvania, U. of....................................L
  Pitzer (CA) .... S
  Pomona (CA) .... R
  Rice (TX) .... R
  Skidmore (NY) .... R
▲ Smith (MA) .... R
  South, U. of the (TN) .... R
  Stanford (CA) ....M
  Vanderbilt (TN) .... R
  Washington U. (MO) ....M
  Yale (CT)..M

GROUP II
Very Selective

Arizona, U. of...XL
Beloit (WI) .... R
California, U. of (Santa Cruz) ....M
Colorado, U. of...L
Hamline (MN).. R
Hofstra (NY) ....M
Kansas, U. of...L
Maryland, U. of XL

Oregon, U. of..L
Pittsburgh, U. of (PA) L
Tulsa, U. of (OK) ....M
Washington State L
Washington, U. of XL
Wisconsin, U. of..XL
Wisconsin, U. of (Milwaukee)................L

GROUP III
Selective

Hawaii, U. of..L
New Mexico State U. L
New Mexico, U. of......................................M

Queens (CUNY) (NY) L
Tennessee, U. of....................................XL

ARCHITECTURE

GROUP I
Most Selective

▲Barnard (NY) .... R
Buffalo (SUNY) (NY) L
California, U. of (Berkeley) XL
Carnegie Mellon (PA) ....M
Columbia (NY) ....M
Cooper Union (NY) .... S
Cornell (NY) L
Florida, U. of XL
Georgia Inst. of Tech. L
Illinois Inst. of Tech. .... R
Illinois, U. of (Urbana-Champaign) XL

Miami U. (OH) L
Michigan, U. of XL
MIT (MA) ....M
Notre Dame (IN) ....M
★ **PRINCETON (NJ)**................................**M**
Rensselaer (NY) ....M
Rice (TX) .... R
Tulane (LA) ....M
Virginia, U. of L
Washington U. (MO) ....M
Yale (CT) ....M

GROUP II
Very Selective

Arizona State XL
Arizona, U. of..XL
Auburn (AL) L
Cal. Poly. State U. (San Luis Obispo)....L
Catholic U. (DC) ....M
Cincinnati, U. of (OH) L
Clemson (SC)..L
Detroit Mercy, U. of (MI) ....M
Drury (MO) .... S
Houston, U. of (TX) L
Kansas State L
Kansas, U. of L
Milwaukee Sch. of Engineering (WI).... R

Montana State L
Nebraska, U. of..L
North Carolina State L
Oklahoma, U. of L
Oregon, U. of L
Pennsylvania State XL
Rhode Island School of Design (RI)...... R
Southern California, U. of......................L
Syracuse (NY) L
Texas A&M XL
Texas, U. of (Austin)..............................XL
Virginia Poly. Inst. L
Washington, U. of XL

GROUP III
Selective

Arkansas, U. of..L
City College (CUNY) (NY) L
Kent State (OH).......................................L
Louisiana State XL
Nevada, U. of (Las Vegas) ....M
Ohio State XL

Pratt Inst. (NY) .... R
Roger Williams (RI) .... R
Texas, U. of (Arlington) L
Tuskegee University (AL) ....M
Woodbury (CA) .... S

Enrollment Code

S = Small (less than 1000 students)   **M** = Medium (3000-8000 students)   **XL** = Extra Large (over 20,000 students)
R = Moderate (1000-3000 students)   **L** = Large (8000-20,000 students)
★ **THE COUNSELORS' CHOICE**   ■ Men Only   ▲ Women Only

ART (STUDIO)

GROUP I
Most Selective

Bard (NY)	R	★ NEW YORK U.	L
Bates (ME)	R	Pennsylvania, U. of	L
Boston U. (MA)	L	R.I. School of Design	R
Brown (RI)	M	Rochester, U. of (NY)	M
▲ Bryn Mawr (PA)	S	▲ Scripps (CA)	S
Carnegie Mellon (PA)	M	Skidmore (NY)	R
Cooper Union (NY)	S	▲ Smith (MA)	R
Cornell (NY)	L	Southwestern (TX)	R
Dallas, U. of (TX)	R	St. Olaf (MN)	R
Dartmouth (NH)	M	Trinity (TX)	R
Drew (NJ)	R	Virginia, U. of	L
Furman (SC)	R	Washington U. (MO)	M
Harvard (MA)	M	▲ Wellesley (MA)	R
Lafayette (PA)	R	Wesleyan (CT)	R
Macalester (MN)	R	Wheaton (IL)	R
Middlebury (VT)	R	Williams (MA)	R
Michigan, U. of	XL	Yale (CT)	M
New Jersey, College of	M		

GROUP II
Very Selective

Arizona, U. of	XL	▲ Hollins (VA)	S
Art Center College of Design (CA)	R	Houghton (NY)	S
Auburn (AL)	L	Hunter (CUNY) (NY)	L
▲ Agnes Scott (GA)	S	Knox (IL)	R
Alma (MI)	R	Lake Forest (IL)	S
Augustana (IL)	R	Loras (IA)	R
Birmingham-Southern (AL)	R	Manhattanville (NY)	S
Bowling Green (OH)	L	Marietta (OH)	R
California Institute of the Arts	S	Maryland Institute–College of Art	S
California, U. of (Irvine)	L	Mass. College of Art	R
California, U. of (Santa Barbara)	L	Messiah (PA)	R
Colorado State	L	▲ Mills (CA)	S
▲ Converse (SC)	S	Missouri, U. of (Kansas City)	M
Delaware, U. of	L	Moore College of Art (PA)	S
Guilford (NC)	R	Moravian (PA)	R
Hamline (MN)	R	Muhlenberg (PA)	R
Hofstra (NY)	M		

GROUP II continues next page

Enrollment Code

S = Small (less than 1000 students)   **M** = Medium (3000-8000 students)   **XL** = Extra Large (over 20,000 students)
R = Moderate (1000-3000 students)   **L** = Large (8000-20,000 students)

★ THE COUNSELORS' CHOICE   ■ Men Only   ▲ Women Only

ART (STUDIO), *continued*

GROUP II, *continued*

Ohio State XL	Southern Methodist (TX) ....M
Ohio U. L	Syracuse (NY) L
Otis Art Institute (CA) ....S	Temple (PA) L
Parsons School of Design (NY) ....R	Washington & Jefferson (PA) ....S
Principia (IL) ....S	Washington, U. of XL
▲ Randolph-Macon Woman's Col. (VA) ... S	▲ Wesleyan Col. (GA) ....S
Redlands, U. of (CA) ....R	Western Washington U. (WA) L
▲ Rosemont (PA) ....R	Wheaton (MA) ....R
Salem College (NC) ....S	Whitworth (WA) ....R
Shepherd (WV) ....R	Wittenberg (OH) ....R

GROUP III
Selective

Arizona State XL	Mercyhurst (PA) ....R
Belhaven (MS) ....R	Millikin (IL) ....R
Bloomsburg (PA) ....M	Mount St. Joseph (OH) ....R
California State U. (Long Beach) L	New Mexico, U. of....................................L
California State U. (San Jose) XL	North Carolina (Greensboro) ....M
▲ Chatham Col. (PA)....................................S	Northern Iowa L
Fairleigh Dickinson (NJ) ....M	Old Dominion (VA) L
Hawaii, U. of..L	Roanoke (VA) ....R
Jacksonville (FL) ....R	Rockford (IL) ....S
Keene State (NH) ....R	▲ Salem College (NC)..................................S
Kent State (OH) L	Santa Fe, College of (NM) ....S
Kutztown (PA) ....M	▲ Seton Hill (PA) ....S
▲ Mary Baldwin (VA) ....S	Virginia Commonwealth U. L
Massachusetts, U. of (Dartmouth) ....M	West Virginia Wesleyan ....R

ART HISTORY

GROUP I
Most Selective

▲Barnard (NY) .... R
  Bowdoin (ME) .... R
  Brown (RI) ....M
▲ Bryn Mawr (PA) ....S
  California, U. of (Los Angeles)............XL
  Case Western Reserve U. (OH) .... R
  Chicago, U. of (IL) .... R
  Columbia (NY) ....M
  Harvard (MA) ....M
  Johns Hopkins (MD)................................. R
  Michigan, U. of XL
▲ Mount Holyoke (MA)............................... R
★ **NEW YORK U.** L

  North Carolina, U. of L
  Oberlin (OH) .... R
  Pennsylvania, U. of...................................L
  Princeton (NJ)...M
  Rochester, U. of (NY) ....M
  Skidmore (NY) .... R
▲ Smith (MA) .... R
  Swarthmore (PA)....................................... R
  Vassar (NY) .... R
  Washington U. (MO) ....M
▲ Wellesley (MA) .... R
  Williams (MA)... R
  Yale (CT)...M

GROUP II
Very Selective

  California, U. of (Riverside)...................M
  California, U. of (Santa Barbara) L
  Colorado State L
  Delaware, U. of L
  Florida State..L
▲ Hollins (VA) ....S
  Kansas, U. of...L
  Lake Forest (IL) ....S
  Manhattanville (NY) ....S

  Minnesota, U. of.....................................XL
  Missouri, U. of XL
  Oregon, U. of L
▲ Rosemont (PA) ....S
▲ Salem College (NC)...................................S
  Southern Methodist (TX).........................M
▲ Sweet Briar (VA) ....S
  Wheaton (MA) .... R
  Wooster (OH) .... R

ASTRONOMY

GROUP I
Most Selective

Boston U. L
★ CALIFORNIA INST. OF TECH. .... S
California, U. of (Berkeley) XL
California, U. of (Los Angeles) XL
Case Western Reserve U. (OH) .... R
Cornell (NY) L
Harvard (MA) .... M
Haverford (PA) .... S
Illinois, U. of (Urbana-Champaign) XL
Michigan, U. of XL

MIT (MA) .... M
North Carolina, U. of L
Northwestern (IL) .... M
Pennsylvania, U. of L
Pennsylvania State XL
Villanova (PA) .... M
Virginia, U. of L
Wesleyan (CT) .... R
Williams (MA) .... R

GROUP II
Very Selective

Arizona, U. of XL
Colorado, U. of L
Hawaii, U. of L
Iowa, U. of XL
Kansas, U. of L

Maryland, U. of XL
Oklahoma, U. of L
Stony Brook (SUNY) (NY) L
Texas, U. of (Austin) XL
Washington, U. of XL

GROUP III
Selective

Louisiana State XL
Lycoming (PA) .... R

Wyoming, U. of L

Enrollment Code
S = Small (less than 1000 students)   **M** = Medium (3000-8000 students)   **XL** = Extra Large (over 20,000 students)
R = Moderate (1000-3000 students)   **L** = Large (8000-20,000 students)
★ THE COUNSELORS' CHOICE   ■ Men Only   ▲ Women Only

BIOCHEMISTRY (MOLECULAR BIOLOGY)

GROUP I
Most Selective

▲Barnard (NY) .... R
Binghamton (SUNY) (NY) L
Bowdoin (ME) .... R
Brandeis (MA) .... R
Brown (RI) ....M
California, U. of (Berkeley)..............XL
California, U. of (Los Angeles)............XL
California, U. of (San Diego) L
Columbia (NY) ....M
Cornell (NY) L
Dallas, U. of (TX) .... R
Geneseo (SUNY) (NY) ....M
★ HARVARD (MA)............................ M

Iowa, U. of XL
Miami, U. of (FL) L
MIT (MA) ....M
▲ Mount Holyoke (MA)........................ R
Pennsylvania, U. of........................L
Princeton (NJ) ....M
Rice (TX) .... R
Rutgers (NJ) L
Rochester, U. of (NY) ....M
Swarthmore (PA)........................ R
Tulane (LA)............................M
Yale (CT)............................M

GROUP II
Very Selective

Albright (PA) .... R
Beloit (WI) .... R
California, U. of (Davis)........................L
California, U. of (Riverside).................M
Colorado, U. of L
Denison (OH) .... R
Florida Inst. of Tech............................ R
Kansas State L
Lewis & Clark (OR) .... R
Louisiana State XL
Michigan State XL

Muhlenberg (PA)........................ R
Pennsylvania State XL
Pittsburgh, U. of (PA) L
Purdue (IN) XL
Regis (CO)............................ R
Ripon (WI) .... R
Skidmore (NY) .... R
St. Andrews Presbyterian (NC) .... S
Stony Brook (SUNY) (NY) L
Virginia Poly. Inst. L
Wisconsin, U. of............................XL

GROUP III
Selective

Ohio Northern............................ R
Oregon State L

Sacred Heart (CT) .... R
Temple (PA)............................L

Enrollment Code

S = Small (less than 1000 students)   **M** = Medium (3000-8000 students)   **XL** = Extra Large (over 20,000 students)
R = Moderate (1000-3000 students)   **L** = Large (8000-20,000 students)

★ THE COUNSELORS' CHOICE   ■ Men Only   ▲ Women Only

BIOLOGY

GROUP I
Most Selective

Albany (SUNY) (NY) L	Miami, U. of (FL) L
Amherst (MA) .... R	Middlebury (VT) .... R
Bates (ME) .... R	Minnesota, U. of (Morris) .... R
Bethany (WV) .... S	MIT (MA) .... M
Boston College (MA) L	▲ Mount Holyoke (MA) .... R
Bowdoin (ME) .... R	New College (FL) .... S
Brandeis (MA) .... R	Occidental (CA) .... R
Brown (RI) .... M	Pomona (CA) .... R
▲ Bryn Mawr (PA) .... S	Princeton (NJ) .... M
Bucknell (PA) .... R	Reed (OR) .... R
California Inst. of Tech. .... S	Rhodes (TN) .... R
California, U. of (Los Angeles) XL	Rice (TX) .... R
California, U. of (San Diego) L	Rochester, U. of (NY) .... M
Carleton (MN) .... R	Rutgers (NJ) L
Chicago, U. of (IL) .... R	Skidmore (NY) .... R
Claremont McKenna (CA) .... S	▲ Smith (MA) .... R
Colby (ME) .... R	South, U. of the (TN) .... R
Colgate (NY) .... R	Southwestern (TX) .... R
Colorado Col. .... R	Stanford (CA) .... M
Cornell (NY) .... R	St. Mary's Col. of Maryland .... R
Dallas, U. of (TX) .... R	St. Olaf (MN) .... R
Dartmouth (NH) .... M	Swarthmore (PA) .... R
Dickinson (PA) .... R	Trinity (CT) .... R
Duke (NC) .... M	Tufts (MA) .... M
Emory (GA) .... R	Tulane (LA) .... M
Franklin & Marshall (PA) .... R	Ursinus (PA) .... R
Geneseo (SUNY) (NY) .... M	Union (NY) .... R
Georgetown (DC) .... M	Vassar (NY) .... R
Gettysburg (PA) .... R	Vermont, U. of L
Grinnell (IA) .... R	Villanova (PA) .... M
Hamilton (NY) .... R	Virginia, U. of L
★ HARVARD (MA) .... M	■ Wabash (IN) .... S
Harvey Mudd (CA) .... S	Wake Forest (NC) .... M
Haverford (PA) .... S	Washington U. (MO) .... M
Holy Cross (MA) .... R	▲ Wellesley (MA) .... R
Illinois Wesleyan .... R	Wesleyan (CT) .... R
Johns Hopkins (MD) .... R	Wheaton (IL) .... R
Kalamazoo (MI) .... R	Whitman (WA) .... R
Kenyon (OH) .... R	Willamette (OR) .... R
Lafayette (PA) .... R	William & Mary (VA) .... M
Lawrence (WI) .... R	Yale (CT) .... M
Macalester (MN) .... R	Yeshiva (NY) .... R

BIOLOGY continues next page

BIOLOGY, *continued*

GROUP II
Very Selective

Albertson (ID) .... S	Loyola (IL) .... M
Albright (PA) .... R	Loyola (MD) .... R
Allegheny (PA) .... R	Marquette (WI) .... M
Alma (MI) .... R	Mary Washington (VA) .... R
Benedictine (IL) .... R	Michigan State XL
Berry (GA) .... R	Millsaps (MS) .... S
California, U. of (Irvine) L	Morningside (IA) .... S
California, U. of (Riverside) ...... M	Muhlenberg (PA) .... R
California, U. of (Santa Cruz) ... M	Nebraska Wesleyan .... R
Concordia (MN) .... R	New Hampshire, U. of L
Connecticut, U. of L	North Central (IL) .... R
Creighton (NE) .... R	Ohio Northern .... R
Delaware, U. of L	Ohio Wesleyan .... R
Denison (OH) .... R	Presbyterian (SC) .... S
Duquesne (PA) .... M	Randolph-Macon (VA) .... R
Earlham (IN) .... R	▲ Randolph-Macon Woman's Col. (VA) ... S
Eckerd (FL) .... R	Ripon (WI) .... R
Erskine (SC) .... S	Roanoke (VA) .... R
Fairfield (CT) .... M	Scranton, U. of (PA) .... M
Georgia, U. of XL	▲ Scripps (CA) .... S
Guilford (NC) .... R	Spring Hill (AL) .... R
Hamline (MN) .... R	St. John's (MN) .... R
■ Hampden-Sydney (VA) .... S	St. Louis (MO) .... M
Hendrix (AR) .... R	Stony Brook (SUNY) (NY) L
Hiram (OH) .... R	Truman State (MO) .... M
Hobart & William Smith (NY) .... R	Washington & Jefferson (PA) ...... S
▲ Hood (MD) .... S	Washington College (MD) .... S
Hope (MI) .... R	Western Maryland .... R
Houghton (NY) .... S	Westminster (PA) .... R
Indiana U. XL	Wheaton (MA) .... R
Juniata (PA) .... R	Winona State U. (MN) .... M
Kansas State L	Wisconsin, U. of (Stevens Point) .... M
Lake Forest (IL) .... S	Wittenberg (OH) .... R
Lewis & Clark (OR) .... R	Wofford (SC) .... R
Linfield (OR) .... R	Wooster (OH) .... R
Loras (IA) .... R	

BIOLOGY continues next page

BIOLOGY, *continued*

GROUP III
Selective

Blackburn (IL) .... S	Puerto Rico (CAYEY), U. of .... M
Carroll (MT) .... R	▲ Spelman (GA) .... R
College of Charleston (SC) .... M	St. Vincent (PA) .... R
Delaware Valley (PA) .... R	Temple (PA) L
Houston Baptist (TX) .... R	Thomas More (KY) .... S
Jacksonville (FL) .... R	Tougaloo (MS) .... S
Long Island U. (Southhampton Col.) (NY)R	Virginia Wesleyan .... R
▲ Meredith (NC) .... R	Wartburg (IA) .... R
Mount St. Mary's (CA) .... R	Xavier University of Louisiana .... R
Northland (WI) .... S	

BOTANY

GROUP I
Most Selective

California, U. of (Berkeley) XL	Florida, U. of XL
Connecticut College .... R	Miami U. (OH) L
Cornell (NY) L	Michigan, U. of XL
★ DUKE (NC) ....M	

GROUP II
Very Selective

California, U. of (Davis) L	Ohio Wesleyan... R
California, U. of (Riverside) ....M	Pennsylvania State XL
Connecticut, U. of L	Purdue (IN) XL
Maine, U. of ....M	Texas, U. of (Austin) XL
Maryland, U. of L	Washington, U. of XL
Michigan State.......................................XL	Wisconsin, U. of......................................XL
Montana, U. of..M	Vermont, U. of..L
North Carolina State L	

GROUP III
Selective

Colorado State L	Oregon State L
Hawaii, U. of...L	Tennessee, U. of...................................XL
Humboldt State (CA) ....M	Wyoming, U. of L
Louisiana State XL	

BUSINESS ADMINISTRATION

GROUP I
Most Selective

Albany (SUNY) (NY) L	Lehigh (PA) ....M
American (DC) ....M	Miami U. (OH) L
Binghamton (SUNY) (NY) L	Michigan, U. of XL
Boston College (MA) L	MIT (MA) ....M
Boston U. (MA) L	Muhlenberg (PA) .... R
Bucknell (PA) .... R	New York U. L
Buffalo (SUNY) (NY) L	North Carolina, U. of L
California, U. of (Berkeley) XL	Notre Dame (IN) ....M
Carnegie Mellon (PA) ....M	Pennsylvania, U. of.................L
Case Western Reserve U. (OH) .... R	Rensselaer (NY) ....M
Claremont McKenna (CA).................S	Richmond, U. of (VA) .... R
Clarkson (NY) ....M	Southwestern (TX) .... R
► Colby (ME) .... R	Syracuse (NY) L
DePauw (IN) .... R	Trinity (TX) .... R
Emory (GA).................R	Tulane (LA).................M
Fairfield (CT).................R	U.S. Air Force Academy (CO) ....M
Florida, U. of XL	Vermont, U. of L
Florida State L	Villanova (PA) ....M
Franklin & Marshall (PA).................R	Virginia Poly. Institute L
Geneseo (SUNY) (NY) ....M	Virginia, U. of L
Georgetown (DC) ....M	Wake Forest (NC) ....M
Gettysburg (PA) .... R	Washington U. (MO) ....M
Gustavus Adolphus (MN) .... R	Washington & Lee (VA) ....M
★ ILLINOIS, U. OF (URBANA-	William & Mary (VA) ....M
CHAMPAIGN XL	Wisconsin, U. of.................XL
Indiana U. XL	Yeshiva (NY) .... R

► *Administrative Science*

GROUP II
Very Selective

Alabama, U. of L	Augustana (IL).................R
Albertson (ID) ....S	Austin (TX) .... R
Albright (PA) .... R	Babson (MA) .... R
Alfred (NY) .... R	Baylor (TX).................M
Alma (MI) .... R	Bentley (MA) ....M
Arizona, U. of XL	Birmingham Southern (AL).................R
Arizona State XL	Bowling Green (OH) L
Asbury (KY) .... R	*GROUP II continues next page*

Enrollment Code

S = Small (less than 1000 students) | **M** = Medium (3000-8000 students) | **XL** = Extra Large (over 20,000 students)
R = Moderate (1000-3000 students) | **L** = Large (8000-20,000 students)

★ THE COUNSELORS' CHOICE ■ Men Only ▲ Women Only

BUSINESS ADMINISTRATION, *continued*

GROUP II, *Continued*

Bryant (RI) .... R	Juniata (PA) .... R
Buena Vista (IA) .... R	Kansas Newman (KS) .... S
Butler (IN) .... R	Kentucky, U. of L
California State (Fullerton) L	LaSalle (PA) .... M
California, U. of (Santa Barbara) L	Lebanon Valley (PA) .... R
Capital U. (OH) .... R	LeMoyne (NY) .... R
Centenary (LA) .... S	LeTourneau (TX) .... R
Christian Brothers (TN) .... R	Lewis & Clark (OR) .... R
Clark (MA) .... R	Longwood (VA) .... R
Coe (IA) .... R	Loras (IA) .... R
Colorado, U. of (Col. Springs) ....M	Lowell, U. of (MA) L
Concordia (MN) .... R	Loyola (MD) .... R
Delaware, U. of L	Loyola (LA) .... R
Denver, U. of (CO) .... M	Loyola Marymount (CA) .... M
DePaul (IL) .... M	Luther (IA) .... R
Drake (IA) .... M	Manhattan (NY) .... M
Eckerd (FL) .... R	Manhattanville (NY) .... R
Elizabethtown (PA) .... R	Marietta (OH) .... R
Erskine (SC) .... S	Marist (NY) .... M
Florida Atlantic .... M	Marquette (WI) .... M
Florida Inst. of Tech. .... R	Maryland, U. of XL
Florida International .... M	Massachusetts, U. of L
Fredonia (SUNY) (NY) .... M	Michigan, U. of (Dearborn) .... M
George Mason (VA) L	Michigan State XL
Gonzaga (WA) .... R	Millersville (PA) .... M
Goucher (MD) .... S	Millsaps (MS) .... S
Grove City (PA) .... R	Minnesota, U. of XL
Guilford (NC) .... R	Mississippi College .... R
Hampton (VA) .... M	Mississippi, U. of .... M
Hanover (IN) .... S	Mississippi U. for Women .... R
Hendrix (AR) .... R	Monmouth (IL) .... S
Hillsdale (MI) .... R	Moravian (PA) .... R
Hofstra (NY) .... M	Nazareth (NY) .... R
▲ Hood (MD) .... S	New Paltz (SUNY) (NY) .... M
Houston, U. of (TX) L	North Carolina, U. of (Greensboro) .... M
Idaho, U. of .... M	North Dakota, U. of .... M
Indiana U. of Pennsylvania L	Northeastern (MA) XL
Iowa, U. of XL	North Florida .... M
James Madison (VA) .... M	Ohio U. L
John Carroll (OH) .... M	*GROUP II continues next page*

BUSINESS ADMINISTRATION, *continued*

GROUP II, *Continued*

Oglethorpe (GA) .... R	Spring Hill (AL) .... R
Oklahoma City U. (OK) .... R	St. Bonaventure (NY) .... R
Oklahoma State L	▲ St. Catherine (MN) .... R
Old Dominion (VA) L	St. John's (MN) .... R
Oregon, U. of L	St. Joseph's U. (PA) .... R
Oswego (SUNY) (NY) ....M	St. Mary's Col. of CA .... R
Pacific Lutheran (WA) .... R	▲ St. Mary's Col. (IN) .... R
Pacific University (OR) .... S	St. Mary's Col. (MN) .... R
Pennsylvania State XL	St. Michael's Col. (VT) .... R
Pepperdine (CA) .... R	St. Norbert (WI) .... R
Pittsburgh, U. of (PA) L	Stetson (FL) .... R
Plattsburgh (SUNY) (NY) ....M	Stockton State (NJ) ....M
Presbyterian (SC) ....S	Stonehill (MA) .... R
Principia (IL) ....S	Susquehanna U. (PA) .... R
Providence (RI) ....M	Texas A&M XL
Puerto Rico, U. of L	Texas A&M at Galveston .... S
Puget Sound (WA) .... R	Texas, U. of (Austin) XL
Queens (NC) ....S	Texas Christian ....M
Redlands, U. of (CA) .... R	Transylvania (KY) .... S
Ripon (WI) .... R	Truman State (MO) ....M
Roanoke (VA) .... R	▲ Trinity (DC) .... S
Rockhurst (MO) .... R	Ursinus (PA) .... R
Rowan (NJ) ....M	Valparaiso (IN) ....M
Salem College (NC) ....S	Virginia Military Inst. .... R
Samford (AL) .... R	Washington State L
San Diego, U. of (CA) ....M	Washington, U. of XL
San Francisco, U. of (CA) ....M	▲ Wells (NY) .... S
Santa Clara, U. of (CA) ....M	▲ Wesleyan College (GA) .... S
Scranton, U. of (PA) ....M	Western Maryland .... R
Seton Hall (NJ) ....M	Western Michigan L
Shaw (NC) .... R	West Virginia U. L
Shepherd (WV) ....M	Wilberforce (OH) .... S
Siena (NY) .... R	William Jewell Col. (MO) .... R
▲ Simmons (MA) .... R	Wisconsin, U. of (Stevens Point) ....M
Skidmore (NY) .... R	Wittenberg (OH) .... R
Southern California, U. of L	Wyoming, U. of L
Southern Methodist (TX) ....M	

BUSINESS ADMINISTRATION, *continued*

GROUP III
Selective

Alaska, U. of (Anchorage)	M		Green Mountain (VT)	S
Alaska, U. of (Fairbanks)	M		Hartford, U. of (CT)	M
American International (MA)	R		Hartwick (NY)	R
Appalachian State (NC)	L		Hastings (NE)	S
Arkansas, U. of	L		Hawaii Pacific	M
Azusa Pacific (CA)	R		Heidelberg (OH)	S
Baker (KS)	S		Hillsdale (MI)	R
Baldwin-Wallace (OH)	R		Howard (DC)	M
Barry (FL)	R		Illinois, U. of (Chicago)	L
Baruch (CUNY) (NY)	L		Indiana State U.	L
Belmont Abbey (NC)	S		Iona (NY)	M
Benedictine (KS)	S		Jacksonville (FL)	R
Benedictine (IL)	R		Kennesaw State (GA)	R
▲ Bennett (NC)	S		Kentucky Wesleyan (KY)	S
Bethel (MN)	R		King's (PA)	R
Bluffton (OH)	S		LaVerne, U. of (CA)	S
Brockport (SUNY) (NY)	M		Lenoir-Rhyne (NC)	R
Caldwell (NJ)	S		▲ Lesley (MA)	S
California Lutheran	R		Linfield (OR)	R
Carthage (WI)	R		Maine (Farmington)	R
Canisius (NY)	M		Maine, U. of	M
Cedarville (OH)	R		Malone (OH)	R
Catawba (NC)	S		Manchester (IN)	R
Chapman (CA)	R		Marshall (WV)	M
▲ Chatham (PA)	S		▲ Mary Baldwin (VA)	S
Colorado State	L		Massachusettes, U. of (Boston)	M
Delaware Valley (PA)	R		Mercer (GA)	R
Dillard (LA)	R		▲ Meredith (NC)	R
Doane (NE)	S		Merrimack (MA)	R
Eastern (PA)	R		Milligan (TN)	S
Elmira (NY)	R		Mercyhurst (PA)	R
Emory & Henry (VA)	S		Montreat (NC)	S
Eureka (IL)	S		■ Morehouse (GA)	R
Fairleigh Dickinson (NJ)	M		Mount Mercy (IA)	S
Ferris State (MI)	L		Mount St. Joseph (OH)	R
Florida A&M	M		Mount St. Mary's (CA)	R
Fisk (TN)	S		Mount St. Mary's (MD)	R
Gannon (PA)	R		Mount Union (OH)	S
Graceland (IA)	R			

GROUP III continues next page

BUSINESS ADMINISTRATION, *continued*

GROUP III, *Continued*

Muskingum (OH) .... R	South Dakota, U. of .... M
Nebraska, U. of L	Southern Illinois L
New Orleans, U. of L	Southern Mississippi L
Niagara (NY) .... R	South Florida, U. of XL
North Carolina, U. of (Charlotte) L	Southwest Texas State L
North Carolina, U. of (Wilmington) ...... M	St. Andrews Presbyterian (NC) .... S
North Georgia .... R	St. Francis (NY) .... R
Northern Arizona L	St. John Fisher (NY) L
Northern Illinois L	St. John's (NY) L
Northern Iowa, U. of L	St. Mary's (TX) .... R
Northwood University (MI) .... R	St. Rose (NY) .... R
Nova Southeastern (FL) .... R	St. Thomas, Col. of (MN) .... M
Ohio State XL	Tampa, U. of (FL) .... R
Ozarks, College of the (MO) .... R	Tennessee, U. of L
Pace (NY) .... R	Texas Wesleyan .... R
Phila. Col. of Textiles & Sci. (PA) .... R	Texas, U. of (San Antonio) L
Point Loma (CA) .... R	Thomas More (KY) .... S
Puerto Rico (CAYEY), U. of .... M	Toledo, U. of L
Quinnipiac (CT) .... R	Towson State (MD) L
Phillips (OK) .... R	Utica College of Syracuse U. (NY) .... R
Radford (VA) .... M	Virginia Wesleyan .... R
Regis (CO) .... R	Wagner (NY) .... R
Roosevelt (IL) .... R	Washington & Jefferson (PA) .... R
Sacred Heart (CT) .... R	West Chester (PA) .... M
San Diego State (CA) XL	West Florida, U. of .... M
Schreiner (TX) .... S	Western Connecticut State .... M
Seattle U. (WA) .... R	Western New England (MA) .... R
Seton Hall (NJ) .... M	Whittier (CA) .... R
Shippensburg (PA) .... M	Wisconsin, U. of (Green Bay) .... M
Simpson (IA) .... S	Woodbury (CA) .... S
Sonoma State (CA) .... M	Xavier (OH) .... R
South Carolina, U. of L	Xavier U. of Louisiana .... R

Enrollment Code

S = Small (less than 1000 students)   **M** = Medium (3000-8000 students)   **XL** = Extra Large (over 20,000 students)
R = Moderate (1000-3000 students)   **L** = Large (8000-20,000 students)

★ THE COUNSELORS' CHOICE   ■ Men Only   ▲ Women Only

CHEMISTRY

GROUP I
Most Selective

Amherst (MA) .... R
▲ Barnard (NY) .... R
Bates (ME) .... R
Bowdoin (ME) .... R
Brown (RI) ....M
▲ Bryn Mawr (PA) .... S
Bucknell (PA) ....M
California Inst. of Tech. .... S
California, U. of (Berkeley) XL
California, U. of (San Diego) L
Carleton (MN) .... R
Carnegie Mellon (PA) ....M
Case Western Reserve U. (OH) .... R
Centre (KY) .... S
Colgate (NY) .... R
Columbia (NY) ....M
Dartmouth (NH) ....M
Davidson (NC) .... R
Drew (NJ) .... R
Duke (NC) ....M
Emory (GA) .... R
Franklin & Marshall (PA) .... R
Furman (SC) .... R
Grinnell (IA) .... R
Hamilton (NY) .... R
Harvard (MA) ....M
Haverford (PA) .... S
★ HARVEY MUDD (CA) .... S
Illinois, U. of (Urbana-Champaign) XL
Johns Hopkins (MD)...................... R
Kalamazoo (MI) .... R

Kenyon (OH) .... R
Lafayette (PA) .... R
Lawrence (WI) .... R
MIT (MA) ....M
▲ Mount Holyoke (MA) .... R
New College (FL) .... S
North Carolina, U. of L
Northwestern (IL) ....M
Notre Dame (IN) ....M
Oberlin (OH) .... R
Occidental (CA) .... R
Pennsylvania State XL
Pomona (CA) .... R
Princeton (NJ) ....M
Reed (OR)................................. R
Rice (TX) .... R
Rochester, U. of (NY) ....M
Rutgers (NJ) L
Skidmore (NY) .... R
Southwestern (TX) .... R
St. Olaf (MN) .... R
Stanford (CA) ....M
Trinity (TX) .... R
Tufts (MA) ....M
Union (NY) .... R
▲ Wellesley (MA) .... R
Wesleyan (CT) .... R
Wheaton (IL) .... R
Whitman (WA) .... R
Willamette (OR) .... R
Williams (MA) .... R

CHEMISTRY continues next page

CHEMISTRY, *continued*

GROUP II
Very Selective

Albertson (ID)	S	Marquette (WI)	M
Alma (MI)	R	Massachusetts, U. of	L
Baylor (TX)	M	Michigan State	XL
Birmingham-Southern (AL)	R	Minnesota, U. of (Morris)	R
California, U. of (Santa Cruz)	M	New Hampshire, U. of	L
Carroll (WI)	R	Ohio Northern	R
Centenary (LA)	S	Ohio University	L
Colorado, U. of	L	Ohio Wesleyan	R
Delaware, U. of	L	Oregon, U. of	L
Duquesne (PA)	M	Purdue (IN)	XL
Earlham (IN)	R	Ripon (WI)	S
Florida State	L	Rochester, U. of (NY)	M
Georgia, U. of	XL	Rockhurst (MO)	R
Goucher (MD)	S	St. John's (MN)	R
Hamline (MN)	R	St. Louis (MO)	M
Hendrix (AR)	R	St. Michael's (VT)	R
Hiram (OH)	R	▲ Spelman (GA)	R
Hobart & William Smith (NY)	R	Spring Hill (AL)	R
Hope (MI)	R	Stetson (FL)	R
Houghton (NY)	S	Stony Brook (SUNY) (NY)	L
Huntingdon (AL)	S	Texas A&M	XL
Indiana U.	XL	Truman State (MO)	M
Ithaca Col.	M	Ursinus (PA)	R
Juniata (PA)	R	Vermont, U. of	L
Kansas, U. of	L	Washington & Jefferson (PA)	S
Knox (IL)	R	Washington, U. of	XL
Lake Forest (IL)	S	Wofford (SC)	R
Linfield (OR)	R	Wooster (OH)	R
Louisiana State	XL		

GROUP III
Selective

College of Charleston (SC)	M	Temple (PA)	L
Delaware Valley (PA)	R	Whittier (CA)	R
Houston Baptist (TX)	R	Wyoming, U. of	L
Louisiana State	XL	Xavier U. of Louisiana	R
▲ Sweet Briar (VA)	S		

CLASSICS

GROUP I
Most Selective

▲ Barnard (NY) .... R
Brown (RI) ....M
▲ Bryn Mawr (PA) .... S
Chicago, U. of (IL) .... R
Columbia (NY) ....M
Dallas, U. of (TX) .... R
Duke (NC) ....M
★ HARVARD (MA)..............................M
Holy Cross (MA) .... R
Johns Hopkins (MD)................... R
Kalamazoo (MI) .... R
Macalester (MN) .... R

Michigan, U. of XL
Middlebury (VT) .... R
New York U. ....M
North Carolina, U. of L
Northwestern (IL) ....M
Pennsylvania, U. of........................L
Princeton (NJ)..................................M
Stanford (CA) ....M
Swarthmore (PA).............................. R
Tufts (MA) ....M
Williams (MA)................................... R
Yale (CT)..M

GROUP II
Very Selective

Beloit (WI) .... R
California, U. of (Santa Barbara) L
Catholic U. (DC) ....M
Florida, U. of XL

Fordham (NY)....................................L
■ Hampden-Sydney (VA) .... S
Montana, U. of...................................L
▲ Randolph-Macon Woman's Col. (VA) ... S

Enrollment Code

S = Small (less than 1000 students)   **M** = Medium (3000-8000 students)   **XL** = Extra Large (over 20,000 students)
R = Moderate (1000-3000 students)   **L** = Large (8000-20,000 students)

★ THE COUNSELORS' CHOICE   ■ Men Only   ▲ Women Only

COMPUTER SCIENCE

GROUP I
Most Selective

Brandeis (MA)	R	Maryland, U. of (Baltimore County)	M
Brown (RI)	M	Michigan, U. of	XL
California, U. of (Berkeley)	XL	★ MIT (MA)	M
California, U. of (Los Angeles)	XL	Missouri, U. of (Rolla)	M
Carnegie Mellon (PA)	M	Pennsylvania State	XL
Case Western Reserve U. (OH)	M	Rensselaer (NY)	M
Cornell (NY)	L	Rice (TX)	R
Dartmouth (NH)	M	Stanford (CA)	M
Furman (SC)	R	Washington, U. of	XL
Georgia Institute of Tech.	M	Washington U. (MO)	M
Grinnell (IA)	R	William & Mary (VA)	M
Harvey Mudd (CA)	S	Williams (MA)	R
Haverford (PA)	R	Wisconsin, U. of	XL
Illinois, U. of	XL	Worcester Poly. Tech. (MA)	R
Iowa State	XL	Yeshiva (NY)	R

GROUP II
Very Selective

Allegheny (PA)	R	Massachusetts, U. of	L
Alma (MI)	R	Michigan, U. of (Dearborn)	M
Bradley (IL)	M	Minnesota, U. of (Morris)	R
Cal. Poly. State U. (San Luis Obispo)	L	Montana, U. of	M
California, U. of (Irvine)	L	Moravian (PA)	R
California, U. of (San Diego)	L	North Central (IL)	R
California, U. of (Santa Barbara)	L	Oklahoma City U.	R
Central (IA)	R	Oregon, U. of	L
Central Florida, U. of	L	Pacific Lutheran (WA)	R
Clarke (IA)	S	Pepperdine (CA)	R
Clemson (SC)	L	Pittsburgh, U. of (Johnstown)	R
DePaul (IL)	M	Potsdam (SUNY) (NY)	M
Drexel (PA)	M	Regis (CO)	R
Goucher (MD)	R	Rhode Island, U. of	L
Hiram (OH)	R	Rochester, U. of (NY)	M
Hunter (CUNY) (NY)	L	Rochester Inst. of Tech. (NY)	L
LaSalle (PA)	M		

GROUP II continues next page

Enrollment Code

S = Small (less than 1000 students)   **M** = Medium (3000-8000 students)   **XL** = Extra Large (over 20,000 students)
R = Moderate (1000-3000 students)   **L** = Large (8000-20,000 students)

★ THE COUNSELORS' CHOICE   ■ Men Only   ▲ Women Only

COMPUTER SCIENCE, *continued*

GROUP II, *Continued*

Rutgers (Camden) (NJ) ....M	Texas, U. of..XL
Santa Clara U. (CA) ....M	Transylvania (KY) ....S
St. Ambrose (IA)...................................... R	Utah, U. of..L
South Carolina, U. of L	Westminster (PA)..................................... R
Stony Brook (SUNY) (NY) L	Wofford (SC) .... R

GROUP III
Selective

Arizona State XL	■ Morehouse (GA).................................... R
California State U. (Chico) L	Mount Union (OH)................................. S
Catawba (NC) .... S	Muskingum (OH) .... R
Colorado, U. of (Col. Springs) ....M	Oakland U. (MI)......................................M
Colorado, U. of (Denver).......................M	Pittsburgh, U. of (Bradford)..................S
Eureka (IL)... S	Quinnipiac (CT) .... R
Evansville (IN) .... R	Rider (NJ)..M
Ferris State (MI)......................................L	San Jose State U. (CA)............................L
Hawaii Pacific ....M	▲ Spelman (GA) .... R
Loyola U. (LA) ....M	West Florida, U. of ....M
Marygrove (MI) .... R	West Virginia Wesleyan .... R
Monmouth (NJ) ....M	Wisconsin (LaCrosse) L

DANCE/DRAMA/THEATER

GROUP I
Most Selective

American Acad. of Dramatic Arts (NY) S	Miami, U. of (FL) L
Amherst (MA).. R	▲ Mount Holyoke (MA) .... R
▲ Barnard (NY) .... R	New York U. L
Boston U. (MA)..L	North Carolina, U. of L
Brandeis (MA) .... R	Northwestern (IL) ....M
California, U. of (Los Angeles)............XL	Princeton (NJ) ....M
Carleton (MN)... R	Sarah Lawrence (NY) ....S
★ CARNEGIE MELLON (PA)..................M	Skidmore (NY) .... R
Columbia (NY) ....M	Southwestern (TX) .... R
Cornell (NY) L	Tufts (MA) ....M
Dartmouth (NH) ....M	Tulane (LA) ....M
Drew (NJ) .... R	Vassar (NY) .... R
Illinois Wesleyan .... R	Wesleyan (CT) .... R
Juilliard (NY)..S	Whitman (WA) .... R
Kenyon (OH)... R	William & Mary (VA) .... R
Macalester (MN) .... R	Yale (CT)...M

GROUP II
Very Selective

Bard (NY) .... R	Muhlenberg (PA).. R
Baylor (TX)...M	No. Carolina School of the Arts ....S
Beloit (WI) .... R	Ohio U...L
Bennington (VT) ....S	Oklahoma State L
Butler (IN) .... R	Purchase (SUNY) (NY) .... R
California, U. of (Irvine) L	Rollins (FL)... R
Catawba (NC) ....S	▲ Scripps (CA) ....S
Catholic U. (DC) ....M	Southern Methodist (TX).........................M
DePaul (IL) ....M	Susquehanna (PA) .... R
Florida State L	Syracuse (NY) L
Fordham (NY)...L	Texas Christian...M
George Mason (VA) L	Texas, U. of..XL
Goucher (MD)..S	Utah, U. of L
Hofstra (NY) ....M	Virginia Commonwealth U. L
Indiana U. XL	Washington, U. of XL
Kansas, U. of...L	West Virginia U. L
Loyola (IL) ....M	Wheaton (MA) .... R
Lyon (AR) ....S	Wooster (OH) .... R

DANCE/DRAMA/THEATER continues next page

Enrollment Code

S = Small (less than 1000 students)	**M** = Medium (3000-8000 students)	**XL** = Extra Large (over 20,000 students)
R = Moderate (1000-3000 students)	**L** = Large (8000-20,000 students)	

★ THE COUNSELORS' CHOICE ■ Men Only ▲ Women Only

DANCE/DRAMA/THEATER, *continued*

GROUP III
Selective

Alaska, U. of (Fairbanks)	M	Northwestern College (IA)	S
Allentown College (PA)	S	Ohio State	XL
Barry (FL)	R	Otterbein (OH)	R
Bethany (WV)	S	Point Park (PA)	R
Catawba (NC)	S	Rockford (IL)	S
Emerson (MA)	R	San Francisco State (CA)	L
Evansville (IN)	R	Santa Fe, College of (NM)	S
Fontbonne (MO)	S	▲ Seton Hill (PA)	S
Franklin (IN)	S	Southern Utah	M
Humboldt State (CA)	M	South Florida, U. of	L
Illinois State	L	St. Mary's (MN)	R
Jacksonville (FL)	R	Temple (PA)	L
Evansville (IN)	R	Webster (MO)	R
Niagara (NY)	R	Western Michigan	L

ECONOMICS

GROUP I
Most Selective

American U. (DC)	M	
Amherst (MA)	R	
▲ Barnard (NY)	R	
Bates (ME)	R	
Boston University (MA)	L	
Bowdoin (ME)	R	
Brandeis (MA)	R	
▲ Bryn Mawr (PA)	S	
Bucknell (PA)	M	
California, U. of (Los Angeles)	XL	
California, U. of (San Diego)	L	
Chicago, U. of (IL)	R	
Claremont McKenna (CA)	S	
Colby (ME)	R	
Columbia (NY)	M	
Cornell (NY)	L	
Dallas, U. of (TX)	R	
Dartmouth (NH)	M	
Duke (NC)	M	
Hamilton (NY)	R	
Harvard (MA)	M	
Haverford (PA)	S	
Holy Cross (MA)	R	
Kalamazoo (MI)	R	
Kenyon (OH)	R	
Lafayette (PA)	R	
Macalester (MN)	R	
Michigan, U. of	XL	

★ MIT (MA)	M
Middlebury (VT)	R
▲ Mount Holyoke (MA)	R
Northwestern (IL)	M
Occidental (CA)	R
Pennsylvania, U. of	L
Pomona (CA)	R
Princeton (NJ)	M
Rhodes (TN)	R
Rochester, U. of (NY)	M
▲ Smith (MA)	R
South, U. of the (TN)	R
Stanford (CA)	M
St. Olaf (MN)	R
Swarthmore (PA)	R
Trinity (CT)	R
Trinity (TX)	R
Vanderbilt (TN)	M
Virginia, U. of	L
Wake Forest (NC)	M
Washington & Lee (VA)	R
▲ Wellesley (MA)	R
Wesleyan (CT)	R
Whitman (WA)	R
Willamette (OR)	R
Williams (MA)	R
Yale (CT)	M

ECONOMICS continues next page

Enrollment Code

S = Small (less than 1000 students)   M = Medium (3000-8000 students)   XL = Extra Large (over 20,000 students)
R = Moderate (1000-3000 students)   L = Large (8000-20,000 students)

★ THE COUNSELORS' CHOICE   ■ Men Only   ▲ Women Only

ECONOMICS, *continued*

GROUP II
Very Selective

▲ Agnes Scott (GA)	S	Randolph-Macon (VA) .... R
Albion (MI)	R	Ripon (WI) .... S
Allegheny (PA)	R	▲ Salem Col. (NC) .... S
Beloit (WI)	R	San Francisco, U. of .... M
Centre (KY)	S	St. John's (MN) .... R
Denison (OH)	R	St. Lawrence (NY) .... R
George Mason (VA)	L	Texas A&M XL
Hendrix (AR)	R	Ursinus (PA) .... R
Hobart & William Smith (NY)	R	Virginia Military Inst. .... R
Illinois Col.	S	Washington & Jefferson (PA) .... S
Lake Forest (IL)	S	Washington, U. of XL
Manhattanville (NY)	R	Westminster Col. (MO) .... S
Maryland, U. of	XL	Westmont Col. (CA) .... R
Michigan State	XL	Wheaton (MA) .... R
North Carolina State	L	Wofford (SC) .... R
Ohio Wesleyan (OH)	R	Wooster (OH) .... R
Oneonta (SUNY) (NY)	M	

GROUP III
Selective

Heidelberg (OH)	S	Whittier (CA) .... R
St. Anselm (NH)	R	▲ Wilson (PA) .... S
Washington State	L	Wyoming, U. of L

EDUCATION

GROUP I
Most Selective

Boston U. (MA)	L	Occidental (CA)	R
Bucknell (PA)	R	Pennsylvania, U. of	L
Buffalo (SUNY) (NY)	L	Rutgers (NJ)	L
Connecticut Col.	R	Skidmore (NY)	R
Dallas, U. of (TX)	R	Swarthmore (PA)	S
Earlham (IN)	R	Trinity (TX)	R
Illinois, U. of	XL	➤ Tufts (MA)	M
Iowa, U. of	XL	★ VANDERBILT (TN)	M
Miami U. (OH)	L	▲ Wellesley (MA)	R
Michigan, U. of	XL	Wheaton (IL)	R
New Jersey, College of	M	William & Mary (VA)	M
North Carolina, U. of	L		

➤ *Child Study*

GROUP II
Very Selective

Adelphi (NY)	M	Concordia (MN)	R
Adrian (MI)	S	Dayton, U. of (OH)	M
Albertson (ID)	S	Delaware, U. of	L
Alfred (NY)	R	Drake (IA)	M
Alma (MI)	R	Eastern Michigan	L
Arizona, U. of	XL	Erskine (SC)	S
Auburn (AL)	L	Florida State	L
Augustana (IL)	R	Fredonia (SUNY) (NY)	M
Augustana (SD)	R	Georgia, U. of	XL
Austin (TX)	R	Goucher (MD)	R
Baylor (TX)	L	Guilford (NC)	R
Berry (GA)	R	Hanover (IN)	S
Birmingham Southern (AL)	R	Hillsdale (MI)	R
Buena Vista (IA)	R	Hiram (OH)	R
Butler (IN)	R	▲ Hood (MD)	S
California, U. of (Santa Barbara)	L	Houghton (NY)	S
Calvin (MI)	M	Hunter (CUNY) (NY)	L
Capital U. (OH)	R	Indiana, U.	XL
Carroll (WI)	R	Indiana, U. of (PA)	L
Centenary (LA)	S	Iowa State	XL
Central (IA)	R	James Madison (VA)	M
Coe (IA)	R	Juniata (PA)	R
Connecticut, U. of	L		

GROUP II continues next page

Enrollment Code

S = Small (less than 1000 students) **M** = Medium (3000-8000 students) **XL** = Extra Large (over 20,000 students)
R = Moderate (1000-3000 students) **L** = Large (8000-20,000 students)

★ THE COUNSELORS' CHOICE ■ Men Only ▲ Women Only

EDUCATION, *continued*

GROUP II, *continued*

Kentucky, U. of	L
Loras (IA)	R
Luther (IA)	R
Lyon (AR)	S
Manhattan (NY)	M
Manhattanville (NY)	R
Maryland, U. of	XL
Messiah (PA)	R
Michigan State	XL
▲ Mills (CA)	S
Minnesota, U. of	XL
Moravian (PA)	R
Nazareth (NY)	R
New Paltz (SUNY) (NY)	M
North Carolina, U. of (Asheville)	R
North Dakota, U. of	M
North Florida	M
Ohio U.	L
Oregon, U. of	L
Pennsylvania State	XL
Principia (IL)	S
Puerto Rico, U. of	L
Queens (CUNY) (NY)	L
Redlands, U. of (CA)	R
Regis (CO)	R
Rowan (NJ)	M
St. Louis (MO)	M

St. Mary's Col. (CA)	R
▲ St. Mary's Col. (IN)	R
St. Mary's Col. (MN)	R
St. Michael's (VT)	R
Shepherd (WV)	M
Shippensburg (PA)	M
Southwest Missouri	L
Stetson (FL)	R
Tennessee, U. of	XL
Texas A&M	XL
Texas, U. of (Austin)	XL
Truman State (MO)	M
Ursinus (PA)	R
Washington & Jefferson (PA)	R
Washington, U. of	XL
▲ Wells (NY)	S
Western Maryland College	R
Western Michigan	L
Western Washington U.	L
Whitworth (WA)	R
William Jewell Col. (MO)	R
Wisconsin, U. of	XL
Wisconsin, U. of (Milwaukee)	L
Wisconsin, U. of (Stevens Point)	M
Wittenberg (OH)	R
Wofford (SC)	R
York (PA)	M

GROUP III
Selective

Alaska, U. of (Anchorage)	M
Appalachian State (NC)	L
Arkansas, U. of	L
Arizona State	XL
Augsburg (MN)	R
Averett (VA)	R
Baldwin-Wallace (OH)	R
Beaver (PA)	R
▲ Bennett (NC)	S

Berea (KY)	R
Bethany (WV)	S
Bethel (MN)	R
Bowling Green (OH)	L
Bloomsburg (PA)	M
Brockport (SUNY) (NY)	M
Caldwell (NJ)	S
California Lutheran	R

GROUP III continues next page

Enrollment Code

S = Small (less than 1000 students) **M** = Medium (3000-8000 students) **XL** = Extra Large (over 20,000 students)
R = Moderate (1000-3000 students) **L** = Large (8000-20,000 students)

★ THE COUNSELORS' CHOICE ■ Men Only ▲ Women Only

EDUCATION, *continued*

GROUP III, *continued*

Catawba (NC)	S	Montevallo (AL)	R
Cedarville (OH)	R	Mount St. Joseph (OH)	R
Central Michigan U.	L	Muskingum (OH)	R
City Col. (CUNY) (NY)	L	Nevada, U. of (Reno)	M
College of Charleston (SC)	M	New Mexico, U. of	M
▲ Converse (SC)	S	Northern Arizona	L
Dordt (IA)	S	Northern Iowa	L
Dubuque, U. of (IA)	S	Northwestern (IA)	R
East Carolina (NC)	L	Northwestern (MN)	R
Edgewood (WI)	S	Ohio State	L
Elmira (NY)	R	Oklahoma Baptist	R
Flagler (FL)	R	Ozarks, College of the (MO)	R
Florida A&M U.	M	Peru State (NE)	R
Florida Atlantic	M	Point Loma (CA)	R
Franklin (IN)	S	Puerto Rico (CAYEY), U. of	M
Geneva (PA)	R	Radford (VA)	M
George Fox (OR)	S	Saint Rose (NY)	R
Georgia Southern	L	St. Joseph's (IN)	S
Gordon (MA)	R	St. Joseph's (ME)	S
Graceland (IA)	R	▲ St. Joseph's Col. (CT)	S
Hastings (NE)	S	Seton Hall (NJ)	M
Heidelberg (OH)	S	Simpson (IA)	S
Huntingdon (AL)	S	Southern Oregon State College	M
Illinois State	L	Southern Utah	M
Jacksonville State (AL)	M	Southwest Baptist (MO)	R
Keene State (NH)	R	Texas Tech. U.	L
Kent State (OH)	L	Texas Wesleyan	R
Kutztown (PA)	M	Tougaloo (MS)	S
▲ Lesley (MA)	S	Utah State	L
Linfield (OR)	R	Wagner (NY)	R
Lock Haven (PA)	M	Wartburg (IA)	R
Longwood (VA)	R	Westfield State (MA)	M
Mansfield (PA)	R	West Florida, U. of	M
Marshall (WV)	M	West Virginia Wesleyan	R
Mass. St. Col. System	M	Western Kentucky	L
Millikin (IL)	R	▲ Wheelock (MA)	S
Mississippi State	L	Whittier (CA)	R
Monmouth (IL)	S	Wilmington (OH)	S
Montclair State (NJ)	M	Wisconsin, U. of (Platteville)	M

Enrollment Code

S = Small (less than 1000 students)   **M** = Medium (3000-8000 students)   **XL** = Extra Large (over 20,000 students)
R = Moderate (1000-3000 students)   **L** = Large (8000-20,000 students)

★ THE COUNSELORS' CHOICE   ■ Men Only   ▲ Women Only

ENGINEERING

GROUP I
Most Selective

Boston U. (MA)	L	Missouri, U. of (Rolla)	M
Brown (RI)	M	New Mexico Inst. of Mining & Tech.	S
Bucknell (PA)	M	New Jersey, College of	M
Buffalo (SUNY) (NY)	L	Northwestern (IL)	M
California Inst. of Tech.	S	Notre Dame (IN)	M
California, U. of (Berkeley)	XL	Pennsylvania State	XL
California, U. of (Davis)	L	Pennsylvania, U. of	L
California, U. of (Los Angeles)	XL	Princeton (NJ)	M
California, U. of (San Diego)	L	Rensselaer (NY)	M
California, U. of (Santa Barbara)	L	Rice (TX)	R
Carnegie Mellon (PA)	M	Rose-Hulman (IN)	R
Case Western Reserve U. (OH)	R	Rutgers (NJ)	L
Clarkson (NY)	M	Southern California, U. of	L
Colorado School of Mines	R	★ STANFORD (CA)	**M**
Cooper Union (NY)	S	Stevens Inst. of Tech. (NJ)	R
Cornell (NY)	L	Swarthmore (PA)	R
Dartmouth (NH)	M	Trinity (CT)	R
Duke (NC)	M	Tufts (MA)	M
General Motors Inst. (MI)	R	Tulane (LA)	M
Georgia Inst. of Tech.	M	Union (NY)	R
Harvey Mudd (CA)	S	U.S. Air Force Academy (CO)	M
Illinois Inst. of Tech.	R	U.S. Coast Guard Academy (CT)	S
Illinois, U. of (Urbana-Champaign)	XL	U.S. Military Academy (NY)	M
Iowa State	XL	U.S. Naval Academy (MD)	M
Iowa, U. of	XL	Vanderbilt (TN)	M
Johns Hopkins (MD)	R	Villanova (PA)	M
Lafayette (PA)	R	Virginia, U. of	L
Lehigh (PA)	M	Washington U. (MO)	M
MIT (MA)	M	Washington, U. of	L
Michigan, U. of	XL	Worcester Poly. Tech. (MA)	R

GROUP II
Very Selective

Alabama, U. of	L	California Maritime Academy	S
Alfred (NY)	R	Cal. Poly. State U. (San Luis Obispo)	L
Arizona, U. of	XL	Calvin (MI)	M
Arizona State	XL	Catholic U. (DC)	M
Arkansas, U. of	L	Central Florida, U. of	L
Auburn (AL)	L	Christian Brothers (TN)	R
Bradley (IL)	M	Cincinnati, U. of (OH)	L
California, U. of (Irvine)	L	Clemson (SC)	L
California, U. of (Riverside)	M	

GROUP II continues next page

ENGINEERING, *continued*

GROUP II, *continued*

Colorado, U. of............................L	New Mexico State U. L
Colorado, U. of (Col. Springs) .... R	New Orleans, U. of..............................L
Dayton, U. of (OH) ....M	North Carolina State............................L
Delaware, U. of L	North Dakota State L
Detroit Mercy (MI) ....M	Northeastern (MA) XL
East Carolina (NC) L	Oakland U. (MI) ....M
Florida Inst. of Tech. ....R	Ohio State XL
Gannon (PA) ....R	Ohio U. L
Geneva (PA) ....R	Oklahoma, U. of L
Grove City (PA) ....R	Oklahoma State L
Houston, U. of (TX)........................L	Pacific, U. of the (CA)..........................R
Idaho, U. of ....M	Pennsylvania State XL
Kansas, U. of L	Pittsburgh, U. of L
Kansas State L	Pittsburgh, U. of (Johnstown) .... R
Kentucky, U. of L	Polytechnic Univ. of NY .... R
Letourneau College (TX)....................S	Portland, U. of (OR) .... R
Louisville (KY)..............................L	Purdue (IN) XL
Lowell, U. of (MA).........................L	Rhode Island, U. of............................L
Loyola (MD) ....R	Rochester Inst. of Tech. (NY) L
Loyola Marymount (CA) ....M	Santa Clara, U. of (CA) ....M
Maine, U. of ....M	Seattle Pacific (WA)........................... R
Manhattan (NY)............................M	South Carolina, U. of L
Marquette (WI) ....M	So. Dakota School of Mines................... R
Massachusetts, U. of.......................L	Southern Maine, U. of........................M
Massachusetts, U. of (Boston) ....M	Texas A&M XL
Massachusetts, U. of (Lowell) ....M	Texas, U. of (Arlington) L
Mass. Maritime Academy ....S	Tulsa, U. of (OK) .... R
Michigan State XL	Tuskegee University (AL) ....M
Michigan Tech. ....M	Utah, U. of L
Michigan, U. of (Dearborn) ....M	Virginia Military Inst. .... R
Milwaukee Sch. of Eng, (WI) .... R	Virginia Poly. Inst. L
Minnesota, U. of...........................XL	Washington State L
Mississippi State L	Wayne State (MI) L
Montana College of Min. Sci. & Tech.. R	Western New England (MA).................. R
Montana State L	Wisconsin, U. of...............................XL
Nevada, U. of (Las Vegas) ....M	Wisconsin, U. of (Platteville) ....M
New Jersey Inst. of Tech. ....M	Wyoming, U. of L

Enrollment Code

S = Small (less than 1000 students) M = Medium (3000-8000 students) XL = Extra Large (over 20,000 students)
R = Moderate (1000-3000 students) L = Large (8000-20,000 students)

★ THE COUNSELORS' CHOICE ■ Men Only ▲ Women Only

ENGLISH

GROUP I
Most Selective

Amherst (MA) .... R	Macalester (MN) .... R
Bard (NY) .... R	Middlebury (VT) .... R
▲ Barnard (NY) .... R	▲ Mount Holyoke (MA) .... R
Boston Col. (MA) L	North Carolina, U. of L
Bowdoin (ME) .... R	New Jersey, College of .... M
Brandeis (MA) .... R	Northwestern (IL) .... M
▲ Bryn Mawr (PA) .... S	Oberlin (OH) .... R
Buffalo (SUNY) (NY) L	Pennsylvania, U. of L
California, U. of (Berkeley) XL	Pomona (CA) .... R
California, U. of (Los Angeles) XL	Princeton (NJ) .... M
Carleton (MN) .... R	Reed (OR) .... R
Chicago, U. of (IL) .... R	Rhodes (TN) .... R
Claremont McKenna (CA) .... S	Richmond, U. of (VA) .... R
Colby (ME) .... R	Rutgers (NJ) L
Colgate (NY) .... R	Sarah Lawrence (NY) .... S
Colorado College .... R	Skidmore (NY) .... R
Columbia (NY) .... M	▲ Smith (MA) .... R
Connecticut Col. .... R	South, U. of the (TN) .... R
★ CORNELL (NY) L	Southwestern (TX) .... R
Dallas, U. of (TX) .... R	Stanford (CA) .... M
Dartmouth (NH) .... M	St. Olaf (MN) .... R
Davidson (NC) .... R	Swarthmore (PA) .... R
Dickinson (PA) .... R	Trinity (TX) .... R
Duke (NC) .... M	Tufts (MA) .... M
Emory (GA) .... R	Vanderbilt (TN) .... M
Florida, U. of XL	Vassar (NY) .... R
Franklin & Marshall (PA) .... R	Virginia, U. of L
Georgetown (DC) .... M	Wake Forest (NC) .... M
Gettysburg (PA) .... R	Washington & Lee (VA) .... R
Grinnell (IA) .... R	Washington U. (MO) .... M
Hamilton (NY) .... R	▲ Wellesley (MA) .... R
Haverford (PA) .... S	Wesleyan (CT) .... R
Holy Cross (MA) .... R	Wheaton (IL) .... R
Iowa, U. of XL	Whitman (WA) .... R
Kalamazoo (MI) .... R	Willamette (OR) .... R
Kenyon (OH) .... R	Williams (MA) .... R
Knox (IL) .... R	Wisconsin, U. of XL
Lafayette (PA) .... R	Yale (CT) .... M
Lawrence (WI) .... R	

ENGLISH continues next page

ENGLISH, *continued*

GROUP II
Very Selective

▲ Agnes Scott (GA) .... S	Massachusetts, U. of L
Albany (SUNY) (NY) L	Millsaps (MS) .... S
Albion (MI) .... R	Mississippi, U. of .... M
Alfred (NY) .... R	New Hampshire, U. of L
Arizona, U. of XL	Ohio U. L
Baylor (TX) .... M	Oklahoma, U. of L
Beloit (WI) .... R	Pittsburgh, U. of (PA) L
Bennington (VT) .... S	Presbyterian (SC) .... S
Birmingham-Southern (AL) .... R	Principia (IL) .... S
California, U. of (Davis)....................... L	Puget Sound (WA) .... R
Cal Poly State U. (San Luis Obispo) L	Purchase (SUNY) (NY) .... R
Calvin (MI) .... M	Queens (NC) .... S
Cornell Col. (IA) .... R	Randolph-Macon (VA) .... R
Denison (OH) .... R	▲ Randolph-Macon Woman's Col. (VA) ... S
Denver, U. of (CO) .... M	Redlands, U. of (CA)............................ R
Emmerson (MA) .... R	Ripon (WI) .... S
Fordham (NY)...................................... L	Rochester, U. of (NY) .... M
George Mason (VA) L	Rollins (FL) .... R
Georgia, U. of XL	Rutgers (Camden) NJ .... M
Gonzaga (WA) .... R	Salem College (NC) .... S
Goucher (MD)...................................... R	▲ Scripps (CA) .... S
Grand Valley (MI) L	Spring Hill (AL) .... R
Guilford (NC) .... R	St. Lawrence (NY) .... R
Hamline (MN)...................................... R	▲ St. Mary's Col. (IN) .... R
■ Hampton-Sydney (VA) .... S	Stetson (FL) .... R
Hiram (OH) .... R	Stony Brook (SUNY) (NY) L
Hobart & Wm. Smith (NY) .... R	Warren Wilson (NC)............................. S
▲ Hollins (VA) .... S	Washington & Jefferson (PA) .... R
Hunter (CUNY) (NY) L	▲ Wells (NY) .... S
Lake Forest (IL) .... S	Wheaton (MA) .... R
Loras (IA) .... R	Winona State U. (MN) .... M
Marietta (OH) .... R	Wittenberg (OH) .... R
Marquette (WI).................................... M	Wofford (SC) .... S

ENGLISH continues next page

ENGLISH, *continued*

GROUP III
Selective

Adrian (MI) .... S	Rockford (IL) .... S
Arkansas, U. of L	▲ Rosemont (PA) .... S
Baldwin-Wallace (OH) .... R	St. Mary (KS) .... S
▲ Chestnut Hill (PA) .... S	▲ Salem Col. (NC) .... S
Fairleigh Dickinson (NJ) .... M	San Francisco State (CA) L
Fort Lewis (CO) .... M	▲ Spelman (GA) .... R
Longwood (VA) .... R	Temple (PA) L
Montevallo (AL) .... R	Tennessee, U. of XL
Niagara (NY) .... R	Utah, U. of L
North Carolina, U. of (Wilmington) ...... M	Whittier (CA) .... R
Rhode Island, U. of L	Wisconsin, U. of (Milwaukee) .... R

FOREIGN LANGUAGES

GROUP I
Most Selective

▲ Barnard (NY) .... R
Bowdoin (ME) .... R
Brown (RI) ....M
▲ Bryn Mawr (PA) .... S
California, U. of (Berkeley) XL
California, U. of (Los Angeles) XL
Carleton (MN) .... R
Colby (ME) .... R
Columbia (NY) ....M
Dallas, U. of .... R
Dartmouth (NH) ....M
Dickinson (PA) .... R
Drew (NJ) .... R
Emory (GA) .... R
Georgetown (DC) ....M
Grinnell (IA) .... R
Gustavus Adolphus (MN) .... R
Harvard (MA) ....M
Illinois, U. of (Urbana-Champaign) XL
Kalamazoo (MI) .... R
Lawrence (WI) .... R

Michigan, U. of XL
Middlebury (VT) .... R
▲ Mt. Holyoke (MA) .... R
New York U. ....M
North Carolina, U. of L
Pennsylvania, U. of.................................L
Pomona (CA) .... R
Princeton (NJ) ....M
Rochester, U. of (NY) ....M
Rutgers (NJ) L
Skidmore (NY) .... R
▲ Smith (MA) .... R
South, U. of the (TN) .... R
Southwestern (TX) .... R
Tulane (LA) ....M
Wake Forest (NC) ....M
Washington & Lee (VA) .... R
Washington U. (MO) ....M
▲ Wellesley (MA) .... R
Whitman (WA) .... R
Yale (CT) ....M

FOREIGN LANGUAGES continues next page

Enrollment Code

S = Small (less than 1000 students)   **M** = Medium (3000-8000 students)   **XL** = Extra Large (over 20,000 students)
R = Moderate (1000-3000 students)   **L** = Large (8000-20,000 students)

★ **THE COUNSELORS' CHOICE**   ■ Men Only   ▲ Women Only

FOREIGN LANGUAGES, *continued*

GROUP II
Very Selective

▲ Agnes Scott (GA) .... S
  Beloit (WI) .... R
  Boston College (MA) L
  Brigham Young (UT) XL
  California, U. of (Santa Barbara) L
  Calvin (MI) .... M
  Catholic (DC) .... M
  Central (IA) .... R
  Clark (MA) .... R
  Drake (IA) .... M
  Earlham (IN) .... R
  Eckerd (FL) .... R
  Georgia, U. of XL
  Hawaii, U. of L
▲ Hollins (VA) .... S
★ **INDIANA U.** XL
  Iowa, U. of XL
  James Madison (VA) L

  Kansas, U. of L
  Lewis & Clark (OR) .... R
  Linfield (OR) .... R
▲ Mills (CA) .... S
  Minnesota, U. of (Morris) .... R
  Moravian (PA) .... R
  Pacific University (OR) .... S
  Pepperdine (CA) .... R
▲ Sweet Briar (VA) .... S
  Texas, U. of (Austin) XL
▲ Trinity (DC) .... S
  Truman State (MO) .... M
  Utah, U. of L
  Vermont, U. of L
▲ Wells (NY) .... S
  Wheaton (MA) .... R
  Wisconsin, U. of XL
  Wofford (SC) .... R

GROUP III
Selective

  Bethany (WV) .... S
  Emory & Henry (VA) .... S
  Montana State L
  New Mexico, U. of L

  Southern Oregon State College .... M
  South Florida, U. of L
  Wayne State (MI) L

FOREIGN LANGUAGES continues next page

FOREIGN LANGUAGES, *continued*

Some Recommendations by Specific Departments
Compiled initially with the help of Minnesota's Jeff Sheehan, Secondary School Counselor.

FRENCH

California, U. of (Berkeley) XL	▲ Mount Holyoke (MA)..............................R
Columbia (NY) ....M	Northwestern (IL) ....M
Dartmouth (NH) ....M	Princeton (NJ)..M
Emory (GA)..R	Tufts (MA) ....M
Georgetown (DC) ....M	Tulane (LA)..M
Harvard (MA) ....M	Washington U. (MO) ....M
Indiana U. XL	▲ Wellesley (MA) ....R
▲ Mills (CA) ....S	

GERMAN

Brown (RI) ....M	Princeton (NJ)..M
California, U. of (Santa Barbara)............L	Stanford (CA) ....M
Illinois, U. of (Urbana-Champaign) XL	Texas, U. of (Austin)............................XL
Indiana U. XL	Williams (MA)..R
Michigan State.......................................XL	Wisconsin, U. of....................................XL
Penn State XL	Wofford (SC) ....R
Pennsylvania, U. of.................................L	

JAPANESE

Brigham Young (UT) XL	Oregon, U. of..L
Harvard (MA) ....M	Pennsylvania, U. of.................................L
Hawaii, U. of (Manoa) L	Pittsburgh, U. of (PA) L
Ohio State L	Washington, U. of..................................XL

SPANISH

Buffalo (SUNY) (NY) L	Kansas, U. of..L
California, U. of (Irvine) ....M	Pittsburgh, U. of L
California, U. of (San Diego) L	Rutgers (NJ)..L
California, U. of (Santa Barbara)...........L	Utah, U. of...L
Indiana U. XL	Wisconsin, U. of.....................................XL

Enrollment Code

S = Small (less than 1000 students) | **M** = Medium (3000-8000 students) | **XL** = Extra Large (over 20,000 students)
R = Moderate (1000-3000 students) | **L** = Large (8000-20,000 students) |

★ THE COUNSELORS' CHOICE ■ Men Only ▲ Women Only

FORESTRY

GROUP I
Most Selective

California, U. of (Berkeley) XL
Florida, U. of XL
Michigan, U. of XL

★ **NORTH CAROLINA STATE** L
SUNY Coll. of Env. Sci. & Forestry ..... R

GROUP II
Very Selective

Arizona, U. of XL
Auburn (AL) L
Berry (GA) .... R
Clemson (SC) L
Colorado State L
Georgia, U. of L
Iowa State XL
Maine, U. of .... M
Michigan State XL
Michigan Tech .... M
Minnesota, U. of XL

Missouri, U. of XL
Montana State L
Pennsylvania State XL
Purdue (IN) XL
South, U. of the (TN) .... R
Syracuse (NY) L
Texas A&M XL
Virginia Poly. Inst. L
Washington, U. of XL
West Virginia U. L
Wisconsin, U. of XL

GROUP III
Selective

Humboldt State (CA) .... M
Idaho, U. of .... M
Montana, U. of .... M
Northern Arizona XL

Oregon State L
Stephen F. Austin (TX) L
Utah State L

GEOGRAPHY

GROUP I
Most Selective

Buffalo (SUNY) (NY) L	Florida, U. of XL
California, U. of (Berkeley) XL	George Washington (DC) ....M
California, U. of (Los Angeles) XL	Johns Hopkins (MD) ....R
Chicago, U. of (IL) ....R	Macalester (MN) ....R
★ **CLARK (MA)** ....R	Michigan, U. of XL
Colgate (NY) ....R	Middlebury (VT) ....R
Dartmouth (NH) ....M	Minnesota, U. of XL

GROUP II
Very Selective

Arizona State XL	Michigan State XL
Bemidji State (MN) ....M	Ohio State XL
California, U. of (Santa Barbara) L	Oregon, U. of L
Colorado, U. of L	Pennsylvania State XL
Colorado, U. of (Colorado Springs) ....M	Radford (VA) ....M
Indiana U. XL	Texas, U. of (Austin) XL
Kansas, U. of L	Vermont, U. of L
Louisiana State XL	Wisconsin, U. of (Madison) XL
Mary Washington (VA) ....R	Wittenberg (OH) ....R

GROUP III
Selective

California State U. (Chico) L	Salem State (MA) ....M
Mansfield (PA) ....R	Sonoma State (CA) ....M

Enrollment Code
S = Small (less than 1000 students)   M = Medium (3000-8000 students)   XL = Extra Large (over 20,000 students)
R = Moderate (1000-3000 students)   L = Large (8000-20,000 students)
★ THE COUNSELORS' CHOICE   ■ Men Only   ▲ Women Only

GEOLOGY

GROUP I
Most Selective

Amherst (MA)	R	Franklin & Marshall (PA)	R
▲ Barnard (NY)	R	Furman (SC)	R
Bates (ME)	R	Geneseo (SUNY) (NY)	M
Brown (RI)	M	Harvard (MA)	M
Bowdoin (ME)	R	Lafayette (PA)	R
▲ Bryn Mawr (PA)	R	Lehigh (PA)	M
California Inst. of Tech.	S	MIT (MA)	M
★ CARLETON (MN)	R	Pennsylvania, U. of	L
Chicago, U. of (IL)	R	Pomona (CA)	R
Colgate (NY)	R	Princeton (NJ)	M
Colorado Col.	R	Rochester, U. of (NY)	M
Colorado School of Mines	R	Washington & Lee (VA)	R
Columbia (NY)	M	Washington U. (MO)	M
Dartmouth (NH)	M	William & Mary (VA)	M

GROUP II
Very Selective

Albany (SUNY) (NY)	L	Michigan Tech	M
Alabama, U. of	L	Millsaps (MS)	S
Allegheny (PA)	R	Minnesota, U. of	XL
Arizona, U. of	XL	New Mexico Inst. of Mining & Tech.	S
Beloit (WI)	R	Oklahoma, U. of	L
California, U. of (Davis)	L	Purdue (IN)	XL
California, U. of (Santa Barbara)	L	St. Lawrence (NY)	R
Centenary College (LA)	S	Stony Brook (SUNY) (NY)	L
Colorado State	L	Texas A&M	XL
Colorado, U. of	L	Texas Christian	M
Cornell Col. (IA)	R	Texas, U. of (Austin)	XL
Denison (OH)	R	Tulsa, U. of (OK)	M
Earlham (IN)	R	Vermont, U. of	M
Guilford (NC)	R	Washington, U. of	XL
Hope (MI)	R	Wisconsin, U. of	XL
Indiana U.	XL	Wooster, College of (OH)	R

GROUP III
Selective

Brooklyn Col. (CUNY) (NY)	L	Louisiana State	XL
Fort Lewis (CO)	M	Wyoming, U. of	L
Hartwick (NY)	R		

HISTORY

GROUP I
Most Selective

Albion (MI)	R	Kenyon (OH) .... R
Amherst (MA)	R	Lafayette (PA) .... R
▲ Barnard (NY)	R	Lawrence (WI) .... R
Bates (ME)	R	Macalester (MN) .... R
Boston Col. (MA)	L	Middlebury (VT) .... R
Boston U. (MA)	L	▲ Mount Holyoke (MA) .... R
Bowdoin (ME)	R	North Carolina, U. of L
Brandeis (MA)	R	Northwestern (IL) .... M
Brown (RI)	M	Pennsylvania, U. of L
▲ Bryn Mawr (PA)	S	Pomona (CA) .... R
Bucknell (PA)	M	Princeton (NJ) .... M
California, U. of (Berkeley)	XL	Reed (OR) .... R
California, U. of (Los Angeles)	XL	Rice (TX) .... R
Carleton (MN)	R	▲ Smith (MA) .... R
Chicago, U. of (IL)	R	South, U. of the (TN) .... R
Claremont McKenna (CA)	S	Southwestern (TX) .... R
Colgate (NY)	R	Stanford (CA) .... M
Colorado Col.	R	Swarthmore (PA) .... R
Columbia (NY)	M	Texas Christian U. (TX) .... M
Connecticut Col.	R	Trinity (TX) .... R
Cornell (NY)	L	Tufts (MA) .... M
Dallas, U. of (TX)	R	Tulane (LA) .... M
Davidson (NC)	R	Union (NY) .... R
Dickinson (PA)	R	Vanderbilt (TN) .... R
Drew (NJ)	R	Vassar (NY) .... R
Duke (NC)	M	Virginia, U. of L
Emory (GA)	R	■ Wabash (IN) .... S
George Washington (DC)	M	Wake Forest (NC) .... M
Georgetown (DC)	M	Washington & Lee (VA) .... R
Gettysburg (PA)	R	▲ Wellesley (MA) .... R
Grinnell (IA)	R	Wesleyan U. (CT) .... R
Hamilton (NY)	R	Whitman (WA) .... R
★ HARVARD (MA)	M	Williams (MA) .... R
Haverford (PA)	S	William & Mary (VA) .... M
Holy Cross (MA)	R	Yale (CT) .... M
Kalamazoo (MI)	R	Yeshiva (NY) .... R

HISTORY continues next page

Enrollment Code

S = Small (less than 1000 students)   **M** = Medium (3000-8000 students)   **XL** = Extra Large (over 20,000 students)
R = Moderate (1000-3000 students)   **L** = Large (8000-20,000 students)

★ THE COUNSELORS' CHOICE   ■ Men Only   ▲ Women Only

HISTORY, *continued*

GROUP II
Very Selective

▲ Agnes Scott (GA) .... S
  Albion (MI) .... R
  Allegheny (PA) .... R
  Alma (MI) .... R
  Baylor (TX) ....M
  Birmingham-Southern (AL) .... R
  California, U. of (Davis) L
  Calvin (MI) ....M
  Coe (IA) .... R
  Covenant (GA) .... S
  Denison (OH) .... R
  Erskine (SC) .... S
  Goucher (MD) .... S
■ Hampden-Sydney (VA) .... S
  Hanover (IN) .... R
  Hillsdale (MI) .... R
  Hiram (OH) .... R
  Hobart & William Smith (NY) .... R
  Kansas, U. of..L
  Kentucky, U. of L
  Knox (IL) .... R
  Lake Forest (IL) .... S
  Marquette (WI) ....M
  Maryland, U. of XL

  Mary Washington (VA) .... R
  Massachusetts, U. of...............................L
  Miami, U. of (FL) ....M
  Millersville (PA) ....M
  Missouri, U. of XL
  Muhlenberg (PA) .... R
  North Carolina (Asheville) .... R
  Ohio U. L
  Oklahoma, U. of L
  Queens (NC) .... S
  Rutgers (Camden) (NJ) ....M
  Spring Hill (AL)..................................... R
  Stetson (FL) .... R
  Texas, U. of (Austin)............................XL
  Vermont, U. of.......................................L
  Warren Wilson (NC)............................... S
  Washington College (MD) .... S
▲ Wells (NY) .... S
  Wheaton (MA) .... R
  Willamette (OR) .... R
  Wisconsin, U. of...................................XL
  Wittenberg (OH) .... R
  Wofford (SC) .... R
  Wooster (OH) .... R

GROUP III
Selective

Alabama, U. of L
Charleston, U. of (WV) .... S
New Mexico, U. of.................................... L

St. Mary's (MN) .... R
Toledo, U. of..L

HOME ECONOMICS

GROUP I
Most Selective

★ **CORNELL (NY)** L
Illinois, U. of (Urbana-Champaign) XL

Iowa State XL

GROUP II
Very Selective

Brigham Young (UT) XL
California, U. of (Davis).........................L
Connecticut, U. of................................L
Delaware, U. of L
Drexel (PA) ....M
Florida State..L
Georgia, U. of XL
▲ Hood (MD) ....S
Indiana U. (PA) L
James Madison (VA) L
➤ Kansas State L
Kentucky, U. of L
Maine, U. of ....M
Maryland, U. of XL

Massachusetts, U. of................................L
Michigan State XL
Minnesota, U. of....................................XL
Oneonta (SUNY) (NY).........................M
Pennsylvania State XL
Purdue (IN) XL
Rockhurst (MO)...................................... R
Rowan (NJ) ....M
St. Olaf (MN) .... R
Seattle Pacific (WA)............................... R
Western Washington U. L
Wisconsin, U. of....................................XL
Wisconsin, U. of (Stevens Point) ....M

GROUP III
Selective

Arizona State XL
Berea (KY) .... R
Central Michigan...................................L
Dominican (IL) ....S
Fontbonne (MO) ....S
Herbert Lehman (CUNY) (NY) L
▲ Judson (AL)..S
Linfield (OR) .... R
Mass. State College (Framingham)........M
▲ Meredith (NC) .... R

Montclair State (NJ) ....M
Montevallo (AL) .... R
Nebraska, U. of......................................L
North Carolina, U. of (Greensboro).......M
Ohio State XL
Oregon State L
Point Loma (CA) .... R
▲+ Seton Hill (PA) ....S
Texas Tech. U...L

➤ *Nutritional & Exercise Sciences*
+ *Family Studies*

JOURNALISM/COMMUNICATIONS

GROUP I
Most Selective

American U. (DC)	M	North Carolina, U. of	L
Boston U. (MA)	L	★ **NORTHWESTERN (IL)**	M
California, U. of (Los Angeles)	XL	Ohio U.	L
Creighton (NE)	R	Southwestern (TX)	R
Florida, U. of	XL	Stanford (CA)	M
Gettysburg (PA)	R	Trinity (TX)	R
Illinois, U. of (Urbana-Champaign)	XL	Villanova (PA)	M
Macalester (MN)	R	Wheaton (IL)	R
Miami, U. of (FL)	L	Wisconsin, U. of	XL
Michigan, U. of	XL		

GROUP II
Very Selective

Arizona State	XL	Marist (NY)	M
Arizona, U. of	XL	Maryland, U. of	XL
Central Florida, U. of	L	Massachusetts, U. of	L
Chapman (CA)	R	Michigan State	L
Colorado, U. of	L	▲ Mills College (CA)	S
Delaware, U. of	L	Minnesota, U. of	XL
Drake (IA)	M	Mississippi, U. of	M
Duquesne (PA)	M	Missouri, U. of	XL
Fairfield (CT)	M	Moravian (PA)	R
Fordham (NY)	M	Muhlenberg (PA)	R
Georgia, U. of	XL	Nevada, U. of (Reno)	M
Gonzaga (WA)	R	New Hampshire, U. of	L
Hanover (IN)	S	North Central (IL)	R
Illinois College	S	Ohio Wesleyan	R
Indiana U.	XL	Pepperdine (CA)	R
Iowa, U. of	XL	▲ Randolph-Macon Woman's Col. (VA)	S
John Carroll (OH)	M	Rowan (NJ)	M
Kansas, U. of	L	Santa Clara U. (CA)	M
Kansas State	L	Scranton, U. of (PA)	M
Kentucky, U. of	L	▲ Simmons (MA)	R
Louisiana State	XL	South Carolina, U. of	L
Loyola Marymount (CA)	M	*GROUP II continues next page*	

GROUP II continues next page

Enrollment Code

S = Small (less than 1000 students)   **M** = Medium (3000-8000 students)   **XL** = Extra Large (over 20,000 students)
R = Moderate (1000-3000 students)   **L** = Large (8000-20,000 students)

★ THE COUNSELORS' CHOICE   ■ Men Only   ▲ Women Only

JOURNALISM/COMMUNICATIONS continues next page

JOURNALISM/COMMUNICATIONS, *continued*

GROUP II, *Continued*

Southern California L	Temple (PA) L
Southern Methodist (TX)...........M	Texas A&M (Galveston)..............S
Spring Hill (AL)......................R	Texas Christian U. ....M
St. Ambrose (IA)......................R	Texas, U. of (Austin).................XL
St. Bonaventure (NY)................R	Tulsa, U. of (OK) ....R
St. Louis (MO)........................M	West Virginia U. L
St. Michael's (VT) ....R	Western Washington U. L
Susquehanna U. (PA) ....R	Winona State U. (MN) L
Syracuse (NY) L	Wisconsin, U. of (Stevens Point) ....M

GROUP III
Selective

Appalachian State (NC) L	Loyola (IL) ....M
Arkansas, U. of........................L	Loyola U. (LA) ....M
Augsburg (MN) ....R	Lynchburg (VA) ....R
Bemidji State (MN) ....M	Lyndon State (VT) ....R
Bethany (WV) ....S	Montana, U. of........................M
Buena Vista (IA) ....R	Morningside (IA) ....S
Butler (IN)..............................R	Montevallo (AL) ....R
California State U. (Fullerton) L	Nebraska, U. of........................L
California State U. (Long Beach) L	North Carolina, U. of (Greensboro).......M
Elon (NC) ....R	Oakland U. (MI) ....M
Flagler (FL) ....R	Oklahoma City U. ....R
Florida Southern......................R	Regis (CO)..............................R
Franklin (IN) ....S	St. John Fisher (NY)..................R
Hofstra (NY) ....M	St. Mary's College (MN) ....R
Howard (DC)...........................M	Samford (AL)..........................R
Hunter (CUNY) (NY)................L	San Diego State (CA) XL
Idaho, U. of ....M	Santa Fe, College of (NM) ....S
Jacksonville (FL) ....R	Seton Hall (NJ)........................M
Johnson C. Smith (NC) ....R	Tampa, U. of (FL).....................R
Keene State (NH) ....R	Texas Wesleyan.......................R
Kent State (OH)........................L	Xavier (OH) ....R

MATHEMATICS

GROUP I
Most Selective

American U. (DC) ....M	MIT (MA) ....M
▲ Barnard (NY) ....R	▲ Mount Holyoke (MA) ....R
Bates (ME) ....R	New College (FL) ....S
Binghamton (SUNY) (NY) L	New York U. L
Bowdoin (ME) ....R	Northwestern (IL) ....M
Bucknell (PA) ....M	Occidental (CA) ....R
California Inst. of Tech. ....S	Pomona (CA) ....R
California, U. of (Berkeley) XL	Princeton (NJ) ....M
California, U. of (Los Angeles) XL	Rensselaer (NY) ....M
California, U. of (San Diego) L	Rice (TX)..R
Carleton (MN) ....R	Stanford (CA) ....M
Case Western Reserve U. (OH) ....R	St. Mary's Col. of Maryland ....R
Chicago, U. of (IL) ....R	St. Olaf (MN)..R
Colgate (NY)..R	Trinity (CT)...R
Columbia (NY) ....M	Tulane (LA) ....M
Dartmouth (NH) ....M	Union (NY) ....R
Davidson (NC) ....R	■ Wabash (IN) ....S
Duke (NC) ....M	Washington U. (MO) ....M
Florida, U. of XL	▲ Wellesley (MA) ....R
★ HARVARD (MA)......................................M	Wesleyan (CT) ....R
Harvey Mudd (CA) ....S	Wheaton (IL) ....R
Holy Cross (MA).......................................R	Whitman (WA) ....R
Illinois Inst. of Tech. ....R	Willamette (OR) ....R
Illinois, U. of (Urbana-Champaign) XL	Wisconsin, U. of.......................................XL
Kenyon (OH)...R	Yale (CT) ....M

MATHEMATICS continues next page

MATHEMATICS, *continued*

GROUP II
Very Selective

Albion (MI)	R		Muhlenberg (PA)	R
Arizona State	XL		North Carolina State	L
Birmingham-Southern (AL)	R		Ohio U.	L
California, U. of (Irvine)	L		Oregon, U. of	L
California, U. of (Riverside)	M		Potsdam (SUNY) (NY)	R
California, U. of (Santa Cruz)	M		▲ Simmons (MA)	R
Cincinnati, U. of (OH)	L		Southern California, U. of	L
Colorado, U. of	L		Southwest Missouri	L
Concordia (MN)	R		Stetson (FL)	R
Earlham (IN)	R		▲ Sweet Briar (VA)	S
Fairfield (CT)	M		Texas, U. of (Austin)	XL
Hiram (OH)	R		▲ Trinity (DC)	S
Kansas State	L		Valparaiso (IN)	M
Knox (IL)	S		Washington, U. of	XL
Lebanon Valley (PA)	R		Wofford (SC)	R
Michigan State	XL		Wooster (OH)	R
Millsaps (MS)	S			

GROUP III
Selective

Fisk (TN)	S		Malone (OH)	R
Fontbonne (MO)	S		Texas Tech. U.	L
Louisiana State	XL			

Enrollment Code

S = Small (less than 1000 students)   **M** = Medium (3000-8000 students)   **XL** = Extra Large (over 20,000 students)
R = Moderate (1000-3000 students)   **L** = Large (8000-20,000 students)

★ THE COUNSELORS' CHOICE   ■ Men Only   ▲ Women Only

MUSIC

GROUP I
Most Selective

▲ Barnard (NY) .... R
Beloit (WI) .... R
Boston U. (MA) L
Bowdoin (ME) .... R
Brandeis (MA) .... R
Bucknell (PA) .... R
California, U. of (Berkeley) XL
California, U. of (Los Angeles) XL
California, U. of (San Diego) L
Carnegie-Mellon (PA) ....M
Case Western Reserve U. (OH) .... R
Cleveland Inst. of Music (OH) .... S
Columbia (NY) ....M
Connecticut College .... R
DePauw (IN) .... R
Furman (SC) .... R
Geneseo (SUNY) (NY) ....M
Gustavus Adolphus (MN) .... R
Harvard (MA) ....M
Hofstra (NY) ....M
Illinois, U. of (Urbana-Champaign) XL
Illinois Wesleyan .... R

Iowa, U. of XL
Juilliard (NY).. S
Lawrence (WI) .... R
Miami, U. of (FL) L
Michigan, U. of XL
New York U. L
Northwestern (IL) ....M
★ **OBERLIN (OH)** .... R
Princeton (NJ) ....M
Rice (TX) .... R
Rochester, U. of (NY) ....M
Skidmore (NY) .... R
▲ Smith (MA) .... R
Southwestern (TX) .... R
Stanford (CA) ....M
St. Mary's College of Maryland .... R
St. Olaf (MN) .... R
Vassar (NY) .... R
Wheaton (IL).. R
Whitman (WA) .... R
Willamette (OR) .... R
Yale (CT)..M

GROUP II
Very Selective

Augustana (IL).. R
Bard (NY) .... R
Birmingham-Southern (AL) .... R
Boston Conservatory .... S
Butler (IN) .... R
Cal. Inst. of the Arts .... S
California, U. of (Riverside) ....M
California, U. of (Santa Barbara) L
California, U. of (Santa Cruz) ....M
Capital (OH) .... R
Catholic U. (DC) ....M
Clark (MA) .... R
Coe (IA) .... R

Colorado, U. of L
▲ Converse (SC).. S
Curtis Institute of Music (PA) .... S
Drury (MO) .... S
Florida State...L
Fredonia (SUNY) (NY) ....M
Hope (MI) .... R
Indiana U. XL
Ithaca (NY) ....M
James Madison (VA) L
▲ Judson (AL).. S
Lake Forest (IL) .... S

GROUP II continues next page

Enrollment Code

S = Small (less than 1000 students) | M = Medium (3000-8000 students) | XL = Extra Large (over 20,000 students)
R = Moderate (1000-3000 students) | L = Large (8000-20,000 students)

★ THE COUNSELORS' CHOICE   ■ Men Only   ▲ Women Only

MUSIC, *continued*

GROUP II, *continued*

Lebanon Valley (PA)	R	Purchase (SUNY) (NY)	R
Louisiana State	XL	Rowan (NJ)	M
Luther (IA)	R	San Francisco Conservatory (CA)	S
Manhattanville (NY)	R	Santa Clara, U. of (CA)	M
Manhattan School of Music (NY)	S	Shepherd (WV)	R
▲ Mills (CA)	S	Southern California, U. of	L
Millsaps (MS)	S	▲ St. Catherine (MN)	R
Missouri, U. of (Kansas City)	M	Stetson (FL)	R
Moravian (PA)	R	Temple (PA)	M
New England Consevatory (MA)	S	West Chester (PA)	M
North Florida	M	West Virginia, U. of	L
North Texas	L	William Jewell Col. (MO)	R
Ohio U.	L	Wittenberg (OH)	R
Pacific, U. of the (CA)	R	Whitworth (WA)	R
Potsdam (SUNY) (NY)	M	Wooster, College of (OH)	R

GROUP III
Selective

Arkansas, U. of	L	Humboldt State (CA)	M
Baldwin-Wallace (OH)	R	Jacksonville (FL)	R
Belhaven (MS)	S	Keene State (NH)	R
➤ Belmont (TN)	R	Kent State (OH)	L
Bethany (WV)	R	Loyola (LA)	M
Bowling Green (OH)	L	Massacjusetts, U. of (Boston)	M
California State U. (Fullerton)	L	Massachusetts, U. of (Lowell)	M
Central Washington	L	Memphis, U. of (TN)	L
Duquesne (PA)	M	Northern Colorado	L
East Carolina	L	▲ Meredith (NC)	R
➤ Five Towns College (NY)	S	Rider (NJ)	M
Hartford, U. of (CT)	M	▲ Seton Hill (PA)	S
Hartwick (NY)	R	Southwest Baptist (MO)	R
Heidelberg (OH)	S	Tampa, U. of (FL)	R

➤ *Music Business*

Enrollment Code

S = Small (less than 1000 students) **M** = Medium (3000-8000 students) **XL** = Extra Large (over 20,000 students)
R = Moderate (1000-3000 students) **L** = Large (8000-20,000 students)

★ THE COUNSELORS' CHOICE ■ Men Only ▲ Women Only

NURSING

GROUP I
Most Selective

▲ Barnard (NY) .... R
Binghamton (SUNY) (NY) L
Boston Col. (MA) L
Case Western Reserve U. (OH) ....R
Colorado, U. of L
Columbia (NY) ....M
DePauw (IN) .... R
Duke (NC) ....M
Emory (GA)............................... R
Florida, U. of XL

Gustavus Adolphus (MN) .... R
Illinois, U. of XL
New York U. L
★ PENNSYLVANIA, U. OF L
Rochester, U. of (NY) ....M
St. Olaf (MN) .... R
Vanderbilt (TN).........................M
Villanova (PA)..........................M
Virginia, U. of L
Wisconsin, U. of..........................L

GROUP II
Very Selective

Adelphi (NY) ....M
Arizona, U. of XL
Augustana (SD) .... R
Barry (FL) .... R
Baylor (TX) ....M
Bethel (MN) .... R
Capital (OH) .... R
Carroll (WI) .... R
Catholic U. (DC) ....M
Creighton (NE) .... R
Daemen (NY) .... R
Delaware, U. of L
Detroit Mercy (MI) ....M
Duquesne (PA)...........................M
Evansville (IN) .... R
Fairfield (CT)..........................M
Franciscan U. of Steuberville (OH) .... R
George Mason (VA) ....M
Georgetown (DC) ....M
Gwynedd Mercy (PA)......................S
Hunter (CUNY) (NY) L
Iowa, U. of XL
Lebanon Valley (PA)...................... R
Loyola (IL)..............................M

Luther (IA) .... R
Marquette (WI) ....M
➤ Maryland, U. of (Baltimore County) .....M
Massachusetts, U. of L
Michigan, U. of XL
Minnesota, U. of.........................XL
▲ Mississippi U. for Women.................. R
Morningside (IA) ....S
Mount Mercy (IA) ....S
New Jersey, College of ....M
Pace (NY) ....M
Pacific Lutheran (WA) .... R
Pennsylvania State XL
Pittsburgh, U. of (PA) L
Samford (AL)............................ R
San Diego, U. of (CA) ....M
San Francisco, U. of (CA) ....M
Seattle Pacific (WA).................... R
Seton Hall (NJ) ....M
▲ Simmons (MA) .... R
▲ St. Catherine (MN) .... R
St. Louis (MO)...........................M
▲ St. Mary's College (IN) .... R
GROUP II continues next page

NURSING, *continued*

GROUP II, *continued*

Texas Christian U. ....M	Washington, U. of XL
Truman State (MO)..............................M	William Jewell (MO)............................. R
Union University (TN) .... R	Wisconsin, U. of (Milwaukee)..............XL
Valparaiso U. (IN) ....M	York (PA) ....M

➤ *Health Policy, also*

GROUP III
Selective

Alaska, U. of (Fairbanks) ....M	Mississippi College .... R
Arizona State XL	Mount St. Joseph (OH) .... R
Azusa Pacific (CA) .... R	Mount St. Mary's (CA) ....S
Bellarmine (KY)....................................... R	Mount St. Mary's (NY)............................S
Berea (KY) .... R	North Carolina, U. of (Charlotte)............L
California State U. (Chico) L	North Carolina, U. of (Greensboro).......M
Carroll (MT) .... R	Northeast Louisiana.................................L
▲ Cedar Crest (PA) ....S	Northern Illinois U. L
Cedarville (OH) .... R	Oakland (MI) ....M
D'Youville (NY) .... R	Ohio State XL
East Carolina (NC) L	Pennsylvania State XL
Eastern (PA)... R	Plattsburgh (SUNY) (NY) ....M
Edgewood (WI) ....S	Point Loma (CA) .... R
Goshen (IN).. R	Rhode Island, U. of.................................L
Graceland (IA) .... R	Russell Sage (The Sage Colleges) (NY)... R
Hartwick (NY) .... R	St. Scholastica (MN) .... R
Howard (DC)..M	St. Joseph's (ME)....................................S
Jacksonville (FL) .... R	Seattle U. (WA) .... R
MacMurray (IL)..S	South Dakota, U. of ....M
Marshall (WV)...M	South Florida, U. of................................L
Marycrest (IA) ....S	Southern Maine, U. of.............................M
Maryville (St. Louis) (MO) .... R	St. Anselm (NH)...................................... R
Massachusetts, U. of (Boston) ....M	Tuskegee University (AL) ....M
Massachusetts, U. of (Dartmouth) ....M	Western Connecticut State ....M
Mercy (NY) ....M	Western Kentucky....................................L
Misericordia, College (PA) ....S	Widener (PA) .... R

PHARMACY

GROUP I
Most Selective

Buffalo (SUNY) (NY)	L	Michigan, U. of	XL
Butler (IN)	R	North Carolina, U. of	L
Creighton (NE)	R	Purdue (IN)	XL
Florida, U. of	XL	★ RUTGERS (NJ)	L
Illinois, U. of	XL		

GROUP II
Very Selective

Albany Col. of Pharmacy (NY)	S	Ohio State	XL
Cincinnati, U. of (OH)	L	Ohio Northern U.	R
Connecticut, U. of	L	Pacific, U. of the (CA)	R
Drake (IA)	M	Philadelphia Col. of Pharm. & Science.	R
Duquesne (PA)	M	Pittsburgh, U. of	L
Ferris State (MI)	L	Rhode Island, U. of	L
Georgia, U. of	L	Samford (AL)	R
Kansas, U. of	L	South Carolina, U. of	L
Kentucky, U. of	L	Southern California, U. of	L
Maryland, U. of	XL	St. John's (NY)	L
Mass. College of Pharmacy	R	St. Louis Col. of Pharmacy (MO)	S
Mercer (GA)	R	Temple (PA)	L
Minnesota, U. of	XL	Texas, U. of (Austin)	XL
Mississippi, U. of	M	Toledo, U. of	L
Montana, U. of	M	Virginia Commonwealth U.	L
New Mexico, U. of	M	Washington State	L
Northeast Louisiana	L	Wayne State (MI)	L
North Dakota State	L	Wyoming, U. of	L

Enrollment Code

S = Small (less than 1000 students) M = Medium (3000-8000 students) XL = Extra Large (over 20,000 students)
R = Moderate (1000-3000 students) L = Large (8000-20,000 students)

★ THE COUNSELORS' CHOICE ■ Men Only ▲ Women Only

PHILOSOPHY

GROUP I
Most Selective

▲ Barnard (NY) .... R
Bates (ME) .... R
Boston Col. (MA) L
Boston U. (MA) L
Bowdoin (ME) .... R
Bucknell (PA) ....M
California, U. of (Berkeley) XL
California, U. of (Los Angeles) XL
Chicago, U. of (IL) .... R
Claremont McKenna (CA) .... S
Colgate (NY) .... R
Colorado Col. .... R
Columbia (NY) ....M
Connecticut Col. .... R
Cornell (NY) L
Davidson (NC) .... R
Duke (NC) ....M
Florida State L
Florida, U. of XL
George Washington (DC) ....M
Georgetown (DC) ....M
Hamilton (NY) .... R
Harvard (MA) ....M
Haverford (PA) .... S

Holy Cross (MA) .... R
Johns Hopkins (MD) .... R
Kenyon (OH) .... R
Macalester (MN) .... R
Michigan, U. of XL
New College (FL) .... S
New York U. L
Oberlin (OH) .... R
Pennsylvania, U. of L
Pittsburgh, U. of (PA) L
Pomona (CA) .... R
★ **PRINCETON (NJ)**.......................M
Reed (OR) .... R
Rochester, U. of (NY) ....M
▲ Smith (MA) .... R
St. Olaf (MN) .... R
Swarthmore (PA) .... R
Trinity (CT) .... R
Trinity (TX) .... R
Tulane (LA) ....M
Washington U. (MO) ....M
Wheaton (IL) .... R
Whitman (WA) .... R
Yale (CT) ....M

GROUP II
Very Selective

Allegheny (PA) .... R
Asbury (KY) .... R
Biola (CA) .... R
California, U. of (Santa Barbara) L
Cornell Col. (IA) .... R
Denison (OH) .... R
Fordham (NY) L
Franciscan U. of Steubenville (OH) ...... R
▲ Hood (MD) .... S
Indiana U. XL

Loyola (LA) ....M
Milligan (TN) .... S
Muhlenberg (PA) .... R
Regis (CO) .... R
St. Andrews Presbyterian (NC) .... S
St. Bonaventure (NY) .... R
St. Louis (MO) ....M
Skidmore (NY) .... R
Stony Brook (SUNY) (NY) L
Wofford (SC) .... R

PHYSICS

GROUP I
Most Selective

Amherst (MA)	R	
▲ Barnard (NY)	R	
Bates (ME)	R	
Binghamton (SUNY) (NY)	L	
Boston U. (MA)	L	
▲ Bryn Mawr (PA)	S	
★ CALIFORNIA INST. OF TECH.	S	
California, U. of (Berkeley)	XL	
California, U. of (San Diego)	L	
Carleton (MN)	R	
Case Western Reserve U. (OH)	R	
Centre (KY)	S	
Chicago, U. of (IL)	R	
Colorado School of Mines	R	
Columbia (NY)	M	
Cornell (NY)	L	
Dartmouth (NH)	M	
Florida, U. of	XL	
Franklin & Marshall (PA)	R	
Geneseo (SUNY) (NY)	M	
Georgia Inst. of Tech.	M	
Grinnell (IA)	R	
Gustavus Adolphus (MN)	R	
Harvard (MA)	M	
Harvey Mudd (CA)	S	
Haverford (PA)	S	
Illinois, U. of (Urbana-Champaign)	XL	
Kalamazoo (MI)	R	
Lawrence (WI)	R	
Macalester (MN)	R	
MIT (MA)	M	
New College (FL)	S	
New Mexico Inst. of Mining & Tech.	S	
Occidental (CA)	R	
Princeton (NJ)	M	
Reed (OR)	R	
Rensselaer (NY)	M	
Rice (TX)	R	
▲ Smith (MA)	R	
Stanford (CA)	M	
Swarthmore (PA)	R	
Wake Forest (NC)	M	
Washington U. (MO)	M	
▲ Wellesley (MA)	R	
Wheaton (IL)	R	
Whitman (WA)	R	
William & Mary (VA)	M	
Worcester Poly. Inst. (MA)	R	
Yeshiva (NY)	R	

PHYSICS continues next page

Enrollment Code

S = Small (less than 1000 students)   **M** = Medium (3000-8000 students)   **XL** = Extra Large (over 20,000 students)
R = Moderate (1000-3000 students)   **L** = Large (8000-20,000 students)

★ **THE COUNSELORS' CHOICE**   ■ Men Only   ▲ Women Only

PHYSICS

GROUP II
Very Selective

Adelphi (NY)	M	Mississippi, U. of	M
Beloit (WI)	R	Ohio State	XL
California, U. of (Irvine)	L	Ohio U.	L
California, U. of (Santa Barbara)	L	Oregon State	L
California, U. of (Santa Cruz)	M	Rollins (FL)	R
Colorado, U. of	L	St. John's (MN)	R
Colorado, U. of (Colorado Springs)	M	Stockton State (NJ)	M
Denver, U. of (CO)	M	Stony Brook (SUNY) (NY)	L
Evansville, U. of (IN)	R	Texas, U. of (Austin)	XL
Fairfield (CT)	M	Ursinus (PA)	R
Guilford (NC)	R	Vermont, U. of	M
Lewis & Clark (OR)	R	Wisconsin, U. of	XL
Loyola (IL)	M		

GROUP III
Selective

Brooklyn Col. (CUNY) (NY)	L	Jacksonville (FL)	R
City Col. (CUNY) (NY)	L	Louisiana State	XL
Goshen (IN)	R	Wyoming, U. of	L

POLITICAL SCIENCE

GROUP I
Most Selective

American U. (DC)	M	Macalester (MN)	R
Amherst (MA)	R	MIT (MA)	M
Boston U. (MA)	L	Middlebury (VT)	R
Brandeis (MA)	R	▲ Mount Holyoke (MA)	R
Brown (RI)	M	Northwestern (IL)	M
California, U. of (Los Angeles)	XL	Nortre Dame (IN)	M
California, U. of (San Diego)	L	Occidental (CA)	R
Centre (KY)	S	Pennsylvania, U. of	L
Chicago, U. of (IL)	R	Princeton (NJ)	M
Claremont McKenna (CA)	S	Rochester, U. of (NY)	M
Colby (ME)	R	Rhodes (TN)	R
Colgate (NY)	R	▲ Smith (MA)	R
Colorado Col.	R	South, U. of the (TN)	R
Columbia (NY)	M	Southwestern (TX)	R
Connecticut Col.	R	Stanford (CA)	M
Dartmouth (NH)	M	Swarthmore (PA)	R
Dickinson (PA)	R	Trinity (TX)	R
Drew (NJ)	R	Tufts (MA)	M
Duke (NC)	M	Union (NY)	R
Emory (GA)	R	Ursinus (PA)	R
Franklin & Marshall (PA)	R	■ Wabash (IN)	S
Furman (SC)	R	▲ Wellesley (MA)	R
George Washington (DC)	M	Washington & Lee (VA)	R
Georgetown (DC)	M	Whitman (WA)	R
Grinnell (IA)	R	Willamette (OR)	R
Hamilton (NY)	R	Williams (MA)	R
★ HARVARD (MA)	M	Yale (CT)	M
Johns Hopkins (MD)	R	Yeshiva (NY)	R
Kenyon (OH)	R		

POLITICAL SCIENCE continues next page

Enrollment Code

S = Small (less than 1000 students)	**M** = Medium (3000-8000 students)	**XL** = Extra Large (over 20,000 students)
R = Moderate (1000-3000 students)	**L** = Large (8000-20,000 students)	

★ THE COUNSELORS' CHOICE ■ Men Only ▲ Women Only

POLITICAL SCIENCE, *continued*

GROUP II
Very Selective

Austin (TX) .... R
California, U. of (Davis) L
California, U. of (Riverside) .... M
California, U. of (Santa Barbara) L
Cal. Poly. State U. (San Luis Obispo) L
Creighton (NE) .... R
Dayton, U. of .... M
Denison (OH) .... R
DePaul (IL) .... M
Drake (IA) .... M
Hawaii, U. of L
Hobart & William Smith (NY) .... R
Hofstra (NY) .... M
Hope (MI) .... R
Knox (IL) .... R
Marquette (WI) .... M
Maryland, U. of (Baltimore County) ..... M
Minnesota, U. of XL
North Central (IL) .... R
Oglethorpe (GA) .... S

Ohio Wesleyan .... R
Presbyterian (SC) .... S
Providence (RI) .... M
Randolph Macon (VA) .... R
Redlands, U. of (CA) .... R
Ripon (WI) .... S
Siena (NY) .... R
Skidmore (NY) .... R
Spring Hill (AL) .... R
St. Bonaventure (NY) .... R
St. John's (MN) .... R
St. Lawrence (NY) .... R
Stonehill (MA) .... R
Syracuse (NY) L
▲ Trinity (DC) .... S
Vermont, U. of L
Washington & Jefferson (PA) .... R
Wheaton (MA) .... R
Wilberforce (OH) .... S
Wittenberg (OH) .... R

GROUP III
Selective

Adrian (MI) .... S
Albright (PA) .... R
Arizona State XL
Belmont Abbey (NC) .... S
▲ Chatham (PA) .... S
Hartwick (NY) .... R
Michigan State XL

Mt. St. Mary's (MD) .... R
Radford (VA) .... M
Rhode Island, U. of L
St. Mary's (TX) .... R
▲ Spelman (GA) .... R
Virginia Wesleyan .... R
Whittier (CA) .... R

Enrollment Code

S = Small (less than 1000 students)   **M** = Medium (3000-8000 students)   **XL** = Extra Large (over 20,000 students)
R = Moderate (1000-3000 students)   **L** = Large (8000-20,000 students)

★ **THE COUNSELORS' CHOICE**   ■ Men Only   ▲ Women Only

PRE-LAW

Author's Note: *Law School Associations usually recommend that a student choose a major dependent upon one's own individual intellectual interests and upon "the quality of undergraduate education" provided by various departments and colleges. The above recommended colleges have been taken primarily from our recommended departments in English, Economics, and Political Science.*

GROUP I
Most Selective

Albany (SUNY) (NY)	L	Florida, U. of	XL
Allegheny (PA)	R	Franklin & Marshall (PA)	R
American U. (DC)	M	Furman (SC)	R
Amherst (MA)	R	George Washington (DC)	M
Bard (NY)	R	Georgetown (DC)	M
▲ Barnard (NY)	R	Gettysburg (PA)	R
Bates (ME)	R	Grinnell (IA)	R
Binghamton (SUNY) (NY)	L	Hamilton (NY)	R
Boston Col. (MA)	L	★ HARVARD (MA)	M
Boston U. (MA)	L	Haverford (PA)	S
Bowdoin (ME)	R	Holy Cross (MA)	R
Brandeis (MA)	R	Iowa, U. of	XL
Brown (RI)	M	Johns Hopkins (MD)	R
▲ Bryn Mawr (PA)	S	Kalamazoo (MI)	R
Bucknell (PA)	M	Kenyon (OH)	R
Buffalo (SUNY) (NY)	L	Lafayette (PA)	R
California, U. of (Berkeley)	XL	Macalester (MN)	R
California, U. of (Los Angeles)	XL	Maryland, U. of (Baltimore County)	M
California, U. of (San Diego)	L	MIT (MA)	M
Carleton (MN)	R	Michigan, U. of	XL
Centre (KY)	S	Middlebury (VT)	R
Chicago, U. of (IL)	R	▲ Mount Holyoke (MA)	R
Claremont McKenna (CA)	S	Muhlenberg (PA)	R
Clark (MA)	R	New Jersey, College of	M
Colby (ME)	R	North Carolina, U. of	L
Colgate (NY)	R	Northwestern (IL)	M
Colorado Col.	R	Notre Dame (IN)	M
Columbia (NY)	M	Oberlin (OH)	R
Connecticut Col.	R	Occidental (CA)	R
Dallas, U. of (TX)	R	Pennsylvania, U. of	L
Dartmouth (NH)	M	Pomona (CA)	R
Davidson (NC)	R	Princeton (NJ)	M
Dickinson (PA)	R	Providence (RI)	M
Drew (NJ)	R	Reed (OR)	R
Duke (NC)	M	Rhodes (TN)	R
Emory (GA)	R		

GROUP I continues next page

Enrollment Code

S = Small (less than 1000 students)   **M** = Medium (3000-8000 students)   **XL** = Extra Large (over 20,000 students)
R = Moderate (1000-3000 students)   **L** = Large (8000-20,000 students)

★ THE COUNSELORS' CHOICE   ■ Men Only   ▲ Women Only

PRE-LAW, *continued*

GROUP I, *continued*

Rice (TX) .... R	Tufts (MA) .... M
Richmond, U. of (VA) .... M	Union (NY) .... R
Rochester, U. of (NY) .... M	Ursinus (PA) .... R
Rutgers (NJ) L	Vanderbilt (TN) .... M
Sarah Lawrence (NY) .... S	Vassar (NY) .... R
Skidmore (NY) .... R	Virginia, U. of L
▲ Smith (MA) .... R	■ Wabash (IN) .... S
South, U. of the (TN) .... R	Wake Forest (NC) .... M
Southwestern (TX) .... R	Washington & Lee (VA) .... R
Stanford (CA) .... M	Washington U. (MO) .... M
St. Olaf (MN) .... R	▲ Wellesley (MA) .... R
Swarthmore (PA) .... R	Wesleyan U. (CT) .... R
Trinity (CT) .... R	Wheaton (IL) .... R
Trinity (TX) .... R	Whitman (WA) .... R

GROUP II
Very Selective

▲ Agnes Scott (GA) .... S	DePaul (IL) .... M
Albany (SUNY) (NY) L	Drake (IA) .... M
Albion (MI) .... R	Evansville (IN) .... R
Alfred (NY) .... R	Fordham (NY) L
Alma (MI) .... R	George Mason (VA) L
Arizona, U. of XL	Georgia, U. of XL
Baylor (TX) .... R	Gonzaga (WA) .... R
Bennington (VT) .... S	Goucher (MD) .... R
Birmingham-Southern (AL) .... R	Grand Valley (MI) L
Butler (IN) .... R	Guilford (NC) .... R
California, U. of (Davis) L	Hamline (MN) .... R
California, U. of (Irvine) L	■ Hampden-Sydney (VA) .... S
California, U. of (Riverside) .... M	Hartwick (NY) .... R
California, U. of (Santa Barbara) L	Hobart & Wm. Smith (NY) .... R
Calvin (MI) .... M	Hofstra (NY) .... M
Catholic (DC) .... R	Hope (MI) .... R
Clark (MA) .... R	Hunter (CUNY) (NY) L
Cornell Col. (IA) .... R	Illinois College .... S
Creighton (NE) .... R	Knox (IL) .... S
Denison (OH) .... R	Lake Forest (IL) .... R
Denver, U. of (CO) .... M	*GROUP II continues next page*

GROUP II continues next page

Enrollment Code

S = Small (less than 1000 students) | **M** = Medium (3000-8000 students) | **XL** = Extra Large (over 20,000 students)
R = Moderate (1000-3000 students) | **L** = Large (8000-20,000 students)

★ THE COUNSELORS' CHOICE   ■ Men Only   ▲ Women Only

PRE-LAW, *continued*

GROUP II, *continued*

Lawrence (WI)	R
Loras (IA)	R
Marietta (OH)	R
Marquette (WI)	M
Massachusetts, U. of	L
Michigan State	XL
Millersville (PA)	M
Millsaps (MS)	S
Minnesota, U. of	XL
Minnesota, U. of (Morris)	R
Mississippi, U. of	M
New Hampshire, U. of	L
North Carolina State	L
North Central (IL)	R
Oglethorpe (GA)	S
Ohio U.	L
Ohio Wesleyan	R
Oklahoma, U. of	L
Oneonta (SUNY) (NY)	M
Pittsburgh, U. of (PA)	L
Presbyterian (SC)	S
Principia (IL)	S
Puget Sound (WA)	R
Purchase (SUNY) (NY)	R
Queens (NC)	S
Randolph-Macon (VA)	R
▲ Randolph-Macon Woman's Col. (VA)	S
Redlands, U. of (CA)	R
Ripon (WI)	S
Rutgers (Camden) (NJ)	M

▲ Salem College (NC)	S
San Francisco, U. of (CA)	M
Santa Clara (CA)	R
▲ Scripps (CA)	S
Siena (NY)	R
Spring Hill (AL)	R
St. Bonaventure (NY)	R
St. John's (MN)	R
St. Lawrence (NY)	R
▲ St. Mary's Col. (IN)	R
Stetson (FL)	R
Stonehill (MA)	R
Stony Brook (SUNY) (NY)	L
Syracuse (NY)	L
▲ Trinity (DC)	S
Ursinus (PA)	R
Vermont, U. of	L
Virginia Commonwealth U.	L
Virginia Military Inst.	R
Warren Wilson (NC)	S
Washington, U. of	XL
Washington & Jefferson (PA)	S
▲ Wells (NY)	S
Westminster Col. (MO)	S
Westmont (CA)	R
Wheaton (MA)	R
Wilberforce (OH)	S
Wittenberg (OH)	R
Wofford (SC)	R
Wooster (OH)	R

PRE-LAW continues next page

PRE-LAW, *continued*

GROUP III
Selective

Adrian (MI)	S	Niagara (NY)	R
Albright (PA)	R	North Carolina, U. of (Wilmington)	M
Arkansas, U. of	L	Radford (VA)	M
Baldwin-Wallace (OH)	R	Roanoke (VA)	R
Belmont Abbey (NC)	S	Rhode Island, U. of	L
▲ Bennett (NC)	S	Rockford (IL)	S
▲ Chatham (PA)	S	San Francisco State (CA)	L
▲ Chestnut Hill (PA)	S	▲ Spelman (GA)	R
Emerson (MA)	R	St. Anselm (NH)	R
Fairleigh Dickinson (NJ)	M	Temple (PA)	L
Fisk (TN)	S	Tennessee, U. of	XL
Florida A&M	M	Utah, U. of	L
Fort Lewis (CO)	M	Virginia Wesleyan	R
Hawaii, U. of	L	Whittier (CA)	R
Heidelberg (OH)	S	▲ Wilson (PA)	S
▲ Hollins (VA)	S	Wisconsin, U. of (Milwaukee)	L
Longwood (VA)	R	Wyoming, U. of	L
Mt. St. Mary's (MD)	R		

PRE-MED/PRE-DENTAL

Author's Note: *In addition to general college requirements and requirements of their major department, premedical and predental students must usually pass with a good grade the following: general chemistry, zoology, organic chemistry, general biology, English composition or literature, and general physics.*

Other required or highly recommended courses are: advanced biology, psychology or sociology, physical chemistry, calculus, and quantitative chemistry. Of course, the wise path to follow is to consult the exact course requirements of the school you expect to apply to. The recommended colleges below are taken primarily from our recommended departments in biology and chemistry.

GROUP I
Most Selective

Albany (SUNY) (NY)	L	Emory (GA)	R
Allegheny (PA)	R	Fairfield (CT)	M
Amherst (MA)	R	Franklin & Marshall (PA)	R
Bates (ME)	R	Furman (SC)	R
Binghamton (SUNY) (NY)	L	Geneseo (SUNY) (NY)	M
Boston Col. (MA)	L	Georgetown (DC)	M
Bowdoin (ME)	R	Gettysburg (PA)	R
Brandeis (MA)	R	Grinnell (IA)	R
Brown (RI)	M	Hamilton (NY)	R
▲ Bryn Mawr (PA)	S	Harvard (MA)	M
Bucknell (PA)	M	Harvey Mudd (CA)	S
Buffalo (SUNY) (NY)	L	Haverford (PA)	S
California Inst. of Tech.	S	Holy Cross (MA)	R
California, U. of (Berkeley)	XL	Illinois, U. of (Urbana-Champagne)	XL
California, U. of (Los Angeles)	XL	Illinois Wesleyan	R
California, U. of (San Diego)	L	Iowa, U. of	XL
Carleton (MN)	R	★ JOHNS HOPKINS (MD)	R
Carnegie-Mellon (PA)	M	Kalamazoo (MI)	R
Case Western Reserve U. (OH)	R	Kenyon (OH)	R
Centre (KY)	S	Knox (IL)	R
Chicago, U. of (IL)	R	Lafayette (PA)	R
Claremont McKenna (CA)	S	Lawrence (WI)	R
Clark (MA)	R	Macalester (MN)	R
Colby (ME)	R	Miami, U. of (FL)	L
Colgate (NY)	R	MIT (MA)	M
Colorado Col.	R	Michigan, U. of	XL
Colorado School of Mines	R	Middlebury (VT)	R
Cornell (NY)	L	▲ Mount Holyoke (MA)	R
Dallas, U. of (TX)	R	New College (FL)	S
Dartmouth (NH)	M	New Jersey, College of	M
Davidson (NC)	R	North Carolina, U. of	L
Dickinson (PA)	M	Northwestern (IL)	M
Duke (NC)	R		

GROUP I continues next page

Enrollment Code

S = Small (less than 1000 students) | M = Medium (3000-8000 students) | XL = Extra Large (over 20,000 students)
R = Moderate (1000-3000 students) | L = Large (8000-20,000 students)

★ THE COUNSELORS' CHOICE ■ Men Only ▲ Women Only

PRE-MED/PRE-DENTAL, *continued*

GROUP I, *continued*

Notre Dame (IN)	M	Trinity (TX)	R
Oberlin (OH)	R	Tufts (MA)	M
Occidental (CA)	R	Tulane (LA)	M
Pomona (CA)	R	Union (NY)	R
Princeton (NJ)	M	Ursinus (PA)	R
Reed (OR)	R	Vanderbilt (TN)	M
Rhodes (TN)	R	Villanova (PA)	M
Rice (TX)	R	■ Wabash (IN)	S
Rochester, U. of (NY)	M	Wake Forest (NC)	M
Rutgers (NJ)	L	Washington U. (MO)	M
Skidmore (NY)	R	▲ Wellesley (MA)	R
▲ Smith (MA)	R	Wesleyan (CT)	R
South, U. of the (TN)	R	Wheaton (IL)	R
Southwestern (TX)	R	Whitman (WA)	R
Stanford (CA)	M	Willamette (OR)	R
Stetson (FL)	R	Williams (MA)	R
St. Mary's College of Maryland	R	William & Mary (VA)	M
St. Olaf (MN)	R	Yale (CT)	M
Swarthmore (PA)	S	Yeshiva (NY)	R
Trinity (CT)	R		

GROUP II
Very Selective

Albertson (ID)	S	Colorado, U. of	L
Albright (PA)	R	Concordia (MN)	R
Alma (MI)	R	Connecticut, U. of	L
Arizona State	XL	Creighton (NE)	R
Austin (TX)	R	Delaware, U. of	L
Baylor (TX)	M	Denison (OH)	R
Bethany (WV)	S	Duquesne (PA)	M
Berry (GA)	R	Earlham (IN)	R
Birmingham-Southern (AL)	R	Eckerd (FL)	R
Butler (IN)	R	Erskine (SC)	S
California, U. of (Davis)	L	Florida State	L
California, U. of (Irvine)	L	Fordham (NY)	M
California, U. of (Riverside)	M	Georgia, U. of	XL
California, U. of (Santa Cruz)	M	Guilford (NC)	R
Carroll (WI)	R	Hamline (MN)	R
College of Charleston (SC)	M		

GROUP II continues next page

Enrollment Code

S = Small (less than 1000 students) **M** = Medium (3000-8000 students) **XL** = Extra Large (over 20,000 students)
R = Moderate (1000-3000 students) **L** = Large (8000-20,000 students)

★ THE COUNSELORS' CHOICE   ■ Men Only   ▲ Women Only

PRE-MED/PRE-DENTAL, *continued*

GROUP II, *continued*

■ Hampden-Sydney (VA)	S	Ohio Wesleyan .... R
Heidelberg (OH)	R	Pacific Lutheran (OR) .... R
Hendrix (AR)	R	Pennsylvania State XL
Hiram (OH)	R	Pittsburgh, U. of (PA) L
Hobart & Wm. Smith (NY)	R	Presbyterian (SC) .... S
Hofstra (NY)	M	Randolph-Macon (VA) .... R
▲ Hood (MD)	S	▲ Randolph-Macon Woman's Col. (VA)... S
Hope (MI)	R	Regis (CO) .... R
Houghton (NY)	S	Ripon (WI) .... S
Houston Baptist (TX)	R	San Francisco, U. of (CA) .... M
Huntingdon (AL)	S	Scranton, U. of (PA) .... M
Indiana U.	XL	▲ Scripps (CA) .... S
Ithaca Col. (NY)	M	Siena (NY) .... R
Juniata (PA)	R	Spring Hill (AL) .... R
Kansas, U. of	L	St. John's (MN) .... R
Kansas State	L	St. Louis (MO) .... M
Kentucky, U. of	L	Saint Thomas, U. of (MN) .... S
Knox (IL)	S	Stetson (FL) .... R
Lake Forest (IL)	S	Stony Brook (SUNY) (NY) L
Lewis & Clark (OR)	R	Transylvania (KY) .... S
Loyola (IL)	M	Truman State (MO) .... M
Loyola (LA)	R	Texas A&M XL
Loyola (MD)	M	Vermont, U. of L
Marquette (WI)	M	Washington & Jefferson (PA) ..... S
Mary Washington (VA)	R	Washington, U. of XL
Massachusetts, U. of	L	▲ Wells (NY) .... S
Michigan State	XL	Western Maryland .... R
Millsaps (MS)	R	Westminster (PA) .... R
Minnesota, U. of (Morris)	R	Westmont (CA) .... R
Morningside (IA)	S	Wheaton (MA) .... R
Muhlenberg (PA)	R	Winona State U. (MN) .... M
Nebraska Wesleyan	R	Wisconsin, U. of XL
New Hampshire, U. of	L	Wittenberg (OH) .... R
New York U.	L	Wofford (SC) .... R
North Central (IL)	R	Wooster (OH) .... R
Ohio State	XL	Wyoming, U. of L

PRE-MED/PRE-DENTAL continues next page

Enrollment Code

S = Small (less than 1000 students)   **M** = Medium (3000-8000 students)   **XL** = Extra Large (over 20,000 students)
R = Moderate (1000-3000 students)   **L** = Large (8000-20,000 students)

★ THE COUNSELORS' CHOICE   ■ Men Only   ▲ Women Only

PRE-MED/PRE-DENTAL, *continued*

GROUP III
Selective

American International (MA) .... R	Louisiana State XL
Benedictine (IL) .... R	Mt. St. Mary's (MD) .... R
▲ Bennett (NC) .... S	▲ Spelman (GA) .... R
Blackburn (IL) .... S	St. Mary's (TX) .... R
Brooklyn Col. (SUNY) (NY) L	St. Vincent (PA) .... R
Carroll (MT) .... R	Temple (PA) L
Delaware Valley (PA) .... R	Thomas More (KY) .... S
DePaul (IL) .... M	Virginia Commonwealth L
East Carolina (NC) L	Virginia Wesleyan .... R
Florida A&M .... M	Wartburg (IA) .... R
Florida Southern .... R	Wayne State (MI) L
Heidelberg (OH) .... S	Xavier U. of Louisiana .... R
Jacksonville (FL) .... R	

PSYCHOLOGY

GROUP I
Most Selective

Allegheny (PA)	R	
Amherst (MA)	R	
▲ Barnard (NY)	R	
Bates (ME)	R	
Binghamton (SUNY) (NY)	L	
Boston U. (MA)	L	
Brandeis (MA)	R	
▲ Bryn Mawr (PA)	S	
Bucknell (PA)	M	
California, U. of (Berkeley)	XL	
California, U. of (Los Angeles)	XL	
California, U. of (San Diego)	L	
Carnegie-Mellon (PA)	M	
Chicago, U. of (IL)	R	
Claremont McKenna (CA)	S	
Colby (ME)	R	
Columbia (NY)	M	
Connecticut Col.	R	
Drew (NJ)	R	
Duke (NC)	M	
Emory (GA)	R	
Furman (SC)	R	
George Washington (DC)	M	
Gettysburg (PA)	R	
Grinnell (IA)	R	
Gustavus Adolphus (MN)	R	
Harvard (MA)	M	
Haverford (PA)	S	
Illinois, U. of (Urbana-Champaign)	XL	
Kenyon (OH)	R	
Lafayette (PA)	R	
Macalester (MN)	R	
Michigan, U. of	XL	
▲ Mount Holyoke (MA)	R	
New College (FL)	S	
New Jersey, College of	M	
New York U.	L	
North Carolina, U. of	L	
Occidental (CA)	R	
Pennsylvania, U. of	L	
Pitzer (CA)	S	
Reed (OR)	R	
Rhodes (TN)	R	
Rochester, U. of (NY)	M	
▲ Simmons (MA)	R	
▲ Smith (MA)	R	
Southwestern (TX)	R	
★ STANFORD (CA)	M	
St. Mary's College of Maryland	R	
St. Olaf (MN)	R	
Swarthmore (PA)	R	
Tufts (MA)	M	
Union (NY)	R	
Vanderbilt (TN)	M	
Vassar (NY)	R	
Virginia, U. of	L	
■ Wabash (IN)	S	
Wake Forest (NC)	M	
Wesleyan (CT)	R	
Whitman (WA)	R	
Willamette (OR)	R	
Williams (MA)	R	
Yale (CT)	M	
Yeshiva (NY)	M	

PSYCHOLOGY continues next page

Enrollment Code

S = Small (less than 1000 students)   M = Medium (3000-8000 students)   XL = Extra Large (over 20,000 students)
R = Moderate (1000-3000 students)   L = Large (8000-20,000 students)

★ THE COUNSELORS' CHOICE   ■ Men Only   ▲ Women Only

PSYCHOLOGY, *continued*

GROUP II
Very Selective

▲ Agnes Scott (GA) .... S	Luther (IA) .... R
Albany (SUNY) (NY)............................. L	Manhattanville (NY) .... R
Alfred (NY) .... R	Marist (NY) ....M
Arizona, U. of XL	Mary Washington (VA) .... R
Beloit (WI) .... R	Michigan State XL
Berry (GA) .... R	▲ Mills (CA) .... S
California, U. of (Riverside) ....M	Minnesota, U. of...................................XL
California, U. of (Santa Cruz) ....M	New Paltz (SUNY) (NY) ....M
Carroll (WI) .... R	North Carolina (Asheville)..................... R
Chapman (CA) .... R	Ohio U. L
Clark (MA) .... R	Oregon, U. of L
Colorado State L	Oswego (SUNY) (NY) ....M
Concordia (MN) .... R	Pace (NY) ....M
Cornell Col. (IA) .... R	Pittsburgh, U. of (PA) L
Denison (OH).. R	Queens (CUNY) (NY) L
Denver, U. of (CO) ....M	Randolph-Macon (VA).......................... R
Earlham (IN) .... R	Roanoke (VA) .... R
Fairfield (CT)..M	▲ Randolph-Macon Woman's Col. (VA) ... S
Florida Inst. of Tech. .... R	Rollins (FL).. R
Florida International L	Salisbury State (MD) ....M
Florida State L	San Francisco, U. of (CA) ....M
George Mason (VA) L	Santa Clara, U. of (CA) ....M
Grand Valley (MI) L	Shepherd (WV) .... R
Hamline (MN).. R	Southern California L
Hanover (IN) .... S	St. Lawrence (NY) .... R
Herbert Lehman (CUNY) (NY) L	Stetson (FL) .... R
Hobart & Wm. Smith (NY) .... R	Stonehill (MA).. R
Houghton (NY)...................................... S	Stony Brook (SUNY) (NY) L
Hunter (CUNY) (NY).............................L	▲ Sweet Briar (VA) .... S
Indiana U. XL	Syracuse (NY) L
Iowa, U. of XL	Texas, U. of (Austin)............................XL
Lake Forest (IL) .... S	Tulsa, U. of (OK) .... R
Lebanon Valley (PA).............................. R	Virginia Poly. Inst. L
Louisiana State U..................................L	Washington College (MD) .... S
Loyola (IL)..M	*GROUP II continues next page*

PSYCHOLOGY, *continued*

GROUP II, *continued*

Washington & Jefferson (PA)	S	Westmont (CA)	R
Washington, U. of	XL	Wheaton (MA)	R
Webster (MO)	R	Wisconsin, U. of	XL
▲ Wells (NY)	S	Wittenberg (OH)	R
Western Michigan	L	Wofford (SC)	M
Westminster (MO)	S		

GROUP III
Selective

American International (MA)	R	▲ Mary Baldwin (VA)	S
Aquinas (MI)	R	Mercy (NY)	M
Baker (KS)	S	Montclair State (NJ)	M
Beaver (PA)	R	Northern Arizona	L
Bethel (MN)	R	North Carolina (Wilmington)	M
Biola (CA)	R	Otterbein (OH)	R
Blackburn (IL)	S	Ozarks, College of the (MO)	R
Caldwell (NJ)	S	Palm Beach Atlantic (FL)	R
California Lutheran	R	Purchase (SUNY) (NY)	R
Canisius (NY)	M	Regis (CO)	R
Carthage (WI)	R	▲ Rosemont (PA)	S
▲ Cedar Crest (PA)	S	Sacred Heart (CT)	R
Chapman (CA)	R	St. Joseph's (IN)	S
Colorado, U. of (Colorado Springs)	M	St. Vincent (PA)	R
Elmira (NY)	R	Seton Hall (NJ)	M
Franciscan U. of Steubenville (OH)	R	Sonoma State (CA)	M
▲ Hollins (VA)	S	Taylor (IN)	R
▲ Judson (AL)	S	Virginia Commenwealth U.	L
Lindenwood (MO)	S	Virginia Wesleyan	R
Longwood (VA)	R	Western New England (MA)	R
Lyon (AR)	S	Wyoming, U. of	L
Manchester (IN)	R	Xavier University of Louisiana	R

RELIGIOUS STUDIES

GROUP I
Most Selective

▲ Barnard (NY) .... R
Bates (ME) .... R
Brown (RI) ....M
California, U. of (Berkeley) XL
Chicago, U. of (IL) ....M
Colgate (NY)....................................... R
Columbia (NY) ....M
Dartmouth (NH) ....M
Davidson (NC)...................................... R
Dickinson (PA) .... R
Duke (NC) ....M
Emory (GA) .... R
Furman (SC) .... R
Georgetown, (DC)................................M
Hamilton (NY) .... R
Haverford (PA) .... S
Kenyon (OH).. R

Lawrence (WI) .... R
Northwestern (IL) ....M
Oberlin (OH) .... R
Occidental (CA) .... R
Pomona (CA) .... R
Princeton (NJ) ....M
South, U. of the (TN) .... R
Stanford (CA) ....M
Trinity (CT) .... R
★ **VIRGINIA, U. OF** L
Wake Forest (NC) ....M
▲ Wellesley (MA) .... R
Wesleyan (CT) .... R
Wheaton (IL) .... R
William & Mary (VA) ....M
Yale (CT)..M

GROUP II
Very Selective

Arizona State XL
Baylor (TX)...M
Birmingham-Southern (AL) .... R
Brigham Young (UT) XL
California, U. of (Santa Barbara)...........L
Catholic U. (DC) ....M
Florida State...L
Fordham (NY) ....M
Gordon (MA) .... R
Guilford (NC) .... R
Hendrix (AR) .... R
Hiram (OH) .... R

Houghton (NY)..................................... S
Iowa, U. of XL
Loyola (LA) ....M
Roanoke (VA) .... R
Southern Methodist (TX) L
St. Bonaventure (NY) .... R
Stony Brook (SUNY) (NY) L
Texas Christian U. ....M
Westmont (CA)..................................... R
Whitworth (WA) .... R
Wooster (OH) .... R

GROUP III
Selective

Franciscan U. of Steubenville (OH) ...... R
King (TN) .... S
Milligan (TN)....................................... S
Mississippi College .... R
Regis (CO)... R

Taylor (IN) .... R
▲ St. Catherine (MN) .... R R
Southwest Baptist (MO) .... R
Union University (TN) .... R
Virginia Commonwealth U. L

SOCIOLOGY

GROUP I
Most Selective

Amherst (MA)	R
▲ Barnard (NY)	R
▲ Bryn Mawr (PA)	S
California, U. of (Berkeley)	XL
California, U. of (Los Angeles)	XL
★ CHICAGO, U. OF (IL)	R
Clarkson (NY)	M
Colby (ME)	R
Columbia (NY)	M
Dartmouth (NH)	M
Florida, U. of	XL
Franklin & Marshall (PA)	R
Gettysburg (PA)	S
Haverford (PA)	S
Illinois, U. of (Urbana-Champaign)	XL
Kalamazoo (MI)	R
Michigan, U. of	XL
North Carolina, U. of	L
Northwestern (IL)	M
Oberlin (OH)	R
Pennsylvania, U. of	L
Pitzer (CA)	S
Southwestern (TX)	R
Stanford (CA)	M
Wheaton (IL)	R

GROUP II
Very Selective

Asbury (KY)	R
Beloit (WI)	R
Concordia (MN)	R
Cornell Col. (IA)	R
Covenant (GA)	S
Earlham (IN)	R
Hamline (MN)	R
Hanover (IN)	R
Hendrix (AR)	R
Hofstra (NY)	M
Knox (IL)	S
Lewis & Clark (OR)	R
Manhattanville (NY)	R
Minnesota, U. of	XL
Moravian (PA)	R
North Carolina (Asheville)	R
Puget Sound (WA)	R
Roanoke (VA)	R
▲ Salem Col. (NC)	S
St. Lawrence (NY)	R
St. Mary's Col. (CA)	R
Syracuse (NY)	L
▲ Trinity (DC)	S
▲ Wells (NY)	S
Westminster (PA)	R
Western Maryland College	R
Western Washington U.	L
Wheaton (MA)	R
Winona State U. (MN)	M
Wisconsin, U. of	XL
Wisconsin, U. of (Stevens Point)	M
Wooster (OH)	R

SOCIOLOGY continues next page

Enrollment Code
S = Small (less than 1000 students) | M = Medium (3000-8000 students) | XL = Extra Large (over 20,000 students)
R = Moderate (1000-3000 students) | L = Large (8000-20,000 students)
★ THE COUNSELORS' CHOICE ■ Men Only ▲ Women Only

SOCIOLOGY, *continued*

GROUP III
Selective

Adrian (MI) .... S	Massachusetts, U. of (Dartmouth) ....M
Belmont Abbey (NC) .... S	Michigan State XL
Benedictine (KS) .... S	North Carolina, U. of (Wilmington) ......M
Biola (CA) .... R	Northern Colorado L
Doane (NE) .... S	Quincy (IL) .... R
D'Youville (NY) .... R	▲ St. Catherine (MN) .... R
Eastern (PA) .... R	San Francisco State (CA) L
Fisk (TN) .... S	▲ Spelman (GA) .... R
George Fox (OR) .... S	St. Anselm (NH) .... R
Hartwick (NY) .... R	St. Mary's U. of San Antonio (TX) .... R
Johnson C. Smith (NC) .... R	Temple (PA) L
Lenoir-Rhyne (NC) .... R	Virginia Wesleyan .... R
Lynchburg (VA) .... R	Wagner (NY) .... R
▲ Mary Baldwin (VA) .... S	Whitman (WA) .... R
Massachusetts, U. of (Boston) ....M	▲ Wilson (PA) .... S

ZOOLOGY

GROUP I
Most Selective

California, U. of (Berkeley) XL	Michigan, U. of XL
★ CORNELL (NY) L	North Carolina, U. of L
Duke (NC) .... M	Pennsylvania State XL
Florida, U. of XL	Wisconsin, U. of XL
Miami, U. of (OH) L	

GROUP II
Very Selective

Albertson (ID) .... S	Massachusetts, U. of L
California, U. of (Davis) L	North Carolina State L
Connecticut, U. of L	Ohio U. L
Georgia, U. of L	Oklahoma, U. of L
Indiana U. XL	Texas A&M XL
Iowa State XL	Vermont, U. of L
Kansas, U. of L	Washington State L
Kentucky, U. of XL	Washington, U. of XL
Maryland, U. of XL	

GROUP III
Selective

Colorado State L	Southern Illinois U. (Carbondale) L
Howard (DC) .... M	Tennessee, U. of XL
Montana, U. of .... M	Wyoming, U. of L
Oregon State L	

SECTION TWO

MISCELLANEOUS MAJORS

AFRO-AMERICAN STUDIES

Bates (ME)
California, U. of (Berkeley)
California, U. of (Santa Barbara)
Chicago, U. of (IL)
Columbia (NY)
Denison (OH)
Duke (NC)
Earlham (IN)
Emory (GA)
Harvard (MA)
Howard (DC)
Kalamazoo (MI)
Loyola Marymount (CA)
Luther (IA)
Mercer (GA)
New York U.
North Carolina (Chapel Hill)
Oberlin (OH)

Ohio State U.
Pennsylvania, U. of
Pomona (CA)
Princeton (NJ)
Rutgers (NJ)
San Diego State (CA)
San Francisco State (CA)
▲ Spelman (GA)
Stanford (CA)
Tuskegee University (AL)
Vassar (NY)
Washington U. (MO)
▲ Wellesley (MA)
Wesleyan (CT)
Wooster (OH)
Wisconsin, U. of
Xavier (LA)
Yale (CT)

ALTERNATIVE COLLEGES *(see page ix)*

Antioch (OH)
Atlantic, College of the (ME)
Deep Springs (CA)
Eugene Lang (NY)
Evergreen (WA)
Hampshire (MA)
Marlboro (VT)

New College (FL)
New School for Social
   Research (NY)
St. John's (MD)
Shimer (IL)
Simon's Rock (MA)

ARCHAEOLOGY

Baylor (TX)
Boston U. (MA)
Brown (RI)
▲ Bryn Mawr (PA)
Cornell (NY)
Dartmouth (NH)
Evansville (IN)
Haverford (PA)
Hunter (CUNY) (NY)

Kansas, U. of
Michigan, U. of
Missouri, U. of
New York U.
Pennsylvania, U. of
Texas, U. of
Washington U. (MO)
Washington, U. of
Wheaton (IL)

ATMOSPHERIC SCIENCES

Albany (SUNY) (NY)
California, U. of (Davis)
Colorado State
Cornell (NY)
Florida Inst. of Tech.
Florida State
Hawaii
Iowa State
Kansas
Lyndon State (VT)
Massachusetts (Lowell)
Metropolitan State (CO)
North Carolina State

North Dakota, U. of
Northern Illinois
Oklahoma, U. of
Oneonta (SUNY) (NY)
Pennsylvania State
Purdue (IN)
San Jose State (CA)
St. Louis University (MO)
Texas A&M
Utah, U. of
Washington, U. of
Western Connecticut
Wisconsin, U. of

■ Men Only
▲ Women Only

AUDIOLOGY/SPEECH

Arizona
Arizona State
Boston U.
Buffalo (SUNY) (NY)
California, U. of (Santa Barbara)
Florida
Florida State
Geneseo (SUNY) (NY)
George Washington
Hawaii
Hofstra (NY)
James Madison (VA)
Kansas
Longwood (VA)
Michigan State
Montana
Montevallo (AL)
Nebraska

No. Colorado
No. Iowa
No. Michigan
Oklahoma
Purdue (IN)
Rhode Island
S. Dakota, U. of
Tennessee
Texas
Tulsa (OK)
Utah State
Vanderbilt (TN)
Washington, U. of
Wayne State (MI)
Western Washington
Worcester State (MA)
Wisconsin
Wyoming

BUSINESS STATISTICS

Arizona State
Baylor (TX)
Cleveland State (OH)
Cornell (NY)
Illinois (Chicago)
Illinois, U. of

Indiana U.
New Hampshire College
Pennsylvania State
Tennessee, U. of
Wright State (OH)

CERAMICS

Alfred (NY)
California State U. (Long Beach)
Cleveland Institute of Art (OH)
Clemson (SC)
East Carolina (NC)
Florida, U. of
Hartford, U. of (CT)
Iowa State
Illinois, U. of
Kansas City Art Institute (MO)

Maryland Inst. College of Art
Massachusetts College of Art
Otis/Parsons School of Art &
   Design (CA)
Parsons School of Design (NY)
Rhode Island School of Design
Ringling School of Art &
   Design (FL)
Temple (PA)
Washington, U. of

CINEMATOGRAPHY/FILM STUDIES

Boston U. (MA)
Brooks Institute of Photography
   (CA)
California, U. of (Berkeley)
California, U. of (Irvine)
California, U. of (Santa Barbara)
California, U. of (Santa Cruz)
California Institute of the Arts
Carleton (MN)
Colorado, U. of
Cincinnati, U. of (OH)
Columbia (NY)
Delaware, U. of

Duke (NC)
Emerson (MA)
Florida State
Hampshire (MA)
Howard (DC)
Ithaca (NY)
Kansas
Massachusetts College of Art
Memphis State (TN)
New York U.
Northwestern (IL)
Pennsylvania State

CINEMATOGRAPHY/FILM continues next page

■ Men Only
▲ Women Only

CINEMATOGRAPHY/FILM STUDIES, *CONTINUED*

Pittsburgh, U. of (PA)
Purdue (IN)
Rutgers (NJ)
St. Olaf (MN)
Santa Fe (NM)

Southern California
Temple (PA)
Texas, U. of
Wayne State (MI)
Webster (MO)

CREATIVE WRITING

▲ Agnes Scott (GA)
Alabama, U. of
Albertson (ID)
Bard (NY)
▲ Barnard (NY)
Beloit (WI)
Bennington (VT)
Brown (RI)
Carnegie Mellon (PA)
Columbia (NY)
Creighton (NE)
Eckerd (FL)
Emerson (MA)
Florida State
Grinnell (IA)
Hamilton (NY)
Hobart & Wm. Smith (NY)
Iowa
Johns Hopkins (MD)

Michigan, U. of
North Carolina State
Northwestern (IL)
Oberlin (OH)
Pittsburgh, U. of (PA)
Redlands (CA)
St. Andrews (NC)
Santa Fe, College of (NM)
Sarah Lawrence (NY)
▲ Stephens (MO)
Susquehanna (PA)
▲ Sweet Briar (VA)
Temple (PA)
Virginia
Washington College (MD)
Webster (MO)
Wheaton (MA)
Wittenberg (OH)

CRIMINAL JUSTICE

Albany (SUNY) (NY)
Bowling Green (OH)
California State U. (Fresno)
California State U. (Fullerton)
California State U. (Los Angeles)
California State U. (Sacramento)
California, U. of (Irvine)
Dayton, U. of (OH)
Delaware, U. of
Eastern Kentucky
Elmira (NY)
Florida Southern
Florida State
George Washington (DC)
Guilford (NC)
Hamline (MN)
Indiana
Iona (NY)
Kentucky Wesleyan
Lindenwood (MO)
Loyola (LA)
Lycoming (PA)
Madonna (MI)
Mansfield (PA)
Marist (NY)
Marshall (WV)

Massachusetts State College
 (Westfield)
Mercy (NY)
Mercyhurst (PA)
Michigan State
North Carolina (Chapel Hill)
North CarolinaWesleyan
Northeastern (MA)
No. Florida
Ohio Northern
Regis (CO)
Ripon (WI)
Rowan (NJ)
St. Edward's (TX)
Salve Regina—The Newport
 College (RI)
St. John's (NY)
St. Leo (FL)
San Diego State (CA)
Seton Hall (NJ)
Southern Oregon
Southwest Texas
Wilmington (OH)
Wisconsin (Platteville)
Youngstown State (OH)

■ Men Only
▲ Women Only

DESIGN/COMMERCIAL ART

Alfred (NY)
Bradley (IL)
Brigham Young (UT)
Calif. Inst. of the Arts
California State U. (Long
  Beach)
California, U. of (Davis)
California, U. of (Los Angeles)
Columbia (IL)
Cincinnati, U. of (OH)
Cornish (WA)
Drake (IA)
Edgewood (WI)
Fashion Inst. of Tech. (NY)
Flagler (FL)
Illinois Institute of Technology
Illinois, U. of
Kansas City Art Institute (MO)
Kendall Coll. of Art & Design
  (MI)
Kent State (OH)

Maryland, U. of
Massachusetts College of Art
Massachusetts, U. of
  (Dartmouth)
Memphis College of Art
Moravian (PA)
Morningside (IA)
North Carolina State
North Florida, U. of
Ohio State
Otis Art Institute/Parsons (CA)
Parsons School of Design (NY)
Pratt Institute (NY)
Rhode Island School of Design
Rochester Inst. of Tech. (NY)
St. Mary's (MN)
Shepherd (WV)
Southern Illinois U.
Texas Christian
West Virginia Wesleyan

EAST ASIAN STUDIES

▲ Bryn Mawr (PA)
Bucknell (PA)
California, U. of (Davis)
California, U. of (San Diego)
Chicago, U. of (IL)
Columbia (NY)
Cornell (NY)
DePauw (IN)
Furman (SC)
Harvard (MA)
Indiana
Lawrence (WI)
Lewis & Clark (OR)
Macalester (MN)

Manhattanville (NY)
Middlebury (VT)
Oberlin (OH)
Pennsylvania, U. of
Redlands (CA)
Stanford (CA)
Trinity (TX)
Ursinus (PA)
Vassar (NY)
Washington & Lee (VA)
Washington, U. of
▲ Wellesley (MA)
Wesleyan (CT)
Wittenberg (OH)

ENTREPRENEUR STUDIES

Arizona, U. of
Babson (MA)
Ball State U. (IN)
Baylor (TX)
Boise State U. (ID)
Colorado, U. of
Ferris State U. (MI)
Georgia, U. of
Indiana U.
Illinois

Kennesaw (GA)
Michigan
Muhlenberg (PA)
New York U.
Ohio University
Pennsylvania, U. of
Rennselaer (NY)
Southern California, U. of
Texas, U. of
Washington & Jefferson (PA)

■ Men Only
▲ Women Only

ENVIRONMENTAL STUDIES

Adelphi (NY)
Allegheny (PA)
Bates (ME)
Bethany (WV)
Bowdoin (ME)
Brown (RI)
▲ Bryn Mawr (PA)
California, U. of (Davis)
California, U. of (Irvine)
California, U. of (Riverside)
California, U. of (Santa Barbara)
California, U. of (Santa Cruz)
California State U. (Humboldt)
Case Western Reserve (OH)
Centenary (LA)
Chicago, U. of (IL)
Clemson (SC)
Colby (ME)
Colorado, U. of
Connecticut College
Cornell (NY)
Delaware Valley (PA)
Denison (OH)
Dickinson (PA)
Dubuque (IA)
Earlham (IN)
Eckerd (FL)
Findlay (OH)
Florida, U. of
Florida Institute of Technology
Harvard (MA)
Idaho
Kalamazoo (MI)
Kentucky Wesleyan
Lake Forest (IL)
Macalester (MN)
Michigan, U. of
Michigan State
Middlebury (VT)
Millsaps (MS)
Minnesota, U. of
Monmouth (IL)

Montreat (NC)
New Hampshire, U. of
New Mexico State
North Carolina (Asheville)
Northland (WI)
Oberlin (OH)
Ohio Wesleyan
Oregon State
Pennsylvania State
Pennsylvania, U. of
Pittsburgh (Bradford)
Pittsburgh, U. of (PA)
Pitzer (CA)
Ramapo (NJ)
Rutgers (NJ)
Sacred Heart (CT)
Santa Fe, College of (NM)
Sarah Lawrence (NY)
St. Lawrence (NY)
St. Michael's (VT)
San Francisco State (CA)
South Florida
Stanford (CA)
Stockton State (NJ)
SUNY Coll. of Env. Sci. & Forestry
Susquehanna (PA)
Tufts U. (MA)
Valparaiso (IN)
Vermont, U. of
Warren Wilson (NC)
Washington State
Washington, U. of
Webster (MO)
Wesleyan (CT)
Western Washington
West Virginia Wesleyan
Whitman (WA)
Wisconsin, U. of (Stevens Point)
Wyoming, U. of
Yale (CT)

EQUESTRIAN STUDIES

Averett (VA)
Bluefield College (VA)
Centenary (NJ)
Colorado State
Delaware Valley (PA)
Findlay (OH)
Lake Erie (OH)

Otterbein (OH)
St. Andrews (NC)
▲ Stephens (MO)
Truman State (MO)
William Woods (MO)
▲ Wilson (PA)

■ Men Only
▲ Women Only

FASHION DESIGN/MERCHANDISING

Arkansas, U. of
Auburn (AL)
Baylor (TX)
Bradley (IL)
Cincinnati (OH)
Delaware, U. of
Fashion Inst. of Tech. (NY)
Florida State
Indiana (PA)
Iowa State
Kent State (OH)
Madonna (MI)
▲ Meredith (NC)
New Hampshire College
Ohio U.

Oregon State
Philadelphia Col. Tex. & Sci. (PA)
Pratt (NY)
Purdue (IN)
Rhode Island School of Design
Rhode Island, U. of
Sanford (AL)
▲ Stephens (MO)
Texas Christian
Valparaiso (IN)
Vermont, U. of
Virginia Commonwealth
Western Washington
Wisconsin, U. of

HEALTH SERVICES ADMINISTRATION

Alfred (NY)
Appalachian State (NC)
Augustana (SD)
Baylor (TX)
Detroit Mercy (MI)
Eastern Michigan
Fisk (TN)
Herbert Lehman (CUNY) (NY)
Kentucky
Missouri, U. of
North Carolina (Chapel Hill)
Northeastern (MA)

Northern Michigan
Oregon State
Pennsylvania State
Providence College (RI)
Quinnipiac (CT)
Saint Scholastica (MN)
Scranton (PA)
Spring Arbor (MI)
Stonehill (MA)
Washington, U. of
Winona State (MN)

HISPANIC STUDIES

Arizona, U. of
California, U. of (Berkeley)
California, U. of (Santa Barbara)
CUNY (Hunter)
Northern Colorado
Northridge State (CA)
Northwestern (IL)

Rutgers (NJ)
San Francisco State (CA)
Scripps (CA)
Sonoma State (CA)
Wheaton (MA)
Willamette (OR)

HOTEL AND RESTAURANT MANAGEMENT

Ashland (OH)
Auburn (NY)
Cal Poly (Pomona)
Cornell (NY)
Delaware
Denver, U. of (CO)
Fairleigh Dickinson (NJ)
Florida International U.
Florida State
Hawaii, U. of
Houston, U. of (TX)
Illinois, U. of
Iowa State
James Madison (VA)
Kansas State

Massachusetts, U. of
Michigan State
Nevada (Las Vegas)
New Hampshire College
New Hampshire, U. of
Niagara (NY)
Northern Arizona
North Texas
Ohio U.
Oklahoma State
Penn State
Purdue (IN)
Rochester Inst. of Tech. (NY)
St. Leo (FL)

■ Men Only
▲ Women Only

HOTEL/RESTAURANT MGT. continues next page

HOTEL AND RESTAURANT MANAGEMENT, *continued*

South Carolina, U. of
Texas Tech
Transylvania (KY)
Virginia Poly. Inst.

Washington State
Widener (PA)
Wisconsin (Stout)

HUMAN RESOURCES

American (DC)
Bethel (KS)
Boise State (ID)
Bowling Green (OH)
Cal Poly (Pomona)
Duquesne (PA)
Florida State
George Fox (OR)
George Washington (DC)
Indiana (PA)
LeMoyne (NY)
Massachusetts, U. of
   (Dartmouth)
Montana, U. of

Muhlenberg (PA)
New Mexico, U. of
Northeastern (MA)
Ohio State
Palm Beach Atlantic (FL)
Ohio University
Rockhurst (MO)
Susquehanna (PA)
Washington & Jefferson (PA)
Wayne State (MI)
Wilmington (OH)
Winona State (MN)
Wisconsin (Milwaukee)

INDUSTRIAL ARTS

Berea (KY)
California (PA)
California State U. (Fresno)
Cheyney (PA)
Clemson (SC)
Ferris State (MI)
Fitchburg (MA)
Idaho
Millersville (PA)
Montclair (NJ)
Nebraska, U. of

Northern Colorado
Northern Illinois
Oswego (SUNY) (NY)
Pittsburgh, U. of (PA)
Purdue (IN)
Southern Illinois
Texas A&M
Western Michigan
Wisconsin, U. of (Stout)
Wyoming

INTERNATIONAL RELATIONS/STUDIES

▲ Agnes Scott (GA)
Alma (MI)
American U. (DC)
Beloit (WI)
Bethany (WV)
Boston U. (MA)
Brown (RI)
▲ Bryn Mawr (PA)
Bucknell (PA)
☎ Butler (IN)
California State U. (Los Angeles)
California State U. (Sacramento)
California, U. of (Davis)
Claremont McKenna (CA)
Colby (ME)
Colgate (NY)
Colorado
Connecticut College
Dartmouth (NH)

Davidson (NC)
Denison (OH)
Denver, U. of (CO)
DePaul (IL)
☎ Dickinson (PA)
☎ Drake (IA)
☎ Eckerd (FL)
☎ Elizabethtown (PA)
☎ Elmira (NY)
Emory (GA)
Evansville (IN)
☎ Florida International
George Washington (DC)
Georgetown (DC)
Goucher (MD)
Hamline (MN)
☎ Hawaii
☎ Hiram (OH)

INTERNATIONAL RELATIONS continues next page

■ Men Only
▲ Women Only

INTERNATIONAL RELATIONS/STUDIES, *continued*

☎ Husson (ME)
Johns Hopkins (MD)
Juniata (PA)
☎ Illinois
Indiana
Kalamazoo (MI)
Kenyon (OH)
☎ Lenoir-Rhyne (NC)
Lewis & Clark (OR)
Macalester (MN)
Manhattanville (NY)
Miami, U. of (FL)
Middlebury (VT)
Mississippi, U. of
☎ Moravian (PA)
Mt. Holyoke (MA)
Mt. St. Mary's (MD)
Nebraska
North Carolina (Chapel Hill)
Oglethorpe (GA)
Ohio Wesleyan
Pacific, U. of the (CA)
Pennsylvania, U. of
Pepperdine (CA)
Pittsburgh, U. of
Pitzer (CA)
Pomona (CA)
Princeton (NJ)
▲ Randolph-Macon Woman's Col. (VA)

Redlands (CA)
Rhodes (TN)
☎ Rochester Inst. of Tech. (NY)
San Diego, U. of (CA)
☎ Santa Clara U. (CA)
Scranton, U. of (PA)
▲ Scripps (CA)
☎ South Carolina, U. of
Southwestern (TX)
Spring Hill (AL)
☎ St. Andrews (NC)
▲ St. Catherine (MN)
☎ St. Louis U. (MO)
☎ St. Mary's (MN)
☎ St. Norbert (WI)
St. Olaf (MN)
▲ Sweet Briar (VA)
▲ Trinity (DC)
Tufts (MA)
Tulane (LA)
U. S. Air Force Academy (CO)
U. S. Military Academy (NY)
Vassar (NY)
Washington College (MD)
Westminster (MO)
Wheaton (MA)
Whittier (CA)
William & Mary (VA)
Wisconsin, U. of
Wittenberg (OH)

☎ *International Business*

JAPANESE STUDIES

Bucknell (PA)
California, U. of (Los Angeles)
California, U. of (Santa Barbara)
Earlham (IN)
Georgetown (DC)
Hawaii, U. of
Macalester (MN)

Michigan, U. of
Minnesota, U. of
North Central (IL)
Pacific, U. of the (CA)
San Francisco State (CA)
Stanford (CA)
Washington, U. of
Washington U. (MO)

JAZZ

Arizona State
Arizona, U. of
Auburn (AL)
Augustana (IL)
Bennington College (VT)
Berklee College of Music (MA)
California State U. (Los Angeles)
Cincinnati
Delaware
DePaul U. (IL)
Duquesne U. (PA)
Five Towns College (NY)

Hampshire College (MA)
Hartford (CT)
Idaho
Iowa
Indiana U.
Indiana U. (PA)
Loyola U. (New Orleans) (LA)
Manhattan School of Music (NY)
Mannes College of Music (NY)
Marlboro College (VT)
Miami (FL)

■ Men Only
▲ Women Only

JAZZ continues next page

JAZZ, continued

New England Conservatory of
  Music (MA)
New York U. (NY)
North Florida
North Texas
Oberlin College (OH)
Ohio State U. (OH)
Rochester (NY)
Rutgers (NJ)

Shenandoah U. (VA)
South Florida
Temple U. (PA)
Tennessee
Washington, U. of
Webster U. (MO)
Western Michigan U.
Westfield State (MA)

MARINE SCIENCE

Barry (FL)
California State U. (Long
  Beach)
California State U. (Sonoma)
California U. of (Santa Barbara)
California U. of (Santa Cruz)
College of Charleston (SC)
Eckerd (FL)
Farleigh Dickinson (NJ)
Florida Inst. of Technology
Jacksonville U. (FL)
Juniata (PA)
Long Island U. (Southampton)
  (NY)

Miami, U. of (FL)
New College (FL)
North Carolina, U. of
  (Wilmington)
Occidental (CA)
South Carolina, U. of
Spring Hill (AL)
Tampa, U. of (FL)
Texas A&M
Texas A&M (Galveston)
U. S. Coast Guard Academy
  (CT)
Washington, U. of
Wittenberg (OH)

MEDICAL TECHNOLOGY

Bowling Green (OH)
Bradley (IL)
Buffalo (SUNY) (NY)
California State U. (Bakers-
  field)
California, U. of (Davis)
Case Western Reserve U. (OH)
Creighton (NE)
Detroit Mercy (MI)
Florida State
Florida, U. of
▲ Hood (MD)
Humboldt (CA)
Maine, U. of
Marquette (WI)
▲ Mary Baldwin (VA)
Massachusetts, U. of (Dartmouth)
Mercy (NY)
Miami U. (OH)

Michigan State
Minnesota, U. of
Moravian (PA)
New Hampshire, U. of
North Carolina (Chapel Hill)
North Dakota State
North Dakota, U. of
Northeastern (MA)
Quinnipiac (CT)
St. Leo (FL)
▲ St. Mary's (IN)
San Francisco State (CA)
Texas Tech
Utah, U. of
Virginia Commonwealth
Washington & Jefferson (PA)
Washington, U. of
Wisconsin, U. of

NAVAL ARCHITECTURE

California Maritime Academy
Iowa State
Michigan, U. of
Texas A&M (Galveston)
U. S. Coast Guard Academy (CT)

U. S. Merchant Marine
  Academy (NY)
U. S. Naval Academy
Webb Institute (NY)
Wisconsin, U. of

■ Men Only
▲ Women Only

OCCUPATIONAL THERAPY

Boston U. (MA)
Buffalo (SUNY) (NY)
Colorado State
Creighton (NB)
Elizabethtown (PA)
Florida, U. of
Illinois (Chicago)
Kansas, U. of
Minnesota, U. of
Misericordia, College (PA)
New England, U. of (ME)
New Hampshire, U. of
New York University

North Dakota, U. of
Ohio State
Puget Sound (WA)
St. Ambrose (IA)
▲ St. Catherine (MN)
San Jose State (CA)
▲ Texas Woman's
Tufts (MA)
Utica College (NY)
Washington U. (MO)
Washington, U. of
Wayne State (MI)
Western Michigan

PARKS AND RECREATION SERVICES

Arizona State
Aurora (IL)
Ball State (IN)
Bowling Green (OH)
California Poly (Pomona)
California State (Chico)
California State (Fresno)
Catawba (NC)
Clemson (SC)
Colorado State
Delaware, U. of
Florida International
Florida State
Idaho
Illinois, U. of
Indiana U.
Kansas State
Longwood (VA)
Maine, U. of
Michigan State

Minnesota
Montana
North Carolina State
Northern Arizona
Ohio U.
Pennsylvania State
Pepperdine (CA)
Pfeiffer (NC)
Purdue (IN)
Shepherd (WV)
Slippery Rock (PA)
Springfield College (MA)
Texas A&M
Virginia Wesleyan
Western Washington
Wingate (NC)
Winona State (MN)
Wisconsin (LaCrosse)
Wisconsin (Stevens Point)

PHYSICAL EDUCATION

Bemidji State (MN)
California, U. of (Santa Barbara)
Colorado, U. of
Colorado State
Cortland State (NY)
Elon (NC)
Florida State
Florida, U. of
Georgia, U. of
Iowa, U. of
Ithaca (NY)
Johnson C. Smith (NC)
Kansas State
Kansas, U. of
Linfield (OR)
Maine, U. of

Michigan State
Monmouth (IL)
North Carolina, U. of
Norwich (VT)
Oberlin (OH)
Occidental (CA)
Oregon State
Pacific U. (OR)
Pennsylvania State
Purdue (IN)
Rockford (L)
▲ Simmons (MA)
Slippery Rock (PA)
Springfield (MA)
Texas, U. of

PHYSICAL EDUCATION continues next page

■ Men Only
▲ Women Only

PHYSICAL EDUCATION, *continued*

Ursinus (PA)
Washington State
Westerm Washington

Westmont (CA)
William & Mary (VA)
Wisconsin (LaCrosse)

PHYSICAL THERAPY

American International (MA)
Boston U. (MA)
Buffalo (SUNY) (NY)
California State U. (Long Beach)
California State U. (Fresno)
Colorado, U. of
Connecticut, U. of
D'Youville (NY)
Daemen (NY)
Duquesne (PA)
Evansville (IN)
Florida, U. of
Grand Valley (MI)
Hunter (CUNY) (NY)
Ithaca (NY)
Kentucky, U. of
Louisville, U. of (KY)
Marquette (WI)
Maryville (St. Louis) (MO)
Miami, U. of (FL)
Misericordia, College
Montana, U. of
Mount St. Joseph (OH)
Mt. St. Mary's (CA)
Nebraska, U. of
New England, U. of (ME)
Northeastern (MA)

Northwestern (IL)
Oakland (MI)
Ohio University
Pacific U. (OR)
Philadelphia College of Pharmacy & Science
Pittsburgh, U. of (PA)
Puget Sound (WA)
Quinnipiac (CT)
Rockhurst (MO)
Sage Colleges (NY)
Saint Scholastica (MN)
St. Louis U. (MO)
Scranton, U. of (PA)
Seton Hall (NJ)
▲ Simmons (MA)
Slippery Rock (PA)
Southern Oregon
Southwest Texas State
Springfield College (MA)
Temple (PA)
Texas Tech
▲ Texas Woman's
Utah
Vermont, U. of
Washington U. (MO)
Wisconsin (LaCrosse)
Wisconsin, U. of

PRE-VETERINARY

Auburn (AL)
California, U. of (Davis)
Clemson (SC)
Colorado State
Delaware Valley (PA)
Evansville, U. of (IN)
Fort Lewis (CO)
Humboldt State (CA)
Idaho, U. of
Kansas State
Lawrence (WI)
Loyola (CA)
Maryland, U. of
Michigan State
Minnesota, U. of
Montana, U. of
Moravian (PA)
Muskingham (OH)
Nevada, U. of (Reno)

New Hampshire, U. of
New Mexico State
Northland (WI)
Oklahoma State
Purdue (IN)
▲ Russell Sage (The Sage Colleges) (NY)
▲ Salem (NC)
Southern Mississippi, U. of
Susquehanna (PA)
Tennessee, U. of
Utah State
Virginia Wesleyan
Washington & Jefferson (PA)
Washington State
West Virginia Wesleyan
Wilmington (OH)
Wingate (NC)
Winona State (MN)

■ Men Only
▲ Women Only

SOCIAL AND REHABILITATION SERVICES

Arizona, U. of
Assumption (MA)
Auburn (AL)
Boston U. (MA)
California State (Los Angeles)
Florida State
Gustavus Adolphus (MN)
Iowa, U. of
Louisiana State
Marshall WV)

Northern Colorado
North Texas
Ohio State
Seattle (WA)
South Florida, U. of
Springfield College (MA)
Texas, U. of (Austin)
Virginia Commonwealth
Wisconsin
Wright State (OH)

SOCIAL WORK

Augsburg (MN)
Baylor (TX)
Bemidji State (MN)
Colorado State
Cornell (NY)
Gordon (MA)
Hawaii Pacific
Humboldt State (CA)
Illinois College
Juniata (PA)
Madonna (MI)
Marquette (WI)
Marygrove (MI)
Michigan State
Michigan, U. of
New York University
North Carolina State

Penn State
Pittsburgh, U. of (PA)
Radford (VA)
Sacred Heart (CT)
St. Louis (MO)
St. Olaf (MN)
Shepherd (WV)
Shippensburg, U. of (PA)
South Florida, U. of
Tennessee, U. of
Vermont, U. of
Washington U. (MO)
Washington, U. of
Wayne State (MI)
Western New England (MA)
Wisconsin, U. of

SPECIAL EDUCATION

Adelphi (NY)
American International (MA)
Arkansas
Arizona State
Augustana (SD)
Boston U. (MA)
California State (Chico)
California State (Sonoma)
California State (Stanislaus)
Connecticut, U. of
Curry (MA)
Denver, U. of (CO)
Eastern Montana
Flagler (FL)
Florida State
Geneseo (SUNY) (NY)
Hofstra (NY)
Kansas, U. of
Kean (NJ)
Landmark College (VT)
Lenoir-Rhyne (NC)

Lesley (MA)
Loyola (MD)
Maine, U. of (Farmington)
Marygrove (MI)
Maryland, U. of
Muskingum (OH)
Nebraska
Northern Colorado, U. of
Pacific, U. of (CA)
Penn State
Rhode Island College
Rowan (NJ)
▲ Simmons (MA)
Southern Illinois U.
  (Carbondale)
Texas, U. of
Texas Christian
Toledo (OH)
Virginia, U. of
Wisconsin, U. of (Oshkosh)
Wyoming, U. of

■ Men Only
▲ Women Only

SPORTS MEDICINE

Adelphi (NY)
Bethany (WV)
Castleton (VT)
Catawba (NC)
Charleston, U. of (WV)
Colorado State
Denver, U. of (CO)
Guilford (NC)
Heidelberg (OH)
Indiana U.
Manhattan (NY)
Marietta (OH)
Mercyhurst (PA)
New Mexico State
Occidental (CA)

Ohio Northern
Otterbein (OH)
Pacific, U. of the (CA)
Pepperdine (CA)
Radford (VA)
St. Andrews (NC)
Salisbury State (MD)
Sanford (AL)
Springfield (MA)
West Virginia Wesleyan
Wilmington (OH)
Wingate (NC)
Winona State (MN)
Xavier (OH)

SPORTS SCIENCES

Alabama, U. of
Averett (VA)
Bowling Green (OH)
Connecticut, U. of
Denver, U. of (CO)
Florida Southern
Florida, U. of
Guilford (NC)
Husson (ME)
Incarnate Word (TX)
Indiana U.
Kansas, U. of
Massachusetts, U. of
Mount Union (OH)
North Carolina State
Ohio Northern

Pfeiffer (NC)
Robert Morris (PA)
Rutgers (NJ)
Seton Hall (NJ)
Shepherd (WV)
South Carolina, U. of
Springfield (MA)
St. John's (NY)
St. Leo (FL)
St. Thomas U. (FL)
Stetson (FL)
Temple (PA)
Tennessee
Western New England (MA)
Wingate (NC)

URBAN STUDIES

Arizona State
Augburg (MN)
Boston U. (MA)
Brown (RI)
Buffalo (SUNY) (NY)
California Poly (Pomona)
California (San Diego)
Case Western Reserve (OH)
Cleveland State (OH)
Columbia (NY)
Cornell (NY)
Evansville (IN)
Georgia State
Lake Forest (IL)
Macalester (MN)
Maryland, U. of
Michigan State
New York U.
North Carolina (Greensboro)

Pennsylvania, U. of
Pittsburgh, U. of
Rockford (IL)
Rutgers (NJ)
St. Louis (MO)
Seattle Pacific (WA)
Shippensburg (PA)
Stanford (CA)
Tennessee (Knoxville)
Trinity (TX)
Virginia Commonwealth
Virginia Poly
Washington U. (MO)
Wayne State (MI)
Western Washington
Wisconsin, U. of (Green Bay)
Wooster (OH)
Worcester State (MA)
Wright State (OH)

■ Men Only
▲ Women Only

WOMEN'S STUDIES

Arizona, U. of
▲ Barnard (NY)
Bates (ME)
Beloit (WI)
Bowling Green (OH)
Brown (RI)
California, U. of (Berkeley)
California, U. of (Davis)
California, U. of (Santa Barbara)
California, U. of (Santa Cruz)
Carleton (MN)
Chicago, U. of (IL)
Colorado, U. of
DePauw (IN)
Emory (GA)
Florida, U. of
Goucher (MD)
Harvard (MA)
Hobart & William Smith (NY)
Kalamazoo (MI)
Macalester (MN)
Michigan, U. of
Middlebury (VT)

▲ Mills (CA)
▲ Mt. Holyoke (MA)
Northwestern (IL)
Pennsylvania, U. of
Pitzer (CA)
Portland State (OR)
Rochester, U. of (NY)
Rollins (FL)
Sarah Lawrence (NY)
▲ Simmons (MA)
▲ Smith
Southern California
▲ Spelman (GA)
Stanford (CA)
Tennessee, U. of
Texas, U. of
Vanderbilt (TN)
Washington U. (MO)
Washington, U. of
▲ Wellesley (MA)
Wheaton (MA)
Wisconsin, U. of
Wooster (OH)

■ Men Only
▲ Women Only

SECTION THREE

AVERAGE SAT-1/ACT TOTALS
RECOMMENDED MAJORS

ADELPHI COLLEGE (NY) 1050/22
Ed, Nurs, Physics

ADRIAN COLLEGE (MI) 1035/22
Ed, English, Poli Sci, Pre-Law, Soc

AGNES SCOTT COLLEGE (GA) 1180/26
Art, Econ, English, For Lang, Hist, Pre-Law, Psych

ALABAMA, UNIVERSITY OF (AL) 1080/23
Bus Admin, Engine, Geol, Hist

ALASKA, UNIVERSITY OF (ANCHORAGE) (AK) 1063/23
Bus Admin, Ed

ALASKA, UNIVERSITY OF (FAIRBANKS) (AK) 1070/23
Bus Admin, Drama, Nurs

ALBANY COLLEGE OF PHARMACY (NY) 1140/25
Pharm, Pre-Law, Pre-Med/Pre-Dental

ALBERTSON COLLEGE (ID) 1165/26
Bio, Bus Admin, Chem, Ed, Pre-Med/Pre-Dental, Zoo

ALBION COLLEGE (MI) 1185/26
Econ, English, Hist, Math, Pre-Law

ALBRIGHT COLLEGE (PA) 1070/23
Biochem, Bio, Bus Admin, Poli Sci, Pre-Law, Pre-Med/Pre-Dental

ALFRED UNIVERSITY (NY) 1160/26
Bus Admin, Ed, Engine, English, Pre-Law, Psych

ALLEGHENY COLLEGE (PA) 1199/26
Bio, Comp Sci, Econ, Geol, Hist, Philo, Pre-Law, Pre-Med/Pre-Dental, Psych

ALLENTOWN COLLEGE (PA) 1020/22
Drama

ALMA COLLEGE (MI) 1165/26
Art, Bio, Bus Admin, Chem, Comp Sci, Ed, Hist, Pre-Law, Pre-Med/Pre-Dental

AMERICAN ACADEMY OF DRAMATIC ARTS (NY) 1205/27
Drama

AMERICAN INTERNATIONAL COLLEGE (MA) 1000/27
Bus Admin, Pre-Med/Pre-Dental, Psych

AMERICAN UNIVERSITY (DC) 1185/26
Amer St, Bus Admin, Econ, Communic, Math, Poli Sci, Pre-Law

AMHERST COLLEGE (MA) 1385/31
Amer St, Bio, Chem, Drama, Econ, English, Geol, Hist, Physics, Poly Sci, Pre-Law, Pre-Med/Pre-Dental, Psych, Soc

APPALACHIAN STATE UNIVERSITY (NC) 1090/24
Bus Admin, Communic, Ed

AQUINAS COLLEGE (MI) 1033/22
Psych

ARIZONA, UNIVERSITY OF (AZ) 1100/24
*Ag, Amer St, Anthro, Arch, Art, Astro, Bus Admin, Communic, Ed, Engin, English,
Forest, Geol, Pre-Law, Psych*

ARIZONA STATE UNIVERSITY (AZ) 1090/24
Arch, Art, Bus Admin, Communic, Comp Sci, Ed, Engine, Home Ec, Math, Nurs, Pre-Med

ARKANSAS, UNIVERSITY OF (AR) 1095/24
Ag, Arch, Bus Admin, Communic, Ed, Engine, English, Music, Pre-Law

ART CENTER COLLEGE OF DESIGN (CA) 1100/24
Art

ASBURY COLLEGE (KY) 1100/24
Bus Admin, Philo, Soc

AUBURN UNIVERSITY (AL) 1140/25
Ag, Arch, Art, Ed, Engine, Forest

AUGSBURG COLLEGE (MN) 1040/22
Communic, Ed

AUGUSTANA COLLEGE (IL) 1150/25
Art, Bus Admin, Ed, Music

AUGUSTANA COLLEGE (SD) 1105/24
Ed, Nurs

AUSTIN COLLEGE (TX) 1160/26
Bus Admin, Ed, Poly Sci, Pre-Med/Pre-Dental

AVERETT COLLEGE (VA) 1075/23
Ed

AZUSA PACIFIC (CA) 1060/23
Bus Admin, Nurs

BABSON COLLEGE (MA) 1150/25
Bus Admin

BAKER UNIVERSITY 1075/23
Bus Admin, Psych

BALDWIN-WALLACE COLLEGE (OH) 1075/23
Busis Admin, Ed, English, Music, Pre-Law

BARD COLLEGE (NY) 1270/28
Art, Drama, English, Music, Pre-Law

BARRY UNIVERSITY (FL) 1100/24
Bus Admin, Drama

BATES COLLEGE (ME) 1300/29
*Art, Bio, Chem, Econ, Geol, Hist, Math, Philo, Physics, Pre-Law, Pre-Med/Pre-Dental, Psych,
Rel Stu*

BAYLOR UNIVERSITY (TX) 1145/25
Bus Admin, Chem, Drama, Ed, English, Hist, Nurs, Pre-Law, Pre-Med/Pre-Dental, Reli Stu

BEAVER COLLEGE (PA) 1060/23
Ed. Psych

BELHAVEN COLLEGE (MS) 1099/24
Art, Music

BELLARMINE COLLEGE (KY) 1095/24
Nurs

BELMONT ABBEY COLLEGE (NC) 1040/22
Bus Admin, Poli Sci, Pre-Law, Soc

BELMONT UNIVERSITY (TN) 1080/23
Music

BELOIT COLLEGE (WI) 1199/26
Anthro, Biochem, Classics, Drama, Econ, English, For Lang, Geol, Music, Physics, Psych, Soc

BEMIDJI STATE UNIVERSITY (MN) 1035/22
Communic

BENEDICTINE COLLEGE (KS) 1050/22
Bus Admin, Soc

BENEDICTINE UNIVERSITY (IL) 1030/22
Bio, Bus Admin, Pre-Med/Pre-Dental

BENNETT COLLEGE (NC) 1000/21
Bus Admin, Ed, Pre-Law, Pre-Med/Pre-Dental

BENNINGTON COLLEGE (VT) 1150/25
Drama, English, Pre-Law

BENTLEY COLLEGE (MA) 1100/24
Bus Admin

BEREA COLLEGE (KY) 1050/23
Ag, Ed, Home Ec, Nurs

BERRY COLLEGE (GA) 1155/25
Bio, Ed, Forest, Pre-Med/Pre-Dental, Psych

BETHANY COLLEGE (WV) 1080/23
Bio, Communic, Drama, Ed, For Lang, Music, Pre-Med/Pre-Dental

BETHEL COLLEGE (MN) 1099/24
Bus Admin, Ed, Nurs, Psych

BIOLA UNIVERSITY (CA) 1099/24
Philo, Psych, Soc

BIRMINGHAM-SOUTHERN COLLEGE (AL) 1180/26
Art, Bus Admin, Chem, Ed, English, Hist, Math, Music, Pre-Law, Pre-Med/Pre-Dental, Reli Stu

BLACKBURN COLLEGE (IL) 1000/21
Bio, Pre-Med/Pre-Dental, Psych

BLOOMSBURG UNIVERSITY (PA) 1085/23
Art, Ed

BLUFFTON COLLEGE (OH) 1070/23
Bus Admin

BOSTON COLLEGE (MA) 1270/28
Bio, Bus Admin, English, For Lang, Hist, Nurs, Philo, Pre-Med/Pre-Dental

BOSTON CONSERVATORY OF MUSIC (MA) 1050/22
Music

BOSTON UNIVERSITY (MA) 1260/28
*Art, Astro, Bus Admin, Communic, Drama, Econ, Ed, Engine, Hist, Music, Philo, Physics,
Poli Sci, Pre-Law, Psych*

BOWDOIN COLLEGE (ME) 1330/30
*Art Hist, Biochem, Bio, Chem, Econ, English, For Lang, Geol, Hist, Math, Music, Philo,
Pre-Law, Pre-Med/Pre-Dental*

BOWLING GREEN STATE UNIVERSITY (OH) 1040/22
Art, Bus Admin, Ed, Music

BRADLEY UNIVERSITY (IL) 1150/25
Comp Sci, Engine

BRANDEIS UNIVERSITY (MA) 1300/29
*Anthro, Biochem, Bio, Comp Sci, Drama, Econ, English, Hist, Music, Poli Sci, Pre-Law,
Pre-Med/Pre-Dental*

BRIGHAM YOUNG UNIVERSITY (UT) 1199/26
For Lang, Home Ec, Reli Stu

BROWN UNIVERSITY (RI) 1370/31
*Art, Art Hist, Bio, Biochem, Chem, Classics, Comp Sci, Engine, For Lang, Geol, Hist, Poli Sci,
Pre-Law, Pre-Med/Pre-Dental, Reli Stu*

BRYANT COLLEGE (RI) 1100/24
Bus Admin

BRYN MAWR COLLEGE (PA) 1320/30
*Art, Art Hist, Bio, Chem, Classics, Econ, English, For Lang, Geol, Hist, Physics, Pre-Law,
Pre-Med/Pre-Dental, Psych, Soc*

BUCKNELL UNIVERSITY (PA) 1250/28
Bio, Bus Admin, Chem, Ed, Engine, Hist, Math, Music, Philo, Pre-Med/Pre-Dental, Psych, Soc

BUENA VISTA COLLEGE (IA) 1120/24
Communic, Ed

BUTLER UNIVERSITY (IN) 1150/25
Bus Admin, Communic, Drama, Ed, Music, Pharm, Pre_Law, Pre-Med/Pre-Dental

CALDWELL COLLEGE (NJ) 1030/22
Bus Admin, Ed, Psych

CALIFORNIA INSTITUTE OF THE ARTS (CA) 1100/24
Art, Music

CALIFORNIA INSTITUTE OF TECHNOLOGY (CA) 1480/33
Astro, Bio, Chem, Engine, Geol, Math, Physics, Pre-Med/Pre-Dental

CALIFORNIA, UNIVERSITY OF, AT
      BERKELEY 1295/29
      Anthro, Arch, Biochem, Bot, Bus Admin, Chem, Comp Sci, Engine, English,
      For Lang, Forest, Geol, Hist, Math, Music, Philo, Physics, Pre-Law,
      Pre-Med/Pre-Dental, Psych, Reli Stu, Soc, Zoo
      DAVIS 1165/26
      Ag, Bio, Biochem, Bot, Chem, Engine, English, Geol, Hist, Home, Ec, Poli Sci,
      Pre-Law, Pre-Med/Pre-Dental, Zoo
      IRVINE 1130/25
      Art, Bio, Comp Sci, Drama, Engine, Math, Physics, Pre-Law, Pre-Med/Pre-Dental
      LOS ANGELES 1240/27
      Art Hist, Astro, Bio, Biochem, Communic, Comp Sci, Drama, Econ, Engine, English,
      For Lang, Geog, Hist, Math, Music, Philo, Poli Sci, Pre-Law, Pre-Med/Pre-Dental,
      Psych, Soc
      RIVERSIDE 1100/24
      Ag, Art Hist, Biochem, Bio, Bot, Engine, Math Music, Poli Sci, Pre-Law,
      Pre-Med/Pre-Dental, Psych
      SAN DIEGO 1210/27
      Amer Stu, Biochem, Bio, Chem, Comp Sci, Econ, Engine, Math, Music, Physics,
      Poly Sci, Pre-Law, Pre-Med/Pre-Dental, Psych
      SANTA BARBARA 1110/24
      Art, Art Hist, Bus Admin, Classics, Comp Sci, Ed, Engine, For Lang, Geog, Geol,
      Music, Philo, Physics, Poli Sci, Pre-Law, Reli Stu, Zoo
      SANTA CRUZ 1140/25
      Amer Stu, Anthro, Bio, Chem, Math, Music, Physics, Pre-Med/Pre-Dental, Psych

CALIFORNIA LUTHERAN UNIVERSITY (CA) 1020/22
Bus Admin, Ed, Psych

CALIFORNIA MARITIME ACADEMY (CA) 1100/24
Engine

CALIFORNIA POLYTECHNIC UNIVERSITY AT SAN LUIS OBISPO (CA) 1160/25
Ag, Arch, Bus Admin, Comp Sci, Communic, Engine, English, Poli Sci

CALIFORNIA STATE UNIVERSITY, AT:
      CHICO 1000/21
      Comp Sci, Geog, Nurs
      FULLERTON 1000/21
      Bus Admin, Communic, Music
      LONG BEACH 1000/21
      Art, Communic
      SAN JOSE 1050/23
      Art, Comp Sci

CALVIN COLLEGE (MI) 1140/25
Ed, Engine, English, For Lang, Hist, Pre-Law

CANISIUS COLLEGE 1080/23
Bus Admin, Psych

CAPITAL UNIVERSITY (OH) 1100/24
Bus Admin, Ed, Music, Nurs

CARLETON COLLEGE (MN) 1335/30
*Bio, Chem, Drama, English, For Lang, Geol, Hist, Math, Physics, Pre-Law,
Pre-Med/Pre-Dental*

CARNEGIE MELLON UNIVERSITY (PA) 1310/29
Arch, Art, Bus Admin, Chem, Comp Sci, Drama, Engine, Music, Pre-Med/Pre-Dental, Psych

CARROLL COLLEGE (WI) 1100/24
Chem, Ed, Nurs, Pre-Med/Pre-Dental, Psych

CARROLL COLLEGE (MT) 1080/23
Bio, Nurs, Pre-Med/Pre-Dental

CARTHAGE COLLEGE (WI) 1099/24
Bus Admin, Psych

CASE WESTERN RESERVE UNIVERSITY (OH) 1310/29
*Art Hist, Astro, Bus Admin, Chem, Comp Sci, Engine, Math, Music, Nurs, Physics,
Pre-Med/Pre-Dental*

CATAWBA COLLEGE (NC) 1000/21
Bus Admin, Comp Sci, Drama, Ed

CATHOLIC UNIVERSITY OF AMERICA (DC) 1170/26
Arch, Classics, Drama, Engine, For Lang, Music, Nurs, Pre-Law, Reli Stu

CEDAR CREST COLLEGE (PA) 1080/23
Nurs, Psych

CEDARVILLE COLLEGE (OH) 1099/24
Bus Admin, Ed

CENTENARY COLLEGE OF LOUISIANA (LA) 1140/25
Bus Admin, Chem, Ed, Geol

CENTRAL COLLEGE OF IOWA (IA) 1120/24
Comp Sci, Ed, For Lang

CENTRAL FLORIDA, UNIVERSITY OF (FL) 1100/24
Comp Sci, Communic, Engine

CENTRAL MICHIGAN UNIVERSITY (MI) 1000/21
Ed, Home Ec

CENTRAL WASHINGTON UNIVERSITY 1000/21
Music

CENTRE COLLEGE (KY) 1220/27
Chem, Econ, Physics, Poli Sci, Pre-Law, Pre-Med/Pre-Dental

CHAPMAN UNIVERSITY (CA) 1150/25
Bus Admin, Communic, Psych

CHARLESTON, COLLEGE OF (SC) 1080/23
Bio, Chem, Ed, Pre-Med/Pre-Dental

CHARLESTON, UNIVERSITY OF (WV) 1045/22
Hist

CHATHAM COLLEGE (PA) 1080/23
Art, Bus Admin, Poli Sci, Pre-Law

CHESTNUT HILL COLLEGE (PA) 1050/22
English, Pre-Law

CHICAGO, UNIVERSITY OF (IL) 1345/30
Anthro, Art Hist, Bio, Classics, Econ, English, Geog, Geol, Hist, Math, Philo, Physics, Poli Sci, Pre-Law, Pre-Med/Pre-Dental, Psych, Reli Stu, Soc

CHRISTIAN BROTHERS UNIVERSITY (TN) 1100/24
Bus Admin, Engine

CINCINNATI, UNIVERSITY OF (OH) 1100/24
Engine, Math, Pharm

CLAREMONT MCKENNA COLLEGE (CA) 1360/30
Bio, Bus Admin, Econ, English, Hist, Philo, Poli Sci, Pre-Law, Pre-Med/Pre-Dental, Psych

CLARK UNIVERSITY (MA) 1155/25
Bus Admin, For Lang, Geog, Music, Pre-Law, Pre-Med/Pre-Dental, Psych

CLARKE COLLEGE (IA) 1120/24
Comp Sci

CLARKSON UNIVERSITY (NY) 1200/26
Bus Admin, Engine, Soc

CLEMSON UNIVERSITY (SC) 1130/25
Ag, Arch, Bus Admin, Comp Sci, Engine, Forest

CLEVELAND INSTITUTE OF MUSIC (OH) 1200/26
Music

COE COLLEGE (IA) 1150/25
Bus Admin, Ed, Hist, Music

COLBY COLLEGE (ME) 1290/29
Bio, Bus Admin, Econ, English, For Lang, Poli Sci, Pre-Law, Pre-Med/Pre-Dental, Psych, Soc

COLGATE UNIVERSITY (NY) 1315/29
Bio, Chem, English, Geog, Geol, Hist, Math, Philo, Poli Sci, Pre-Law, Pre-Med/Pre-Dental, Reli Stu

COLORADO COLLEGE (CO) 1250/28
Anthro, Bio, English, Geol, Hist, Philo, Pre-Law, Pre-Med/Pre-Dental

COLORADO, UNIVERSITY OF (CO) 1180/26
Anthro, Astro, Biochem, Chem, Communic, Engine, Geog, Geol, Math, Music, Nurs, Physics, Pre-Med/Pre-Dental

COLORADO, UNIVERSITY OF (COLORADO SPRINGS) 1065/23
Bus Admin, Comp Sci, Engine, Physics, Psych

COLORADO, UNIVERSITY OF (DENVER) 1075/23
Comp Sci, Psych

COLORADO SCHOOL OF MINES (CO) 1230/27
Comp Sci, Engine, Geol, Physics, Pre-Med/Pre-Dental

COLORADO STATE UNIVERSITY (CO) 1125/25
Ag, Art, Art Hist, Bot, Bus Admin, Forest, Geol, Psych, Zoo

COLUMBIA UNIVERSITY/BARNARD COLLEGE (NY) 1370/31; 1325/30
Anthro, Arch, Art Hist, Biochem, Chem, Classics, Drama, Econ, English, For Lang,
Geol, Hist, Math, Music, Nurs, Philo, Physics, Pre-Law, Psych, Reli Stu, Soc

CONCORDIA COLLEGE-MOORHEAD (MN) 1120/24
Bio, Bus Admin, Ed, Math, Pre-Med/Pre-Dental, Psych, Soc

CONNECTICUT, UNIVERSITY OF (CT) 1115/24
Ag, Bio, Bot, Ed, Home Ec, Pharm, Pre-Law, Zoo

CONNECTICUT COLLEGE (CT) 1270/28
Bot, Ed, English, Hist, Music, Philo, Poli Sci, Pre-Law, Psych

CONVERSE COLLEGE (SC) 1100/24
Art, Ed, Music

THE COOPER UNION (NY) 1440/33
Arch, Art, Engine

CORNELL COLLEGE (IA) 1150/25
English, Geol, Philo, Pre-Law, Psych, Soc

CORNELL UNIVERSITY (NY) 1344/30
Ag, Arch, Art, Astro, Biochem, Bio, Bot, Comp Sci, Drama, Engine, Hist, Home Ec, Philo,
Physics, Pre-Med/Pre-Dental, Zoo

COVENANT COLLEGE (GA) 1150/25
Hist, Soc

CREIGHTON UNIVERSITY 1140/25
Bio, Communic, Nurs, Pharm, Poli Sci, Pre-Law, Pre-Med/Pre-Dental

CURTIS INSTITUTE OF MUSIC (PA) 1100/24
Music

DAEMEN COLLEGE (NY) 1030/22
Nurs

DALLAS, UNIVERSITY OF (TX) 1225/27
Art, Bio, Biochem, Classics, Econ, Ed, English, For Lang, Hist, Pre-Law,
Pre-Med/Pre-Dental

DARTMOUTH COLLEGE (NH) 1372/31
Anthro, Bio, Chem, Comp Sci, Drama, Econ, Engine, English, For Lang, Geog, Geol, Math,
Physics, Poli Sci, Pre-Law, Pre-Med/Pre-Dental, Reli Stu, Soc

DAVIDSON COLLEGE (NC) 1315/29
Chem, English, Hist, Math, Philo, Pre-Law, Pre-Med/Pre-Dental, Reli Stu

DAYTON, UNIVERSITY OF (OH) 1165/26
Ed, Engine, Poli Sci

DELAWARE, UNIVERSITY OF (DE) 1150/25
Art, Art Hist, Bio, Bus Admin, Chem, Communic, Ed, Engine, Home Ec, Nurs, Pre-Med/Pre-Dental

DELAWARE VALLEY COLLEGE (PA) 1030/22
Ag, Bio, Bus Admin, Chem, Pre-Med/Pre-Dental

DENISON UNIVERSITY (OH) 1150/25
Bio, Biochem, Econ, English, Geol, Hist, Philo, Poli Sci, Pre-Law, Pre-Med/Pre-Dental, Psych

DENVER, UNIVERSITY OF (CO) 1115/24
Bus Admin, English, Physics, Pre-Law, Psych

DePAUL UNIVERSITY (IL) 1140/25
Bus Admin, Communic, Comp Sci, Drama, Poli Sci, Pre-Law, Pre-Med/Pre-Dental

DePAUW UNIVERSITY (IN) 1220/27
Bus Admin, Music, Nurs

DETROIT MERCY, UNIVERSITY OF (MI) 1100/24
Engine, Nurs

DICKINSON COLLEGE (PA) 1200/26
Bio, English, For Lang, Hist, Poli Sci, Pre-Law, Pre-Med/Pre-Dental, Reli Stu

DILLARD UNIVERSITY (LA) 1000/21
Bus Admin

DOANE COLLEGE (NE) 1080/23
Bus Admin, Soc

DORDT COLLEGE (IA) 1080/23
Ag, Ed

DOMINICAN UNIVERSITY (IL) 1040/22
Home Ec

DRAKE UNIVERSITY (IA) 1145/25
Bus Admin, Communic, Ed, For Lang, Pharm, Poli Sci, Pre-Law

DREW UNIVERSITY (NJ) 1220/27
Art, Chem, Drama, For Lang, Hist, Poli Sci, Pre-Law, Psych

DREXEL UNIVERSITY (PA) 1110/24
Comp Sci, Home Ec

DRURY COLLEGE (MO) 1140/25
Arch, Music

DUBUQUE, UNIVERSITY OF (IA) 1060/23
Ed

DUKE UNIVERSITY (NC) 1380/31
*Anthro, Bio, Bot, Chem, Classics, Econ, Engine, English, Hist, Math, Nurs, Philo, Poli Sci,
Pre-Law, Pre-Med/Pre-Dental, Psych, Reli Stu, Zoo*

DUQUESNE UNIVERSITY (PA) 1100/24
Bio, Chem, Communic, Nurs, Pharm, Pre-Med/Pre-Dental

D'YOUVILLE COLLEGE (NY) 1025/22
Nurs, Soc

EARLHAM COLLEGE (IN) 1180/26
Bio, Chem, Ed, For Lang, Geol, Math, Pre-Med/Pre-Dental, Psych, Soc

EAST CAROLINA UNIVERSITY (NC) 1030/22
Ed, Engine, Music, Nurs, Pre-Med/Pre-Dental

EASTERN COLLEGE (PA) 1060/23
Bus Admin, Nurs, Soc

EASTERN MICHIGAN UNIVERSITY (MI) 1000/21
Ed

ECKERD COLLEGE (FL) 1160/25
Bio, Bus Admin, For Lang, Pre-Med/Pre-Dental

EDGEWOOD COLLEGE (WI) 1030/22
Ed, Nurs

ELIZABETHTOWN COLLEGE (PA) 1130/25
Bus Admin

ELMHURST COLLEGE (IL) 1000/21
Bio

ELMIRA COLLEGE (NY) 1099/24
Bus Admin, Ed, Psych

ELON COLLEGE (NC)..1075/23
Communic

EMERSON COLLEGE (MA) 1135/25
Drama, English, Pre-Law

EMORY & HENRY COLLEGE (VA) 1040/22
Bus Admin, For Lang

EMORY UNIVERSITY (GA) 1315/30
Bio, Bus Admin, Chem, English, For Lang, Hist, Nurs, Poli Sci, Pre-Law, Pre-Med/Pre-Dental, Psych, Reli Stu

ERSKINE COLLEGE (SC)..1110/24
Bio, Bus Admin, Ed, Hist, Pre-Med/Pre-Dental

EUREKA COLLEGE (IL) 1060/23
Bus Admin, Comp Sci

EVANSVILLE, UNIVERSITY OF (IN) 1150/25
Comp Sci, Drama, Nurs, Physics, Pre-Med/Pre-Dental

FAIRFIELD UNIVERSITY (CT) 1157/25
Bio, Bus Admin, Communic, Math, Nurs, Physics, Pre-Med, Psych

FAIRLEIGH DICKINSON (NJ) 1040/22
Art, Bus Admin, English, Pre-Law

FERRIS STATE UNIVERSITY (MI) 970/20
Bus Admin, Comp Sci, Pharm

FISK UNIVERSITY (TN) 1030/22
Bus Admin, Math, Pre-Law, Soc

FIVE TOWNS COLLEGE (NY) 1000/21
Music

FLAGLER COLLEGE (FL) 1099/23
Communic, Ed

FLORIDA, UNIVERSITY OF (FL) 1230/27
Ag, Anthro, Arch, Bot, Bus Admin, Communic, English, Forest, Geol, Math, Nurs, Pharm,
Philo, Physics, Pre-Law, Soc, Zoo

FLORIDA A&M (FL) 1000/21
Bus Admin, Ed, Pre-Law, Pre-Med/Pre-Dental

FLORIDA ATLANTIC UNIVERSITY (FL) 1054/22
Bus Admin, Ed

FLORIDA INSTITUTE OF TECHNOLOGY (FL) 1185/26
Biochem, Bus Admin, Engine, Psych

FLORIDA INTERNATIONAL UNIVERSITY (FL) 1110/24
Bus Admin, Psych

FLORIDA STATE UNIVERSITY (FL) 1170/26
Art Hist, Bus Admin, Chem, Drama, Ed, Home Ec, Music, Philo, Pre-Med/Pre-Dental,
Psych, Reli Stu

FLORIDA SOUTHERN COLLEGE (FL) 1099/23
Communic, Pre-Med/Pre-Dental

FONTBONNE COLLEGE (MO) 1030/22
Drama, Home Ec, Math

FORDHAM UNIVERSITY (NY) 1145/25
Classics, Communic, Drama, English, Philo, Pre-Law, Pre-Med/Pre-Dental, Reli Stu

FORT LEWIS COLLEGE (CO) 1025/22
English, Geol, Pre-Law

FRANCISCAN UNIVERSITY OF STEUBENVILLE (OH) 1099/24
Nurs, Philo, Psych, Reli Stu

FRANKLIN COLLEGE OF INDIANA (IN) 1100/24
Communic, Drama, Ed

FRANKLIN & MARSHALL COLLEGE (PA) 1250/28
Amer Stu, Bio, Bus Admin, Chem, English, Geol, Physics, Poli Sci, Pre-Law,
Pre-Med/Pre-Dental, Soc

FURMAN UNIVERSITY (SC) 1220/27
Art, Chem, Comp Sci, Geol, Music, Poli Sci, Pre-Law, Pre-Med/Pre-Dental, Psych, Reli Stu

GANNON UNIVERSITY (PA) 1099/24
Bus Admin, Engine

GENERAL MOTORS INSTITUTE (MI) 1220/27
Engine

GENEVA COLLEGE (PA) 1080/23
Ed, Engine

GEORGETOWN UNIVERSITY (DC) 1320/30
Amer St, Bio, Bus Admin, English, For Lang, Hist, Nurs, Philo, Poli Sci, Pre-Law, Pre-Med/Pre-Dental, Reli Stu

GEORGE FOX COLLEGE (OR) 1065/23
Ed, Soc

GEORGE MASON UNIVERSITY (VA) 1120/24
Amer St, Bus Admin, Drama, Econ, English, Nurs, Psych, Pre-Law

GEORGE WASHINGTON UNIVERSITY (DC) 1210/27
Amer St, Geog, Hist, Philo, Poli Sci, Pre-Law, Psych

GEORGIA, UNIVERSITY OF (GA) 1190/26
Ag, Bio, Chem, Communic, Ed, English, For Lang, Forest, Home Ec, Pharm, Pre-Law, Pre-Med/Pre-Dental

GEORGIA INSTITUTE OF TECHNOLOGY (GA) 1300/29
Arch, Comp Sci, Engine, Physics

GEORGIA SOUTHERN UNIVERSITY (GA) 1040/22
Ed

GETTYSBURG COLLEGE (PA) 1200/26
Bio, Bus Admin, English, Hist, Pre-Law, Pre-Med/Pre-Dental, Psych, Soc

GONZAGA UNIVERSITY (WA) 1150/25
Bus Admin, Communic, English, Pre-Law

GORDON COLLEGE (MA) 1120/24
Ed, Reli Stu

GOSHEN COLLEGE (IN) 1090/24
Nurs, Physics

GOUCHER COLLEGE (MD) 1190/26
Bus Admin, Chem, Comp Sci, Drama, Ed, English, Hist, Pre-Law/

GRACELAND COLLEGE (IA) 1040/22
Bus Admin, Ed, Nurs

GRAND VALLEY STATE UNIVERSITY (MI) 1100/24
English, Psych, Pre-Law

GREEN MOUNTAIN COLLEGE (VT) 1000/21
Bus Admin

GRINNELL COLLEGE (IA) 1320/30
Anthro, Bio, Chem, Comp Sci, English, For Lang, Hist, Physics, Poli Sci, Pre-Law,
Pre-Med/Pre-Dental, Psych

GROVE CITY COLLEGE (PA) 1199/26
Bus Admin, Engine

GUILFORD COLLEGE (NC) 1140/25
Art, Bio, Bus Admin, Ed, English, Geol, Physics, Pre-Law, Pre-Med/Pre-Dental, Psych, Reli Stu

GUSTAVUS ADOLPHUS COLLEGE (MN) 1200/26
Bus Admin, For Lang, Music, Nurs, Physics, Psych

GWYNEDD-MERCY COLLEGE (PA) 1040/22
Nurs

HAMILTON COLLEGE (NY) 1250/28
Bio, Chem, English, Hist, Philo, Poli Sci, Pre-Law, Pre-Med/Pre-Dental, Reli Stu

HAMLINE UNIVERSITY (MN) 1150/25
Anthro, Art, Bio, Chem, English, Pre-Law, Pre-Med/Pre-Dental, Psych, Soc

HAMPDEN-SYDNEY COLLEGE (VA) 1150/25
Bio, Classics, English, Hist, Pre-Law, Pre-Med/Pre-Dental

HAMPTON UNIVERSITY (VA) 1020/22
Bus Admin

HANOVER COLLEGE (IN) 1145/25
Bus Admin, Communic, Ed, Hist, Psych, Soc

HARTFORD, UNIVERSITY OF (CT) 1050/23
Bus Admin, Music

HARTWICK COLLEGE (NY) 1099/23
Bus Admin, Geol, Music, Nurs, Poli Sci, Pre-Law, Soc

HARVARD/RADCLIFFE COLLEGES (MA) 1435/32
Amer St, Anthro, Art, Art Hist, Astro, Biochem, Bio, Chem, Classics, Econ, for Lang, Geol,
Hist, Math, Music, Philo, Physics, Poli Sci, Pre-Law, Pre-Med/Pre-Dental, Psych

HARVEY MUDD COLLEGE (CA) 1450/33
Bio, Chem, Comp Sci, Engine, Math, Physics, Pre-Med/Pre-Dental

HASTINGS COLLEGE (NE) 1090/24
Bus Admin, Ed

HAVERFORD COLLEGE (PA) 1365/31
Astro, Bio, Chem, Comp Sci, Econ, English, Hist, Philo, Physics, Pre-Law,
Pre-Med/Pre-Dental, Psych, Reli Stu, Soc

HAWAII, UNIVERSITY OF (HI) 1080/23
Ag, Anthro, Art, Astro, Bot, For Lang, Poli Sci, Pre-Law

HAWAII PACIFIC UNIVERSITY (HI) 1110/24
Bus Admin, Comp Sci

HEIDELBERG COLLEGE (OH) 1000/21
Bus Admin, Ed, Music, Pre-Med

HENDRIX COLLEGE (AR) 1170/26
Bio, Bus Admin, Chem, Econ, Pre-Med/Pre-Dental, Reli Stu, Soc

HILLSDALE COLLEGE (MI) 1170/26
Bus Admin, Ed, Hist

HIRAM COLLEGE (OH) 1180/26
Bio, Chem, Comp Sci, English, Ed, Hist, Math, Pre-Law, Pre-Med/Pre-Dental, Reli Stu

HOBART & WILLIAM SMITH COLLEGE (NY) 1190/26
Amer Stu, Bio, Chem, Econ, English, Hist, Poli Sci, Pre-Law, Pre-Med/Pre-Dental, Psych

HOFSTRA UNIVERSITY (NY) 1120/24
*Anthro, Art, Bus Admin, Communic, Drama, Music, Poli Sci, Pre-Law,
Pre-Med/Pre-Dental, Soc*

HOLLINS COLLEGE (VA) 1130/25
Amer St, Art, Art Hist, English, For Lang, Pre-Law, Psych

HOLY CROSS, COLLEGE OF THE (MA) 1250/28
Bio, Classics, Econ, English, Hist, Math, Philo, Pre-Law, Pre-Med/Pre-Dental

HOOD COLLEGE (MD) 1100/24
Bio, Bus Admin, Ed, Home Ec, Philo, Pre-Med/Pre-Dental

HOPE COLLEGE (MI) 1145/25
Bio, Chem, Geol, Music, Poli Sci, Pre-Law, Pre-Med/Pre-Dental

HOUGHTON COLLEGE (NY) 1170/26
Art, Bio, Chem, Ed, Pre-Med, Psych, Reli Stu

HOUSTON BAPTIST UNIVERSITY (TX) 1060/23
Bio, Chem, Pre-Med/Pre-Dental

HOUSTON, UNIVERSITY OF (TX) 1100/24
Arch, Bus Admin, Engine

HOWARD UNIVERSITY (DC) 1000/21
Bus Admin, Communic, Nurs, Zoo

HUMBOLDT STATE UNIVERSITY (CA) 1075/23
Bot, Drama, Forest, Music

HUNTINGDON COLLEGE (AL) 1080/23
Chem, Ed, Pre-Med/Pre-Dental

IDAHO, UNIVERSITY OF (ID) 1085/24
Ag, Bus Admin, Communic, Engine, Forest

ILLINOIS, UNIVERSITY OF, AT:
      URBANA-CHAMPAIGN 1230/27
        *Ag, Arch, Anthro, Astro, Bus Admin, Chem, Comp Sci, Ed, Engine, For Lang,
        Home Ec, Math, Music, Pharm, Physics, Pre-Med/Pre-Dental, Psych, Soc*
      CHICAGO 1030/22
        Bus Admin

ILLINOIS COLLEGE (IL) 1100/24
Communic, Econ, Pre-Law

ILLINOIS INSTITUTE OF TECHNOLOGY (IL)...1190/26
Arch, Engine, Math

ILLINOIS STATE UNIVERSITY (IL) 1040/22
Drama, Ed

ILLINOIS WESLEYAN UNIVERSITY (IL) 1230/27
Bio, Drama, Music, Pre-Med/Pre-Dental

INDIANA STATE UNIVERSITY (IN) 1000/21
Bus Admin, Ed

INDIANA UNIVERSITY (IN) 1110/24
*Bio, Bus Admin, Chem, Communic, Drama, Ed, For Lang, Geog, Geol, Music,
Pre-Med/Pre-Dental, Psych, Zoo*

INDIANA UNIVERSITY OF PENNSYLVANIA 1100/24
Bus Admin, Ed, Home Ec

IONA UNIVERSITY (NY) 1000/21
Bus Admin

IOWA, UNIVERSITY OF 1130/25
*Astro, Biochem, Bus Admin, Communic, Ed, English, For Lang, Music, Nurs, Pre-Law,
Pre-Med, Psych, Reli Stu*

IOWA STATE UNIVERSITY (IA) 1145/25
Ag, Comp Sci, Ed, Engine, Forest, Home Ec, Zoo

ITHACA COLLEGE (NY) 1125/24
Chem, Music, Pre-Med/Pre-Dental

JACKSONVILLE STATE (AL) 1000/21
Ed

JACKSONVILLE UNIVERSITY (FL) 1060/23
Art, Bio, Bus Admin, Communic, Drama, Music, Nurs, Physics, Pre-Med/Pre-Dental

JAMES MADISON UNIVERSITY (VA) 1199/26
Bus Admin, Ed, For Lang, Home Ec, Music

JOHN CARROLL UNIVERSITY (OH) 1110/24
Bus Admin, Communic

JOHNS HOPKINS UNIVERSITY (MD) 1380/31
Art Hist, Bio, Chem, Classics, Engine, Geog, Philo, Poli Sci, Pre-Law, Pre-Med/Pre-Dental

JOHNSON C. SMITH (NC) 950/20
Communic, Soc

JUDSON COLLEGE (AL) 1000/21
Home Ec, Music, Psych

JULLIARD SCHOOL (NY) 1100/24
Drama, Music

JUNIATA COLLEGE (PA) 1140/25
Bio, Bus Admin, Chem, Ed, Pre-Med/Pre-Dental

KALAMAZOO COLLEGE (MI) 1225/27
*Amer St, Bio, Chem, Classics, Econ, English, For Lang, Hist, Physics, Pre-Law,
Pre-Med/Pre-Dental, Soc*

KANSAS NEWMAN COLLEGE (KS) 1100/24
Bus Admin, Philo

KANSAS, UNIVERSITY OF (KS) 1100/23
*Anthro, Arch, Art Hist, Astro, Chem, Communic, Drama, Engine, For Lang, Geog, Hist,
Pre-Med/Pre-Dental, Zoo*

KANSAS STATE UNIVERSITY (KS) 1100/23
Ag, Arch, Bio, Biochem, Communic, Engine, Home Ec, Math Pre-Law, Pre-Med/Pre-Dental

KEENE STATE COLLEGE (NH) 1000/21
Art, Communic, Ed, Music

KENNESAW STATE COLLEGE (GA) 1045/22
Bus Admin

KENT STATE UNIVERSITY (OH) 1000/21
Arch, Art, Communic, Ed, Music

KENTUCKY, UNIVERSITY OF (KY) 1120/24
Ag, Bus Admin, Communic, Ed, Engine, Hist, Home Ec, Pharm, Pre-Med/Pre-Dental

KENTUCKY WESLEYAN (KY) 1060/23
Bus Admin

KENYON COLLEGE (OH) 1270/28
*Bio, Chem, Drama, Econ, English, Hist, Math, Philo, Poli Sci, Pre-Law, Pre-Med/Pre-Dental,
Psych, Reli Stu*

KING COLLEGE (TN) 1090/24
Reli Stu

KING'S COLLEGE (PA) 1060/23
Bus Admin

KNOX COLLEGE (IL) 1190/26
Art, Chem, English, Hist, Math, Poli Sci, Pre-Law, Pre-Med/Pre-Dental, Soc

KUTZTOWN UNIVERSITY (PA) 1000/21
Art, Ed

LAFAYETTE COLLEGE (PA) 1220/27
*Anthro, Art, Bio, Chem, Econ, Engine, English, Geol, Hist, Pre-Law, Pre-Med/Pre-Dental,
Psych*

LAKE FOREST COLLEGE (IL) 1110/24
Art, Art Hist, Bio, Chem, Econ, English, Hist, Music, Pre-Law, Pre-Med/Pre-Dental, Psych

LA SALLE UNIVERSITY (PA) 1110/24
Bus Admin, Comp Sci

LA VERNE, UNIVERSITY OF (CA) 1000/21
Bus Admin

LAWRENCE UNIVERSITY (WI) 1240/28
Bio, Chem, English, For Lang, Hist, Music, Physics, Pre-Law, Pre-Med/Pre-Dental, Reli Stu

LEBANON VALLEY COLLEGE (PA) 1105/24
Bus Admin, Math, Music, Nurs, Psych

LEHIGH UNIVERSITY (PA) 1220/27
Bus Admin, Engine, Geol

LEMOYNE COLLEGE (NY) 1100/24
Bus Admin

LENOIR-RHYNE COLLEGE (NC) 1000/21
Bus Admin, Soc

LESLEY COLLEGE (MA) 1000/21
Bus Admin, Ed

LETOURNEAU COLLEGE (TX) 1130/25
Bus Admin, Engine

LEWIS & CLARK COLLEGE (OR) 1199/27
Bio, Biochem, Bus Admin, For Lang, Physics, Pre-Med/Pre-Dental, Soc

LINDENWOOD COLLEGE (MO) 1060/23
Psych

LINFIELD COLLEGE (OR) 1140/25
Bio, Bus Admin, Chem, Ed, For Lang, Home Ec

LOCK HAVEN UNIVERSITY (PA) 1060/23
Ed

LONG ISLAND UNIVERSITY (SOUTHAMPTON) (NY) 1050/22
Bio

LONGWOOD COLLEGE (VA) 1060/23
Bus Admin, Ed, English, Pre-Law, Psych

LORAS COLLEGE (IA) 1070/23
Art, Bio, Bus Admin, Ed, English, Pre-Law

LOUISIANA STATE UNIVERSITY (LA) 1075/23
Ag, Arch, Astro, Biochem, Chem, Communic, Geog, Geol, Math, Music, Physics,
Pre-Med/Pre-Dental, Psych

LOUISVILLE, UNIVERSITY OF (KY) 1000/21
Engine

LOWELL, UNIVERSITY OF MASSACHUSETTS AT (MA) 1050/22
Bus Admin, Engine, Music

LOYOLA COLLEGE (MD) 1175/26
Bio, Bus Admin, Engine, Pre-Law

LOYOLA MARYMOUNT UNIVERSITY (CA) 1105/24
Bus Admin, Engine, Journal

LOYOLA UNIVERSITY OF CHICAGO (IL) 1105/24
Bio, Communic, Drama, Nurs, Physics, Pre-Med/Pre-Dental, Psych

LOYOLA UNIVERSITY OF NEW ORLEANS (LA) 1145/25
Bus Admin, Comp Sci, Communic, Music, Philo, Pre-Law, Reli Stu

LUTHER COLLEGE (IA) 1155/22
Bus Admin, Ed, Music, Nurs, Psych

LYCOMING COLLEGE (PA) 1090/24
Astro

LYNCHBURG COLLEGE (VA) 1000/21
Communic, Soc

LYON COLLEGE (AR) 1150/25
Drama, Ed, Psych

MACALESTER COLLEGE (MN) 1310/29
*Anthro, Art, Bio, Classics, Communic, Drama, Econ, English, Geog, Hist, Philo, Poli Sci,
Pre-Law, Pre-Med/Pre-Dental, Psych*

MacMURRAY COLLEGE (IL) 1010/21
Nurs

MAINE, UNIVERSITY OF (ME) 1100/24
Ag, Bot, Bus Admin, Engine, Forest, Home Ec

MAINE, UNIVERSITY OF (FARMINGTON) (ME) 1020/22
Bus Admin

MALONE COLLEGE (OH) 1040/22
Bus Admin, Math

MANCHESTER COLLEGE (IN) 1045/22
Bus Admin, Psych

MANHATTAN COLLEGE (NY) 1100/24
Bus Admin, Ed, Engine

MANHATTANVILLE COLLEGE (NY) 1120/24
Art, Art Hist, Bus Admin, Econ, Ed, Music, Psych, Soc

MANHATTAN SCHOOL OF MUSIC (NY) 1100/24
Music

MANSFIELD UNIVERSITY OF PENNSYLVANIA (PA) 1040/22
Ed, Geog

MARIETTA COLLEGE (OH) 1115/24
Art, Bus Admin, English, Pre-Law

MARIST COLLEGE (NY) 1150/25
Bus Admin, Communic, Psych

MARQUETTE UNIVERSITY (WI) 1150/25
Bio, Bus Admin, Chem, English, Engine, Hist, Nurs, Poli Sci, Pre-Law, Pre-Med/Pre-Dental

MARSHALL UNIVERSITY (WV) 1000/21
Bus Admin, Ed, Nurs

MARY BALDWIN COLLEGE (VA) 1060/23
Art, Bus Admin, Communic, Psych, Soc

MARYCREST INTERNATIONAL UNIVERSITY (IA) 1000/21
Nurs

MARYGROVE COLLEGE (MI) 1000/21
Comp Sci

MARYLAND INSTITUTE-COLLEGE OF ART (MD) 1130/25
Art

MARYLAND, UNIVERSITY OF (MD) 1185/26
Ag, Anthro, Astro, Bot, Bus Admin, Communic, Econ, Ed, Hist, Home Ec, Pharm, Pre-Law, Zoo

MARYLAND, UNIVERSITY OF (BALTIMORE COUNTY) (MD) 1210/27
Comp Sci, Nurs, Poli Sci, Pre-Law

MARYVILLE UNIVERSITY-ST. LOUIS (MO) 1060/23
Nurs

MARY WASHINGTON COLLEGE (VA) 1195/26
Amer St, Bio, Geog, Hist, Pre-Med/Pre-Dental, Psych

MASSACHUSETTS, UNIVERSITY OF (MA) 1140/25
*Bus Admin, Chem, Communic, Comp Sci, Engine, English, Hist, Home Ec, Nurs, Pre-Law,
Pre-Med/Pre-Dental, Zoo*

MASSACHUSETTS, UNIVERSITY OF (BOSTON) (MA) 1040/22
Bus Admin, Engine, Music, Nurs, Soc

MASSACHUSETTS, UNIVERSITY OF (DARTMOUTH) (MA) 1080/23
Art, Nurs, Soc

MASSACHUSETTS COLLEGE OF ART (MA) 1070/23
Art

MASSACHUSETTS COLLEGE OF PHARMACY (MA) 1000/21
Pharm

MASSACHUSETTS INSTITUTE OF TECHNOLOGY (MA) 1440/32
*Arch, Astro, Biochem, Bio, Bus Admin, Chem, Comp Sci, Econ, Geol, Math, Physics, Poli Sci,
Pre-Law, Pre-Med/Pre-Dental*

MASSACHUSETTS MARITIME ACADEMY (MA) 1005/21
Engine

MASSACHUSETTS STATE COLLEGE SYSTEM (MA) 1005/21
Ed

MEMPHIS, UNIVERSITY OF (TN) 1040/22
Music

MERCER UNIVERSITY (GA) 1099/24
Bus Admin, Pharm

MEREDITH COLLEGE (NC) 1000/21
Bio, Bus Admin, Home Ec, Music

MERCY COLLEGE (NY) 1000/21
Nurs, Psych

MERCYHURST COLLEGE (PA) 1080/23
Art, Bus Admin

MERRIMACK COLLEGE (MA) 1050/22
Bus Admin

MESSIAH COLLEGE (PA) 1150/25
Art, Ed

MIAMI UNIVERSITY (OH) 1160/25
Arch, Bot, Bus Admin, Ed, Zoo

MIAMI, UNIVERSITY OF (FL) 1180/26
Bio, Biochem, Communic, Drama, Hist, Music, Pre-Med/Pre-Dental

MICHIGAN, UNIVERSITY OF (MI) 1275/27
*Amer St, Anthro, Arch, Art, Art Hist, Astro, Bot, Bus Admin, Classics, Communic, Econ, Ed,
Engine, For Lang, Geog, Music, Nurs, Pharm, Philo, Pre-Law, Pre-Med/Pre-Dental,
Psych, Soc, Zoo*

MICHIGAN, UNIVERSITY OF (DEARBORN) (MI) 1100/24
Bus Admin, Comp Sci, Engine

MICHIGAN STATE UNIVERSITY (MI) 1100/24
*Ag, Biochem, Bio, Bot, Bus Admin, Chem, Communic, Econ, Ed, Forest, Geog, Home Ec, Math,
Poli Sci, Pre-Law, Pre-Med/Pre-Dental, Psych, Soc*

MICHIGAN TECHNOLOGICAL UNIVERSITY (MI) 1199/26
Ag, Engine, Forest, Geol

MIDDLEBURY COLLEGE (VT) 1350/30
Art, Bio, Classics, Econ, English, For Lang, Geog, Hist, Poli Sci, Pre-Law, Pre-Med/Pre-Dental

MILLERSVILLE UNIVERSITY OF PENNSYLVANIA (PA) 1100/24
Bus Admin, Hist, Pre-Law

MILLIGAN COLLEGE (TN) 1045/22
Bus Admin, Philo, Reli Stu

MILLIKIN UNIVERSITY (IL) 1080/23
Art, Ed

MILLS COLLEGE (CA) 1150/25
Art, Communic, Ed, For Lang, Music, Psych

MILLSAPS COLLEGE (MS) 1190/26
Bio, Bus Admin, English, Geol, Math, Music, Pre-Law, Pre-Med/Pre-Dental

MILWAUKEE SCHOOL OF ENGINEERING (WI) 1130/25
Arch, Engine

MINNESOTA, UNIVERSITY OF (MN) 1150/25
Ag, Amer St, Art Hist, Bus Admin, Communic, Ed, Engine, Forest, Geol, Home Ec, Nurs,
Poli Sci, Pre-Law, Psych, Soc

MINNESOTA, UNIVERSITY OF (MORRIS) (MN) 1199/26
Bio, Chem, Comp Sci, For Lang, Pre-Law, Pre Med/Pre-Dental

COLLEGE MISERICORDIA (PA) 1010/21
Nurs

MISSISSIPPI COLLEGE (MS) 1060/23
Bus Admin, Nurs, Reli Stu

MISSISSIPPI STATE UNIVERSITY (MS) 1050/22
Ag, Ed, Engine

MISSISSIPPI, UNIVERSITY OF (MS) 1099/24
Bus Admin, Communic, English, Pharm, Physics, Pre-Law

MISSISSIPPI UNIVERSITY FOR WOMEN (MS) 1115/24
Bus Admin, Nurs

MISSOURI, UNIVERSITY OF (MO) 1150/25
Ag, Art Hist, Communic, Forest, Hist

MISSOURI, UNIVERSITY OF (KANSAS CITY) (MO) 1015/24
Art, Music

MISSOURI, UNIVERSITY OF (ROLLA) (MO) 1255/28
Comp Sci, Engine

MONMOUTH COLLEGE (IL) 1065/23
Bus Admin, Ed

MONMOUTH UNIVERSITY (NJ) 1000/21
Comp Sci

MONTANA COLLEGE OF MINERAL SCIENCE & TECHNOLOGY (MT) 1120/24
Comp Sci, Engine

MONTANA, UNIVERSITY OF (MT) 1060/23
Bot, Classics, Communic, Comp Sci, Forest, Pharm, Zoo

MONTANA STATE UNIVERSITY (MT) 1090/24
Ag, Arch, Engine, For Lang, Forest

MONTCLAIR STATE (NJ) 1099/24
Ed, Home Ec, Psych

MONTEVALLO, UNIVERSITY OF (AL) 1000/21
Communic, Ed, English, Home Ec

MONTREAT COLLEGE (NC) 1070/23
Bus Admin

MORAVIAN COLLEGE (PA) 1135/25
Art, Bus Admin, Communic, Comp Sci, Ed, Soc

MOREHOUSE COLLEGE (GA) 1099/24
Bus Admin, Comp Sci

MORNINGSIDE COLLEGE (IA) 1060/23
Bio, Communic, Nurs, Pre-Med/Pre-Dental

MOUNT HOLYOKE COLLEGE (MA) 1240/28
*Art Hist, Biochem, Bio, Chem, Drama, Econ, English, For Lang, Hist, Math, Poli Sci, Pre-Law,
Pre-Law, Pre-Med/Pre-Dental, Psych*

MOUNT MERCY COLLEGE (IA) 1050/22
Bus Admin, Nurs

MOUNT ST. JOSEPH (OH) 1040/22
Art, Bus Admin, Ed, Nurs

MOUNT ST. MARY'S COLLEGE (NY) 1040/22
Nurs

MOUNT ST. MARY'S COLLEGE (MD) 1070/23
Bus Admin, Poli Sci, Pre-Law, Pre-Med/Pre-Dental

MOUNT ST. MARY'S COLLEGE (CA) 1050/22
Bio, Bus Admin, Nurs

MOUNT UNION COLLEGE (OH) 1099/24
Bus Admin, Comp Sci

MUHLENBERG COLLEGE (PA) 1150/25
*Art, Bio, Biochem, Bus Admin, Communic, Drama, Hist, Math, Philo, Pre-Law,
Pre-Med/Pre-Dental*

MUSKINGUM COLLEGE (OH) 1040/22
Bus Admin, Comp Sci, Ed

NAZARETH COLLEGE OF ROCHESTER (NY) 1110/24
Bus Admin, Ed

NEBRASKA, UNIVERSITY OF (NE) 1085/23
Ag, Arch, Bus Admin, Communic, Home Ec

NEBRASKA WESLEYAN UNIVERSITY (NE) 1110/24
Bio, Pre-Med/Pre-Dental

NEVADA, UNIVERSITY OF, AT:
    LAS VEGAS 1000/21
      Arch, Engine
    RENO 1040/22
      Ag, Communic, Ed

NEW COLLEGE OF THE UNIVERSITY OF SOUTH FLORIDA (FL) 1330/30
Anthro, Bio, Chem, Math, Philo, Physics, Pre-Med/Pre-Dental, Psych

NEW ENGLAND CONSERVATORY (MA) 1100/24
Music

NEW HAMPSHIRE, UNIVERSITY OF (NH) 1130/25
Ag, Bio, Chem, Communic, English, Pre-Med/Pre-Dental, Pre-Law

NEW JERSEY INSTITUTE OF TECHNOLOGY (NJ) 1145/25
Engine

NEW JERSEY, COLLEGE OF (NJ) 1220/27
Art, Ed, Engine, Math, Philo, Pre-Law, Pre-Med/Pre-Dental, Reli Stu

NEW MEXICO INSTITUTE OF MINING (NM) 1180/26
Engine, Geol, Physics

NEW MEXICO STATE UNIVERSITY (NM) 1040/22
Ag, Anthro, Engine

NEW MEXICO, UNIVERSITY OF (NM) 1050/22
Anthro, Art, For Lang, Hist, Pharm

NEW ORLEANS, UNIVERSITY OF (LA) 1000/21
Bus Admin, Engine

NEW YORK, CITY UNIVERSITY OF, AT
      BARUCH COLLEGE 1000/21
      Bus Admin
      BROOKLYN COLLEGE 1040/22
      Geol, Pre-Med/Pre-Dental, Physics
      CITY COLLEGE 1050/22
      Arch, Ed, Physics
      HERBERT LEHMAN COLLEGE 1000/21
      Home Ec, Psych
      HUNTER COLLEGE 1060/23
      Art, Art Hist, Communic, Comp Sci, Ed, English, Nurs, Pre-Law, Psych
      QUEENS COLLEGE 1010/22
      Anthro, Ed, Psych

NEW YORK, STATE UNIVERSITY OF, AT
      ALBANY 1170/26
      Bio, Bus Admin, English, Geol, Pre-Law, Psych
      BINGHAMTON 1220/27
      Biochem, Bus Admin, Math, Nurs, Physics, Pre-Law, Pre-Med/Pre-Dental, Psych
      BROCKPORT, COLLEGE AT 1040/22
      Bus Admin
      BUFFALO 1200/26
      Amer Stu, Anthro, Arch, Bus Admin, Ed, Engine, Geog, Pharm, Pre-Law,
      Pre-Med/Pre-Dental
      FREDONIA, COLLEGE AT 1110/24
      Bus Admin, Ed, Music
      GENESEO, COLLEGE AT 1220/27
      Biochem, Bus Admin, Geol, Music, Physics, Pre-Med/Pre-Dental
      NEW PALTZ, COLLEGE AT 1130/25
      Bus Admin, Ed, Psych
      ONEONTA, COLLEGE AT 1110/24
      Econ, Home Ec, Pre-Law
      OSWEGO, COLLEGE AT 1100/24
      Bus Admin, Home Ec, Psych
      PLATTSBURGH, COLLEGE AT 1070/23
      Bus Admin, Nurs

POTSDAM, COLLEGE AT 1050/22
Comp Sci, Math, Music
PURCHASE, COLLEGE AT 1060/23
Drama, English, Music, Pre-Law, Psych
STONY BROOK 1110/24
Astro, Biochem, Bio, Chem, Comp Sci, English, Geo, Philo, Physics,
Pre-Med/Pre-Dental, Psych, Reli Stu

NEW YORK UNIVERSITY (NY) 1280/29
Art, Art Hist, Bus Admin, Classics, Drama, For Lang, Math, Music, Nurs, Philo,
Pre-Med/Pre-Dental

NIAGARA UNIVERSITY (NY) 1040/22
Bus Admin, Drama, English, Pre-Law

NORTH CAROLINA SCHOOL OF THE ARTS (NC) 1040/22
Drama

NORTH CAROLINA, UNIVERSITY OF, AT
ASHEVILLE 1145/25
Ed, Hist, Soc, Psych
CHAPEL HILL 1215/27
Amer St, Art Hist, Astro, Bus Admin, Chem, Classics, Communic, Drama, Ed,
English, For Lang, Hist, Pharm
CHARLOTTE 1040/22
Bus Admin, Nurs, Pre-Med/Pre-Dental, Pre-Law, Psych, Zoo
GREENSBORO 1050/22
Art, Bus Admin, Communic, Home Ec, Nurs
WILMINGTON 1050/22
Bus Admin, English, Pre-Law, Soc, Psych

NORTH CAROLINA STATE UNIVERSITY (NC) 1155/25
Ag, Arch, Bot, Econ, Engine, Forest, Math, Pre-Law, Zoo

NORTH CENTRAL COLLEGE (IL) 1120/24
Bio, Communic, Comp Sci, Poli Sci, Pre-Med/Pre-Dental, Pre-Law

NORTH DAKOTA STATE UNIVERSITY (ND) 1100/24
Ag, Engine, Pharm

NORTH DAKOTA, UNIVERSITY OF (ND) 1100/24
Bus Admin, Ed

NORTH FLORIDA, UNIVERSITY OF (FL) 1105/24
Bus Admin, Ed, Music

NORTH GEORGIA COLLEGE (GA) 1000/21
Bus Admin

NORTH TEXAS, UNIVERSITY OF (TX) 1080/23
Music

NORTHEASTERN UNIVERSITY (MA) 1100/24
Bus Admin, Engine

NORTHEAST LOUISIANA UNIVERSITY (LA) 1000/21
Bus Admin, Nurs, Pharm

NORTHERN ARIZONA (AZ) 1025/22
Ed, Forest, Psych

NORTHERN COLORADO UNIVERSITY 1030/22
Music, Soc

NORTHERN ILLINOIS UNIVERSITY (IL) 1050/22
Bus Admin, Nurs

NORTHERN IOWA, UNIVERSITY OF (IA) 1080/23
Art, Bus Admin, Ed

NORTHLAND COLLEGE (WI) 1080/23
Bio

NORTHWESTERN COLLEGE (IA) 1075/23
Drama, Ed

NORTHWESTERN COLLEGE (MN) 1085/23
Ed

NORTHWESTERN UNIVERSITY (IL) 1350/30
Anthro, Astro, Chem, Communic, Drama, Econ, Engine, English, Hist, Math, Music, Poli Sci, Pre-Med/Pre-Dental, Pre-Law, Soc

NORTHWOOD UNIVERSITY (MI) 1000/21
Bus Admin

NOTRE DAME, UNIVERSITY OF (IN) 1290/29
Arch, Bus Admin, Chem, Engine, Poli Sci, Pre-Med/Pre-Dental, Pre-Law

NOVA SOUTHEASTERN UNIVERSITY (FL) 1030/22
Bus Admin

OAKLAND UNIVERSITY (MI) 1040/22
Comp Sci, Engine, Nurs

OBERLIN COLLEGE (OH) 1300/29
Art Hist, Chem, English, Music, Philo, Pre-Med/Pre-Dental, Pre-Law, Reli Stu, Soc

OCCIDENTAL COLLEGE (CA) 1200/26
Bio, Chem, Econ, Ed, Math, Physics, Poli Sci, Pre-Med/Pre-Dental, Pre-Law, Psych, Reli Stu

OGLETHORPE UNIVERSITY (GA) 1199/26
Bus Admin, Poli Sci, Pre-Law

OHIO NORTHERN UNIVERSITY (OH) 1115/24
Bio, Chem, Pharm

OHIO STATE UNIVERSITY (OH) 1085/24
Ag, Arch, Art/Studio, Bus Admin, Drama, Engine, Geog, Home Ec, Nurs, Pharm, Physics, Pre-Med/Pre-Dental

OHIO UNIVERSITY (OH) 1120/24
Art, Bus Admin, Communic, Drama, Ed, Engine, English, Hist, Math, Music, Pre-Law, Psych, Zoo

OHIO WESLEYAN UNIVERSITY (OH) 1180/26
Bio, Bot, Chem, Communic, Econ, Poli Sci, Pre-Med/Pre-Dental, Pre-Law, Psych, Zoo

OKLAHOMA BAPTIST UNIVERSITY (OK) 1099/24
Ed

OKLAHOMA CITY UNIVERSITY (OK) 1100/24
Bus Admin, Communic, Comp Sci

OKLAHOMA, UNIVERSITY OF (OK) 1115/24
Arch, Astro, Engine, English, Geol, Hist, Pre-Law, Zoo

OKLAHOMA STATE UNIVERSITY (OK) 1110/24
Ag, Bus Admin, Drama, Engine

OLD DOMINION UNIVERSITY (VA) 1050/22
Art, Bus Admin

OREGON, UNIVERSITY OF (OR) 1120/24
Anthro, Arch, Art Hist, Bus Admin, Chem, Comp Sci, Ed, Geog, Math, Psych

OREGON STATE UNIVERSITY (OR) 1040/22
Ag, Biochem, Bot, Forest, Home Ec, Physics

OTIS ART INSTITUTE/PARSONS (CA) 1000/21
Art

OTTERBEIN COLLEGE (OH) 1099/24
Drama, Psych

OZARKS, COLLEGE OF THE (MO) 1050/22
Bus Admin, Ed, Psych

PACE UNIVERSITY (NY) 1140/25
Bus Admin, Nurs, Psych

PACIFIC LUTHERAN UNIVERSITY (WA) 1105/24
Bus Admin, Nurs

PACIFIC UNIVERSITY (OR) 1110/24
Bus Admin, For Lang

PACIFIC, UNIVERSITY OF THE (CA) 1110/24
Engine, Music, Pharm

PALM BEACH ATLANTIC COLLEGE (FL) 1060/23
Psych

PARSONS SCHOOL OF DESIGN (NY) 1070/23
Art

PENNSYLVANIA, UNIVERSITY OF (PA) 1350/30
Amer St, Anthro, Art, Art Hist, Astro, Biochem, Bus Admin, Classics, Econ, Engine, English, For Lang, Geol, Hist, Nurs, Philo, Poli Sci, Pre-Law, Psych, Soc

PENNSYLVANIA STATE UNIVERSITY (PA) 1199/26
Ag, Arch, Biochem, Bot, Bus Admin, Chem, Comp Sci, Ed, Engine, Forest, Geog, Home Ec, Nurs, Pre-Med/Pre-Dental

PEPPERDINE UNIVERSITY (CA) 1160/25
Bus Admin, Communic, Comp Sci, For Lang

PERU STATE COLLEGE (NE) 1000/21
Ed

PHILADELPHIA COLLEGE OF ART (PA) 1000/21
Art

PHILADELPHIA COLLEGE OF PHARMACY AND SCIENCE (PA) 1140/25
Pharm

PHILADELPHIA COLLEGE OF TEXTILES AND SCIENCE (PA) 1050/22
Bus Admin

PITTSBURGH, UNIVERSITY OF (PA) 1140/25
Anthro, Bio Chem, Bus Admin, Engine, English, Nurs, Philo, Pre-Med/Pre-Dental, Pre-Law, Psych

PITTSBURGH, UNIVERSITY OF (BRADFORD) (PA) 1060/23
Comp Sci

PITTSBURGH, UNIVERSITY OF (JOHNSTOWN) (PA) 1100/24
Comp Sci, Engine

PITZER COLLEGE (CA) 1190/26
Anthro, Psych, Soc

POINT LOMA (CA) 1000/21
Bus Admin, Ed, Home Ec, Nurs

POINT PARK COLLEGE (PA) 1000/21
Drama

POLYTECHNIC UNIVERSITY OF NEW YORK (NY) 1195/26
Engine

POMONA COLLEGE (CA) 1410/32
*Amer St, Anthro, Bio, Chem, Econ, English, For Lang, Geol, Hist, Math, Philo,
Pre-Med/Pre-Dental, Pre-Law, Reli Stu*

PORTLAND, UNIVERSITY OF (OR) 1126/25
Engine

PRATT INSTITUTE (NY) 1040/22
Arch

PRESBYTERIAN COLLEGE (SC) 1130/25
Bio, Bus Admin, English, Poli Sci, Pre-Med/Pre-Dental, Pre-Law

PRINCETON UNIVERSITY (NJ) 1430/32
*Arch, Art Hist, Bio, Biochem, Chem, Classics, Drama, Econ, Engine, English, For Lang, Geol,
Hist, Math, Music, Philo, Physics, Poli Sci, Pre-Med/Pre-Dental, Pre-Law, Reli Sci*

PRINCIPIA COLLEGE (IL) 1100/24
Art, Bus Admin, Ed, English, Pre-Law

PROVIDENCE COLLEGE (RI) 1165/26
Bus Admin, Poli Sci, Pre-Law

PUERTO RICO, UNIVERSITY OF (PR) 1100/24
Bus Admin, Ed

PUERTO RICO, UNIVERSITY OF (CAYEY) (PR) 1000/21
Bio, Bus Admin, Ed

PUGET SOUND, UNIVERSITY OF (WA) 1199/26
Bus Admin, English, Pre-Law, Soc

PURDUE UNIVERSITY (IN) 1120/24
Ag, Biochem, Bot, Bus Admin, Chem, Engine, Forest, Geol, Home Ec, Pharm

QUEENS COLLEGE (NC) 1140/25
Bus Admin, English, Hist, Pre-Law

QUINCY UNIVERSITY (IL) 1080/23
Bus Admin, Soc

QUINNIPIAC COLLEGE (CT) 1099/24
Bus Admin, Comp Sci

RADFORD UNIVERSITY (VA) 1000/21
Bus Admin, Ed, Geog, Poli Sci, Pre-Law

RANDOLPH-MACON COLLEGE (VA) 1140/25
Bio, Econ, English, Poli Sci, Pre-Law, Pre-Med/Pre-Dental, Psych

RANDOLPH-MACON WOMAN'S COLLEGE (VA) 1150/25
Art, Bio, Classics, Communic, English, Pre-Law, Pre-Med/Pre-Dental, Psych

REDLANDS, UNIVERSITY OF (CA) 1100/24
Art, Bus Admin, Ed, English, Music, Poli Sci, Pre-Law

REED COLLEGE (OR) 1310/29
Bio, Chem, English, Hist, Philo, Physics, Pre-Law, Pre-Med/Pre-Dental, Psych

REGIS UNIVERSITY (CO) 1100/24
Bio Chem, Bus Admin, Communic, Comp Sci, Ed, Philo, Pre-Med/Pre-Dental, Psych, Reli Stu

RENSSELAER POLYTECHNIC INSTITUTE (NY) 1230/27
Arch, Bus Admin, Comp Sci, Engine, Math, Physics

RHODE ISLAND SCHOOL OF DESIGN (RI) 1100/24
Arch, Art

RHODE ISLAND, UNIVERSITY OF (RI) 1080/23
Comp Sci, Engine, English, Nurs, Pharm, Poli Sci, Pre-Law

RHODES COLLEGE (TN) 1260/28
Bio, Econ, English, Hist, Poli Sci, Pre-Law, Pre-Med/Pre-Dental, Psych

RICE UNIVERSITY (TX) 1400/31
Anthro, Arch, Biochem, Bio, Chem, Comp Sci, Engine, Hist, Math, Music, Physics, Pre-Law, Pre-Med/Pre-Dental

RICHMOND, UNIVERSITY OF (VA) 1270/28
Bus Admin, English, Pre-Law

RIDER UNIVERSITY (NJ) 1010/21
Comp Sci, Music

RIPON COLLEGE (WI) 1130/25
Bio, Biochem, Bus Admin, Chem, Econ, English, Poli Sci, Pre-Law, Pre-Med/Pre-Dental

ROANOKE COLLEGE (VA) 1150/25
Art, Bio, Bus Admin, Psych, Pre-Law, Reli Stu, Soc

ROCHESTER, UNIVERSITY OF (NY) 1270/28
*Art, Art Hist, Biochem, Bio, Chem, Comp Sci, Econ, English, For Lang, Geol, Music, Nurs,
Philo, Poli Sci, Pre-Law, Pre-Med/Pre-Dental*

ROCHESTER INSTITUTE OF TECHNOLOGY (NY) 1150/25
Comp Sci, Engine

ROCKFORD COLLEGE (IL) 1040/22
Art, Drama, English, Pre-Law

ROCKHURST COLLEGE (MO) 1120/24
Bus Admin, Chem, Home Ec

ROGER WILLIAMS UNIVERSITY (RI) 1065/23
Arch

ROLLINS COLLEGE (FL) 1140/25
Classics, Drama, English, Physics, Psych

ROOSEVELT UNIVERSITY (IL) 1000/21
Bus Admin

ROSE-HULMAN INSTITUTE OF TECHNOLOGY 1330/30
Engine

ROSEMONT COLLEGE (PA) 1100/24
Art, Art Hist, English, Psych

ROWAN UNIVERSITY OF NEW JERSEY (NJ) 1140/25
Bus Admin, Communic, Ed, Home Ec, Music

RUSSELL SAGE COLLEGE (THE SAGE COLLEGES) (NY) 1065/23
Nurs

RUTGERS UNIVERSITY (NJ) 1200/26
Ag, Biochem, Bio, Chem, Ed, Engine, English, For Lang, Pharm, Pre-Law, Pre-Med/Pre-Dental

RUTGERS UNIVERSITY (CAMDEN) (NJ) 1160/25
Comp Sci, English, Hist, Pre-Law

SACRED HEART UNIVERSITY (CT) 1060/23
Biochem, Bus Admin, Psych

ST. AMBROSE COLLEGE (IA) 1050/22
Communic, Comp Sci

ST. ANDREWS PRESBYTERIAN COLLEGE (NC) 1030/22
Biochem, Bus Admin, Philo

ST. ANSELM COLLEGE (NH) 1080/23
Econ, Nurs, Pre-Law, Soc

ST. BONAVENTURE UNIVERSITY (NY) 1110/24
Bus Admin, Communic, Ed, Philo, Poli Sci, Pre-Law, Reli Stu

ST. CATHERINE, COLLEGE OF (MN) 1060/23
Music, Nurs, Reli Stu, Soc

ST. FRANCIS COLLEGE (NY) 1000/21
Bus Admin

ST. JOHN FISHER COLLEGE (NY) 1060/23
Bus Admin, Communic

ST. JOHN'S UNIVERSITY (NY) 1040/22
Bus Admin, Pharm

SAINT JOHN'S UNIVERSITY/COLLEGE OF SAINT BENEDICT (MN) 1120/24
Bio, Bus Admin, Chem, Econ, Physics, Physics, Poli Sci, Pre-Law, Pre-Med/Pre-Dental

SAINT JOSEPH'S COLLEGE (CT) 1000/21
Ed

ST. JOSEPH'S COLLEGE (IN) 1040/22
Ed, Psych

ST. JOSEPH'S COLLEGE (ME) 1050/22
Ed, Nurs

SAINT JOSEPH'S UNIVERSITY (PA) 1150/25
Bus Admin

ST. LAWRENCE UNIVERSITY (NY) 1185/26
Econ, English, Geol, Poli Sci, Pre-Law, Psych, Soc

ST. LOUIS COLLEGE OF PHARMACY (MO) 1115/24
Pharm, Pre-Med/Pre-Dental

SAINT LOUIS UNIVERSITY (MO) 1135/25
Bio, Chem, Communic, Ed, Nurs, Philo, Pre-Med/Pre-Dental

SAINT MARY COLLEGE (KS) 1000/21
English

SAINT MARY'S COLLEGE (IN) 1110/24
Bus Admin, Ed, English, Nurs, Pre-Law

SAINT MARY'S COLLEGE OF CALIFORNIA (CA) 1100/24
Bus Admin, Ed, Soc

ST. MARY'S COLLEGE OF MARYLAND (MD) 1250/28
Bio, Math, Music, Pre-Med/Pre-Dental, Psych

ST. MARY'S UNIVERSITY OF MINNESOTA (MN) 1030/22
Bus Admin, Communic, Drama, Ed, Hist

ST. MARY'S UNIVERSITY OF SAN ANTONIO (TX) 1050/22
Bus Admin, Poli Sci, Pre-Law, Soc

SAINT MICHAEL'S COLLEGE (VT) 1115/24
Bus Admin, Chem, Communic, Ed

ST. NORBERT COLLEGE (WI) 1120/24
Bus Admin

ST. OLAF COLLEGE (MN) 1200/26
Amer St, Art, Bio, Chem, Econ, English, Home Ec, Math, Music, Nurs, Philo, Pre-Law, Pre-Med/Pre-Dental, Psych

SAINT ROSE, COLLEGE OF (NY) 1050/22
Bus Admin, Ed

SAINT SCHOLASTICA, COLLEGE OF (MN) 1070/23
Nurs

SAINT THOMAS, UNIVERSITY OF (MN) 1099/24
Bus Admin

SAINT THOMAS, UNIVERSITY OF (TX) 1160/25
Pre-Med/Pre-Dental

ST. VINCENT COLLEGE (PA) 1090/24
Bio, Pre-Med/Pre-Dental, Psych

SALEM COLLEGE (NC) 1120/24
Art, Art Hist, Bus Admin, Econ, English, Pre-Law, Soc

SALEM STATE COLLEGE (MA) 1000/21
Geog

SALISBURY STATE UNIVERSITY (MD) 1140/25
Ed, Psych

SAMFORD UNIVERSITY (AL) 1115/24
Bus Admin, Communic, Nurs, Pharm

SAN DIEGO STATE UNIVERSITY (CA) 1000/21
Bus Admin, Communic

SAN DIEGO, UNIVERSITY OF (CA) 1120/24
Bus Admin, Nurs, Reli Stu

SAN FRANCISCO CONSERVATORY OF MUSIC (CA) 1150/25
Music

SAN FRANCISCO, UNIVERSITY OF (CA) 1100/24
Bus Admin, Nurs, Psych

SAN FRANCISCO STATE UNIVERSITY (CA) 1000/21
Drama, English, Pre-Law, Soc

SAN JOSE STATE UNIVERSITY (CA) 1000/21
Comp Sci

SANTA CLARA UNIVERSITY (CA) 1175/26
Bus Admin, Comp Sci, Music, Pre-Law

SANTA FE, COLLEGE OF (NM) 1100/24
Art, Communic, Drama

SARAH LAWRENCE COLLEGE (NY) 1200/26
Amer St, Drama, English, Pre-Law

SCHREINER COLLEGE (TX) 1070/23
Bus Admin

SCRANTON, UNIVERSITY OF (PA) 1170/26
Bio, Bus Admin, Communic, Pre-Med/Pre-Dental

SCRIPPS COLLEGE (CA) 1225/27
Art, Bio, Drama, English, Pre-Law, Pre-Med/Pre-Dental

SEATTLE UNIVERSITY (WA) 1090/24
Bus Admin, Nurs

SEATTLE PACIFIC UNIVERSITY (WA) 1100/24
Engine, Home Ec, Nurs

SETON HALL UNIVERSITY (NJ) 1050/23
Bus Admin, Communic, Ed, Nurs, Psych

SETON HILL COLLEGE (PA) 1040/22
Art, Drama, Home Ec, Music

SHAW UNIVERSITY (NC) 1010/21
Bus Admin

SHEPHERD COLLEGE (WV) 1170/26
Art, Bus Admin, Ed, Music, Psych

SHIPPENSBURG UNIVERSITY (PA) 1100/24
Bus Admin, Ed

SIENA COLLEGE (NY) 1115/24
Bus Admin, Poli Sci, Pre-Law, Pre-Med/Pre-Dental

SIMMONS COLLEGE (MA) 1100/24
Bus Admin, Communic, Math, Nurs, Psych

SIMPSON COLLEGE (IA) 1080/23
Bus Admin, Ed

SKIDMORE COLLEGE (NY) 1200/26
Amer St, Anthro, Art, Art Hist, Bio, Biochem, Bus Admin, Chem, Drama, Ed, English, For Lang, Music, Philo, Poli Sci, Pre-Law, Pre-Med/Pre-Dental

SMITH COLLEGE (MA) 1300/27
Amer St, Anthro, Art, Art Hist, Bio, Econ,English, For Lang, Hist, Music, Philo, Physics, Poli Sci, Pre-Law, Pre-Med/Pre-Dental, Psych

SONOMA STATE UNIVERSITY (CA) 1020/22
Bus Admin, Geog, Psych

SOUTH, UNIVERSITY OF THE (TN) 1220/27
Anthro, Bio, Econ, English, For Lang, Hist, Poli Sci, Pre-Law, Pre-Med/Pre-Dental, Reli Stu

SOUTH CAROLINA, UNIVERSITY OF (SC) 1086/23
Bus Admin, Communic, Comp Sci, Engine, Phar

SOUTH DAKOTA, UNIVERSITY OF (SD) 1050/22
Bus Admin, Nurs

SOUTH DAKOTA SCHOOL OF MINES (SD) 1135/25
Engine

SOUTHERN CALIFORNIA, UNIVERSITY OF (CA) 1199/26
Arch, Bus Admin, Communic, Engine, Math, Music, Pharm, Psych

SOUTHERN ILLINOIS UNIVERSITY (CARBONDALE) (IL) 1020/22
Bus Admin, Zoo

SOUTHERN MAINE, UNIVERSITY OF (ME) 1050/22
Engine, Nurs

SOUTH FLORIDA, UNIVERSITY OF (FL) 1075/24
Amer St, Bus Admin, Drama, For Lang, Nurs

SOUTHERN METHODIST UNIVERSITY (TX) 1180/26
Art, Art Hist, Bus Admin, Drama, Communic, Reli Stu

SOUTHERN MISSISSIPPI, UNIVERSITY OF (MS) 1040/22
Bus Admin

SOUTHWEST MISSOURI STATE UNIVERSITY (MO) 1080/23
Ed, Math

SOUTHERN OREGON STATE COLLEGE (OR) 1040/22
Ed, For Lang

SOUTHERN UTAH UNIVERSITY (UT) 1015/22
Drama, Ed

SOUTHWEST BAPTIST UNIVERSITY (MO) 1040/22
Ed, Music, Reli Stu

SOUTHWESTERN UNIVERSITY (TX) 1200/26
Art, Bio, Bus Admin, Chem, Communic, Drama, English, For Lang, Hist, Music, Poli Sci,
Pre-Law, Pre-Med/Pre-Dental, Psych, Soc

SOUTHWEST TEXAS STATE UNIVERSITY (TX) 1010/21
Bus Admin

SPELMAN COLLEGE (GA) 1060/23
Bio, Chem, Comp Sci, English, Poli Sci, Pre-Law, Pre-Med/Pre-Dental, Soc

SPRING HILL COLLEGE (AL) 1100/24
Bio, Bus Admin, Chem, Communic, English, Hist, Poli Sci, Pre-Law, Pre-Med/Pre-Dental

STANFORD UNIVERSITY (CA) 1400/31
Amer St, Anthro, Bio, Chem, Classics, Communic, Comp Sci, Econ, Engine, English, Hist, Math,
Physics, Poli Sci, Pre-Law, Pre-Med/Pre-Dental, Psych, Reli Stu, Soc

STEPHEN F. AUSTIN STATE UNIVERSITY (TX) 1000/21
Forest

STETSON UNIVERSITY (FL) 1120/24
Bus Admin, Chem, Ed, English, Hist, Math, Music, Pre-Law, Pre-Med/Pre-Dental, Psych

STEVENS UNIVERSITY OF TECHNOLOGY (NJ) 1245/28
Engine

STOCKTON STATE (RICHARD STOCKTON COLLEGE OF NEW JERSEY) (NJ) 1140/25
Bus Admin, Physics

STONEHILL COLLEGE (MA) 1120/24
Bus Admin, Poli Sci, Pre-Law, Psych

SUNY COLLEGE OF ENVIRONMENTAL SCIENCE & FORESTRY (NY) 1200/26
Forestry

SUSQUEHANNA UNIVERSITY (PA) 1150/25
Bus Admin, Communic, Drama

SWARTHMORE COLLEGE (PA) 1375/31
Art Hist, Biochem, Bio, Classics, Econ, Ed, Engine, English, Hist, Philo, Physics, Poli Sci,
Pre-Law, Pre-Med/Pre-Dental, Psych

SWEET BRIAR COLLEGE (VA) 1140/25
Art Hist, For Lang, Math, Psych

SYRACUSE UNIVERSITY (NY) 1190/26
Arch, Art, Bus Admin, Communic, Drama, Forest, Poli Sci, Pre-Law, Psych, Soc

TAMPA, UNIVERSITY OF (FL) 1050/22
Bus Admin, Communic, Music

TAYLOR UNIVERSITY (IN) 1099/24
Psych, Reli Stu

TEMPLE UNIVERSITY (PA) 1099/24
Art, Biochem, Bio, Chem, Ciommunic, English, Drama, Music, Pharm, Pre-Law,
Pre-Med/Pre-Dental, Soc

TENNESSEE, UNIVERSITY OF (TN) 1099/24
Ag, Anthro, Bot, Bus Admin, Ed, English, Pre-Law, Zoo

TEXAS, UNIVERSITY OF, AT
      ARLINGTON 1030/22
      Arch, Bus Admin, Engine
      AUSTIN 1190/26
      Amer St, Arch, Astro, Bot, Bus Admin, Comp Sci, Drama, Ed, For Lang, Geog, Geol,
      Hist, Journal, Math, Pharm, Physics, Psych
      SAN ANTONIO 1000/21
      Bus Admin

TEXAS A&M (TX) 1170/26
Ag, Arch, Bus Admin, Chem, Ed, Engine, Forest, Geol, Pre-Med/Pre-Dental, Zoo

TEXAS A&M AT GALVESTON (TX) 1130/25
Bus Admin

TEXAS CHRISTIAN UNIVERSITY (TX) 1140/25
Bus Admin, Communic, Drama, Geol, Hist, Nurs, Reli Stu

TEXAS TECH UNIVERSITY (TX) 1060/23
Ag, Ed, Home Ec, Math

TEXAS WESLEYAN COLLEGE (TX) 1000/21
Bus Admin, Communic, Ed

THOMAS MORE COLLEGE (KY) 1080/23
Bio, Bus Admin, Pre-Med/Pre-Dental

TOLEDO, UNIVERSITY OF (OH) 1040/22
Bus Admin, Econ, Pharm

TOUGALOO COLLEGE (MS) 1000/21
Bio, Ed

TOWSON STATE (MD) 1060/23
Bus Admin

TRANSYLVANIA UNIVERSITY (KY) 1170/26
Bus Admin, Comp Sci, Pre-Med/Pre-Dental

TRINITY COLLEGE (CT) 1255/28
Bio, Bus Admin, Econ, Engine, Math, Philo, Pre-Law, Pre-Med/Pre-Dental, Reli Stu

TRINITY COLLEGE (DC) 1100/24
Bus Admin, For Lang, Math, Poli Sci, Pre-Law, Soc

TRINITY UNIVERSITY (TX) 1250/28
Art, Chem, Communic, Econ, Ed, English, Hist, Philo, Poli Sci, Pre-Law, Pre-Med/Pre-Dental

TRUMAN STATE UNIVERSITY (MO) 1190/26
Bio, Bus Admin, Chem, Ed, For Lang, Nurs, Pre-Med/Pre-Dental

TUFTS UNIVERSITY (MA) 1300/29
*Bio, Chem, Classics, Drama, Ed, Engine, English, Hist, Poli Sci, Pre-Law,
Pre-Med/Pre-Dental, Psych*

TULANE UNIVERSITY (LA) 1255/28
*Amer St, Arch, Bio, Biochem, Bus Admin, Drama, Engine, For Lang, Hist, Math, Philo,
Pre-Med/Pre-Dental, Psych*

TULSA, UNIVERSITY OF (OK) 1180/26
Anthro, Communic, Engine, Geol, Psych

TUSKEGEE INSTITUTE (AL) 1000/21
Ag, Arch, Engine, Nurs

UNION COLLEGE (NY) 1250/28
Bio, Chem, Engine, Hist, Math, Poli Sci, Pre-Law, Pre-Med/Pre-Dental, Psych

UNION UNIVERSITY (TN) 1100/24
Nurs, Reli Stu

U. S. AIR FORCE ACADEMY (CO) 1270/28
Bus Admin, Engine

U. S. COAST GUARD ACADEMY (CT) 1255/28
Engine

U. S. MILITARY ACADEMY (NY) 1265/28
Engine

U. S. NAVAL ACADEMY (MD) 1280/29
Engine

URSINUS COLLEGE (PA) 1170/26
Bio, Bus Admin, Chem, Econ, Ed, Physics, Poli Sci, Pre-Law, Pre-Med/Pre-Dental

UTAH, UNIVERSITY OF (UT) 1115/24
Comp Sci, Drama, Engine, English, For Lang, Pre-Law

UTAH STATE UNIVERSITY (UT) 1040/22
Ag, Ed, Forest

UTICA COLLEGE OF SYRACUSE UNIVERSITY (NY) 1070/23
Bus Admin

VALPARAISO UNIVERSITY (IN) 1160/26
Bus Admin, Math, Nurs

VANDERBILT UNIVERSITY (TN) 1280/29
Anthro, Econ, Ed, Engine, English, Hist, Nurs, Pre-Law, Pre-Med, Psych

VASSAR COLLEGE (NY) 1300/29
Art Hist, Bio, Drama, English, Hist, Music, Pre-Law, Psych

VERMONT, UNIVERSITY OF (VT) 1125/25
Ag, Bio, Bot, Bus Admin, Chem, For Lang, Geog, Geol, Hist, Physics, Poli Sci,
Pre-Law, Pre-Med/Pre-Dental, Zoo

VILLANOVA UNIVERSITY (PA) 1210/27
Astro, Bio, Bus Admin, Communic, Engine, Nurs, Pre-Med/Pre-Dental

VIRGINIA COMMONWEALTH UNIVERSITY (VA) 1040/22
Art, Drama, Pharm, Pre-Med/Pre-Dental, Pre-Law, Psych, Reli Stu

VIRGINIA, UNIVERSITY OF (VA) 1285/29
Amer St, Arch, Art, Astro, Bio, Bus Admin, Econ, English, Hist, Nurs, Reli Stu

VIRGINIA MILITARY INSTITUTE (VA) 1120/23
Bus Admin, Econ, Engine, Pre-Law

VIRGINIA POLYTECHNIC INSTITUTE (VA) 1165/26
Ag, Arch, Biochem, Bus Admin, Engine, Forest, Psych

VIRGINIA WESLEYAN UNIVERSITY (VA) 1030/22
Bio, Bus Admin, Poli Sci, Pre-Law, Pre-Med/Pre-Dental, Psych, Soc

WABASH COLLEGE (IN) 1200/26
Bio, Hist, Math, Poli Sci, Pre-Law, Pre-Med/Pre-Dental, Psych

WAGNER COLLEGE (NY) 1070/23
Bus Admin, Ed, Soc

WAKE FOREST UNIVERSITY (NC) 1310/29
*Bio, Bus Admin, Econ, English, For Lang, Hist, Physics, Pre-Law, Pre-Med/Pre-Dental,
Psych, Reli Stu*

WARREN WILSON COLLEGE (NC) 1125/25
English, Hist, Pre-Law

WARTBURG COLLEGE (IA) 1099/24
Bio, Ed, Pre-Med/Pre-Dental

WASHINGTON COLLEGE (MD) 1150/25
Amer St, Bio, Hist, Pre-Med/Pre-Dental, Psych

WASHINGTON & JEFFERSON COLLEGE (PA) 1110/24
Art, Bio, Bus Admin, Chem, Econ, Ed, English, Pre-Law, Pre-Med/Pre-Dental, Psych

WASHINGTON & LEE UNIVERSITY (VA) 1325/30
Bus Admin, Econ, English, For Lang, Geol, Hist, Poli Sci, Pre-Law

WASHINGTON UNIVERSITY (MO) 1310/29
*Anthro, Arch, Art, Art Hist, Bio, Bus Admin, Comp Sci, Engine, English, For Lang, Geol,
Math, Physics, Pre-Law, Pre-Med/Pre-Dental*

WASHINGTON, UNIVERSITY OF (WA) 1145/25
*Anthro, Art, Bot, Bus Admin, Chem, Comp Sci, Drama, Econ, Ed, Engine, Forest, Geol,
Math, Nurs, Pre-Law, Pre-Med/Pre-Dental, Psych, Zoo*

WASHINGTON STATE UNIVERSITY (WA) 1075/23
Ag, Anthro, Bus Admin, Econ, Engine, Pharm, Zoo

WAYNE STATE UNIVERSITY (MI) 1000/21
Engine, For Lang, Nurs, Pharm, Pre-Med/Pre-Dental

WEBSTER UNIVERSITY (MO) 1090/24
Drama, Psych

WELLESLEY COLLEGE (MA) 1340/30
*Art, Art Hist, Bio, Chem, Econ, Ed, English, For Lang, Hist, Math, Physics, Poli Sci,
Pre-Law, Pre-Med/Pre-Dental, Reli Stu*

WELLS COLLEGE (NY) 1150/25
Amer St, Bus Admin, Ed, English, For Lang, Hist, Pre-Law, Psych, Soc

WESLEYAN COLLEGE (GA) 1100/24
Amer St, Art, Bus Admin

WESLEYAN UNIVERSITY (CT) 1320/30
*Amer St, Art, Astro, Bio, Chem, Drama, Econ, English, Hist, Math, Pre-Law,
Pre-Med/Pre-Dental, Psych, Reli Stu*

WEST CHESTER UNIVERSITY (PA) 1040/22
Bus Admin, Music

WESTERN CONNECTICUT STATE UNIVERSITY (CT) 1000/21
Bus Admin, Nurs

WESTERN KENTUCKY (KY) 1000/21
Ed, Nurs

WESTERN MARYLAND COLLEGE (MD) 1150/25
Bio, Bus Admin, Ed, Pre-Med/Pre-Dental, Soc

WESTERN MICHIGAN UNIVERSITY (MI) 1100/24
Ag, Bus Admin, Drama, Ed, Psych

WESTERN NEW ENGLAND COLLEGE (MA) 1000/21
Bus Admin, Engine, Psych

WESTERN WASHINGTON UNIVERSITY (WA) 1150/25
Art, Communic, Ed, Home Ec, Soc

WESTFIELD STATE COLLEGE (MA) 1010/21
Ed

WEST FLORIDA, UNIVERSITY OF (FL) 1099/24
Bus Admin, Comp Sci, Ed

WESTMINSTER COLLEGE (MO) 1140/25
Econ, Pre-Law, Psych

WESTMONT COLLEGE (CA) 1130/25
Econ, Pre-Law, Pre-Med/Pre-Dental, Psych, Reli Stu

WEST VIRGINIA UNIVERSITY (WV) 1050/22
Bus Admin, Communic, Drama, Forest, Music

WEST VIRGINIA WESLEYAN COLLEGE (WV) 1050/23
Art, Comp Sci, Ed

WHEATON COLLEGE (IL) 1275/28
*Art, Bio, Chem, Communic, Ed, English, Math, Music, Philo, Physics, Pre-Law,
Pre-Med/Pre-Dental, Reli Stu. Soc*

WHEATON COLLEGE (MA) 1160/25
*Art, Art Hist, Bio, Drama, Econ, English, For Lang, Poli Sci, Pre-Law,
Pre-Med/Pre-Dental, Psych, Soc*

WHEELOCK COLLEGE (MA) 1000/21
Ed

WHITMAN COLLEGE (WA) 1285/29
*Bio, Chem, Drama, Econ, English, For Lang, Hist, Math, Music, Philo, Physics, Poli Sci,
Pre-Law, Pre-Med/Pre-Dental, Psych, Soc*

WHITTIER COLLEGE (CA) 1065/23
Bus Admin, Chem, Econ, Ed, English, Poli Sci, Pre-Law

WHITWORTH COLLEGE (WA) 1130/25
Art, Ed, Music, Reli Stu

WIDENER UNIVERSITY (PA) 1060/23
Bus Admin, Nurs

WILBERFORCE UNIVERSITY (OH) 1000/21
Bus Admin, Poli Sci, Pre-Law

WILLAMETTE UNIVERSITY (OR) 1190/26
Bio, Chem, Econ, English, Hist, Math, Music, Poli Sci, Pre-Law, Pre-Med/Pre-Dental, Psych

WILLIAM JEWELL COLLEGE (MO) 1115/24
Bus Admin, Ed, Music, Nurs

WILLIAM & MARY, COLLEGE OF (VA) 1310/29
Amer St, Bio, Bus Admin, Comp Sci, Drama, Ed, Geol, Hist, Physics, Pre-Med/Pre-Dental, Reli Stu

WILLIAMS COLLEGE (MA) 1400/32
Amer St, Art, Art Hist, Astro, Chem, Classics, Comp Sci, Econ, English, Hist, Poli Sci, Pre-Med/Pre-Dental, Psych

WILMINGTON COLLEGE (OH) 1000/21
Ag, Ed

WILSON COLLEGE (PA) 1063/23
Econ, Pre-Law, Soc

WINONA STATE UNIVERSITY (MN) 1050/22
Bio, Communic, English, Pre-Med/Pre-Dental, Soc

WISCONSIN, UNIVERSITY OF, AT
      GREEN BAY 1030/22
      Bus Admin
      LA CROSSE 1080/23
      Comp Sci
      MADISON 1199/26
      Ag, Anthro, Biochem, Bot, Bus Admin, Communic, Comp Sci, Ed, Engine, English, For Lang, Forest, Geol, Hist, Home Ec, Math, Nurs, Physics, Pre-Law, Psych, Soc
      MILWAUKEE 1065/23
      Anthro, Ed, English, Nurs, Pre-Law
      PLATTEVILLE 1050/23
      Ag, Engine, Ed
      STEVENS POINT 1110/24
      Bio, Bus Admin, Communic, Ed, Home Ec, Soc

WITTENBERG UNIVERSITY (OH) 1160/25
Art, Bio, Bus Admin, Ed, English, Geog, Hist, Music, Poli Sci, Pre-Law, Pre-Med/Pre-Dental, Psych

WOFFORD COLLEGE (SC) 1175/26
Bio, Chem, Comp Sci, Econ, Ed, English, For Lang, Hist, Math, Philo, Pre-Law, Pre-Med/Pre-Dental, Psych

WOODBURY UNIVERSITY (CA) 1000/21
Arch, Bus Admin

WOOSTER, COLLEGE OF (OH) 1165/26
Art Hist, Bio, Chem, Drama, Econ, Geol, Hist, Math, Music, Pre-Law, Pre-Med/Pre-Dental, Reli Stu, Soc

WORCESTER POLYTECHNIC INSTITUTE (MA) 1285/29
Comp Sci, Engine, Physics, Pre-Law

WYOMING, UNIVERSITY OF (WY) 1080/23
Ag, Astro, Bot, Bus Admin, Chem, Econ, Engine, Geol, Pharm, Physics, Pre-Law,
Pre-Med/Pre-Dental, Psych

XAVIER UNIVERSITY (OH) 1099/24
Bus Admin, Communic

XAVIER UNIVERSITY OF LOUISIANA (LA) 1020/22
Bio, Bus Admin, Chem, Pharm, Pre-Med/Pre-Dental, Psych

YALE UNIVERSITY (CT) 1405/32
Amer St, Anthro, Arch, Art, Art Hist, Biochem, Bio, Classics, Drama, Econ, English, For Lang,
Hist, Math, Music, Philo, Poli Sci, Pre-Law, Pre-Med/Pre-Dental, Psych, Reli Stu

YESHIVA UNIVERSITY (NY) 1220/27
Bio, Bus Admin, Comp Sci, Hist, Physics, Poli Sci, Pre-Med/Pre-Dental, Psych

YORK COLLEGE OF PENNSYLVANIA (PA) 1110/24
Ed, Nurs

SECTION FOUR

APPENDICES

APPENDIX A
The 760 Colleges Used In This Study

A **Adelphi University**
Garden City, NY 11530

Adrian College
Adrian, Michigan 49221

◆ **Agnes Scott College**
Decatur, Georgia 30030

◆ **Alabama, University of**
Tuscaloosa, Alabama 35487

Alaska, University of
Fairbanks, Alaska 99775

Alaska, University of
Anchorage, Alaska 99508

Albany College of Pharmacy
Albany, New York 12208

Albertson College
Caldwell, Idaho 83605

◆ **Albion College**
Albion, Michigan 49224

Albright College
Reading, Pennsylvania 19612

Alfred University
Alfred, New York 14802

◆ **Allegheny College**
Meadville, Pennsylvania 16335

Allentown College of St. Francis De Sales
Center Valley, Pennsylvania 18034

◆ **Alma College**
Alma, Michigan 48801

American Academy of Dramatic Arts
New York, New York 10016

American International College
Springfield, Massachusetts 01109

◆ **American University**
Washington, DC 20016

◆ **Amherst College**
Amherst, Massachusetts 01002

Appalachian State University
Boone, North Carolina 28608

Aquinas College
Grand Rapids, Michigan 49506

◆ **Arizona, University of**
Tucson, Arizona 85721

◆ **Arizona State University**
Tempe, Arizona 85287

◆ **Arkansas, University of**
Fayetteville, Arkansas 72701

Art Center College of Design
Pasadena, California 91103

Asbury College
Wilmore, Kentucky 40390

Auburn University
Auburn University, Alabama 36849

Augsburg College
Minneapolis, Minnesota 55454

◆ **Augustana College**
Rock Island, Illinois 61201

Augustana College
Sioux Falls, South Dakota 57197

Austin College
Sherman, Texas 75091

Averett College
Danville, Virginia 24541

B **Babson College**
Wellesley, Massachusetts 02157

Baker University
Baldwin City, Kansas 66006

Baldwin-Wallace College
Berea, Ohio 44017

Bard College, Annandale-on-Hudson
New York 12504

Barry University
Miami Shores, Florida 33161

◆ **Bates College**
Lewiston, Maine 04240

◆ **Baylor University**
Waco, Texas 76798

Beaver College
Glenside, Pennsylvania 19038

Belhaven College
Jackson, Mississippi 39202

Bellarmine College
Louisville, Kentucky 40205

Belmont Abbey College
Belmont, North Carolina 28012

Belmont University
Nashville, Tennessee 37212

◆ **Beloit College**
Beloit, Wisconsin 53511

Bemidji State University
Bemidji, Minnesota 56601

◆ Phi Beta Kappa Schools   ▮ Predominantly African-American Institution

Benedictine College
Atchison, Kansas 66002

Benedictine University
Lisle, Illinois 60532

■ Bennett College
Greensboro, North Carolina 27401

Bennington College
Bennington, Vermont 05201

Bentley College
Waltham, Massachusetts 02254

Bethel College
St. Paul, Minnesota 55112

Berea College
Berea, Kentucky 40404

Berry College
Rome, Georgia 30149

Bethany College
Bethany, West Virginia 26032

Biola University
La Mirada, California 91720

◆ Birmingham-Southern College
Birmingham, Alabama 32254

Bloomsburg University
Bloomsburg, Pennsylvania 17815

Bluffton College
Bluffton, Ohio 45817

◆ Boston College
Chestnut Hill, Massachusetts 02167

Boston Conservatory
Boston, Massachusetts 02215

◆ Boston University
Boston, Massachusetts 02215

◆ Bowdoin College
Brunswick, Maine 04011

◆ Bowling Green State University
Bowling Green, Ohio 43403

Bradley University
Peoria, Illinois 61625

◆ Brandeis University
Waltham, Massachusetts 02250

Brigham Young University
Provo, Utah 84602

◆ Brown University
Providence, Rhode Island 02912

Bryant College
Smithfield, Rhode Island 02917

Bryn Mawr College
Bryn Mawr, Pennsylvania 19010

◆ Bucknell University
Lewisburg, Pennsylvania 17837

Buena Vista College
Storm Lake, Iowa 50588

Butler University
Indianapolis, Indiana 46208

C Caldwell College
Caldwell, New Jersey 07006

California Institute of the Arts
Valencia, California 91355

California Institute of Technology
Pasadena, California 91125

California, University of, at
◆ Berkeley, California 94720
◆ Davis, California 95616
◆ Irvine, California 92717
◆ Los Angeles, California 90024
◆ Riverside, California 92521
◆ San Diego, California 92093
◆ Santa Barbara, California 93106
◆ Santa Cruz, California 95064

California Lutheran University
Thousand Oaks, CA 91360

California Maritime Academy
Vallejo, California 94590

California Polytechnic State University
San Luis Obispo, California 93407

California Polytechnic State University
Pomona, California 91768

◆ California State University
Chico, California 95926

California State University
Long Beach, California 90840

Calvin College
Grand Rapids, Michigan 49506

Capital University
Columbus, Ohio 43209

◆ Carleton College
Northfield, Minnesota 55057

◆ Carnegie Mellon University
Pittsburgh, Pennsylvania 15213

Carroll College
Helena, Montana 59601

Carroll College
Waukesha, Wisconsin 53186

Carthage College
Kenosha, Wisconsin 53141

◆ Case Western Reserve University
Cleveland, Ohio 44106

◆ Phi Beta Kappa Schools   ■ Predominantly African-American Institution

Catawba College
Salisbury, North Carolina 28144

Catholic University of America
Washington, DC 20064

Cedar Crest College
Allentown, Pennsylvania 18104

Cedarville College
Cedarville, Ohio 45314

Centenary College of Louisiana
Shreveport, Louisiana 71135

Central Florida, University of
Orlando, Florida 32816

Central Michigan University
Mount Pleasant, Michigan 48859

Central College
Pella, Iowa 50219

◆ **Centre College**
Danville, Kentucky 40422

Chapman College
Orange, California 92666

College of Charleston
Charleston, South Carolina 29424

Charleston, University of
Charleston, West Virginia 25304

◆ **Chatham College**
Pittsburgh, Pennsylvania 15232

Chestnut Hill College
Philadelphia, Pennsylvania 19118

◆ **Chicago, University of**
Chicago, Illinois 60637

Christian Brothers College
Memphis, Tennessee 38104

◆ **Cincinnati, University of**
Cincinnati, Ohio 45221

◆ **Claremont McKenna College**
Claremont, California 91711

◆ **Clark University**
Worcester, Massachusetts 01610

Clarke College
Dubuque, Iowa 52001

Clarkson University
Potsdam, New York 13676

Clemson University
Clemson, South Carolina 29634

Cleveland Institute of Music
Cleveland, Ohio 44106

◆ **Coe College**
Cedar Rapids, Iowa 52402

◆ **Colby College**
Waterville, Maine 04901

◆ **Colgate University**
Hamilton, New York 13346

◆ **Colorado College**
Colorado Springs, Colorado 80903

◆ **Colorado, University of**
Boulder, Colorado 80309

Colorado, University of
Colorado Springs, Colorado 80933

Colorado, University of
Denver, Colorado 80208

Colorado School of Mines
Golden, Colorado 80401

◆ **Colorado State University**
Fort Collins, Colorado 80523

◆ **Columbia University**
New York, New York 10027
  ◆ **Barnard College**, New York, NY 10027

Concordia College
Moorhead, Minnesota 56560

◆ **Connecticut, University of**
Storrs, Connecticut 06268

◆ **Connecticut College**
New London, Connecticut 06320

Converse College
Spartanburg, South Carolina 29301

Cooper Union College, The
New York, New York 10003

◆ **Cornell College**
Mount Vernon, Iowa 52314

◆ **Cornell University**
Ithaca, New York 14853

Covenant College
Lookout Mountain, Georgia 30750

Creighton University
Omaha, Nebraska 68178

Curtis Institute of Music
Philadelphia, Pennsylvania 19103

D **Daemen College**
Amherst, New York 14226

◆ **Dallas, University of**
Irving, Texas 75062

◆ **Dartmouth College**
Hanover, New Hampshire 03755

◆ **Davidson College**
Davidson, North Carolina 28036

◆ Phi Beta Kappa Schools ■ Predominantly African-American Institution

Dayton, University of
Dayton, Ohio 45469

◆ Delaware, University of
Newark, Delaware 19716

Delaware Valley College
Doylestown, Pennsylvania 18901

◆ Denison University
Granville, Ohio 43023

◆ Denver, University of
Denver, Colorado 80208

DePaul University
Chicago, Illinois 60604

◆ DePauw University
Greencastle, Indiana 46135

Detroit Mercy, University of
Detroit, Michigan 48221

◆ Dickinson College
Carlisle, Pennsylvania 17013

■ Dillard University
New Orleans, Louisiana 70122

Doane College
Crete, Nebraska 68333

Dordt College
Sioux Center, Iowa 51250

◆ Drake University
Des Moines, Iowa 50311

◆ Drew University
Madison, New Jersey 07940

Drexel University
Philadelphia, Pennsylvania 19104

Drury College
Springfield, Missouri 65802

◆ Duke University
Durham, North Carolina 27706

Duquesne University
Pittsburgh, Pennsylvania 15219

D'Youville College
Buffalo, New York 14201

E ◆ Earlham College
Richmond, Indiana 47374

Eastern College
St. Davids, Pennsylvania 19087

Eastern Michigan University
Ypsilanti, Michigan 48197

East Carolina University
Greenville, North Carolina 27858

Eckerd College
St. Petersburg, Florida 33733

Edgewood College
Madison, Wisconsin 53711

Elizabethtown College
Elizabethtown, Pennsylvania 17022

Elon College
Elon College, North Carolina 27244

◆ Elmira College
Elmira, New York 14901

Emerson College
Boston, Massachusetts 02116

Emory and Henry College
Emory, Virginia 24327

◆ Emory University
Atlanta, Georgia 30322

Erskine College
Due West, South Carolina 39639

Eureka College
Eureka, Illinois 61530

Evansville, University of
Evansville, Indiana 47722

F ◆ Fairfield University
Fairfield, Connecticut 06430

Fairleigh Dickinson University
Rutherford, New Jersey 07070

Ferris State University
Big Rapids, Michigan 49307

◆■ Fisk University
Nashville, Tennessee 37203

Five Towns College
Dix Hills, New York 11746

Flagler College
St. Augustine, Florida 32085

◆ Florida, University of
Gainesville, Florida 32611

■ Florida A&M University
Tallahassee, FL 32307

Florida Atlantic University
Boca Raton, Florida 33431

Florida Institute of Technology
Melbourne, Florida 32901

Florida International University
Miami, Florida 33199

◆ Florida State University
Tallahassee, Florida 32306

Florida Southern College
Lakeland, Florida 33801

◆ Phi Beta Kappa Schools   ■ Predominantly African-American Institution

Fontbonne College
St. Louis, Missouri 63105

Franklin College of Indiana
Franklin, Indiana 46131

◆ **Fordham University**
Bronx, New York 10458

Fort Lewis College
Durango, Colorado 81301

Franciscan University of Steubenville
Steubenville, Ohio 43952

◆ **Franklin & Marshall College**
Lancaster, Pennsylvania 17604

◆ **Furman University, Greenville**
South Carolina 29613

G **Gannon University, Erie**
Pennsylvania 16541

Geneva College
Beaver Falls, Pennsylvania 15010

General Motors Inst.
Flint, MI 48504

Geneva College
Beaver Falls, Pennsylvania 15010

◆ **Georgetown University**
Washington, DC 20057

George Fox College
Newberg, Oregon 97132

George Mason University
Fairfax, Virginia 22030

◆ **George Washington University**
Washington, DC 20052

◆ **Georgia, University of**
Athens, Georgia 30602

Georgia Institute of Technology
Atlanta, Georgia 30332

Georgia Southern University
Statesboro, Georgia 30460

◆ **Gettysburg College**
Gettysburg, Pennsylvania 17325

Gonzaga University
Spokane, Washington 99258

Gordon College
Wenham, Massachusetts 01984

Goshen College
Goshen, Indiana 46526

◆ **Goucher College**
Towson, Maryland 21204

Graceland College
Lamoni, Iowa 50140

Grand Valley State University
Allendale, Michigan 49401

◆ **Grinnell College**
Grinnell, Iowa 50112

Grove City College
Grove City, Pennsylvania 16127

Guilford College
Greensboro, North Carolina 27410

◆ **Gustavus Adolphus College**
St. Peter, Minnesota 56082

H ◆ **Hamilton College**
Clinton, New York 13323

◆ **Hamline University**
St. Paul, Minnesota 55104

◆ **Hampden-Sydney College**
Hampden-Sydney, Virginia 23943

∎ **Hampton University**
Hampton, Virginia 23668

Hanover College
Hanover, Indiana 47243

Hartford, University of
Hartford, Connecticut 06117

Hartwick College
Oneonta, New York 13820

◆ **Harvard/Radcliffe Colleges**
Cambridge, Massachusetts 02138

Harvey Mudd College
Claremont, California 91711

Hastings College
Hastings, Nebraska 68901

◆ **Haverford College**
Haverford, Pennsylvania 19041

Hawaii Pacific University
Honolulu, Hawaii 96813

◆ **Hawaii, University of**
Manoa, Honolulu, Hawaii 96822

Heidelberg College
Tiffin, Ohio 44883

Hendrix College
Conway, Arkansas 72032

Hillsdale College
Hillsdale, Michigan 49242

◆ **Hiram College**
Hiram, Ohio 44234

◆ **Hobart & William Smith Colleges**
Geneva, New York 14456

◆ Phi Beta Kappa Schools ∎ Predominantly African-American Institution

◆ **Hofstra University**
Hempstead, New York 11550

◆ **Hollins College**
Roanoke, Virginia 24020

◆ **Holy Cross, College of the**
Worcester, Massachusetts 01610

Hood College
Frederick, Maryland 21701

◆ **Hope College**
Holland, Michigan 49423

Houghton College
Houghton, New York 14744

Houston Baptist University
Houston, Texas 77074

Houston, University of
Houston, Texas 77004

◆■ **Howard University**
Washington, DC 20059

Humboldt State University
Arcata, California 95521

Huntingdon College
Montgomery, Alabama 36194

Husson College
Bangor, Maine 04401

■◆ **Idaho, University of**
Moscow, Idaho 83843

Illinois, University of, at
◆ **Urbana-Champaign,** Illinois 61801
◆ **Chicago,** Illinois 60680

◆ **Illinois College**
Jacksonville, Illinois 62650

Illinois Institute of Technology
Chicago, Illinois 60616

Illinois State University
Normal, Illinois 61761

Illinois Wesleyan University
Bloomington, Illinois 61701

Indiana State University
Terre Haute, Indiana 47809

◆ **Indiana University**
Bloomington, Indiana 47401

Indiana University of Pennsylvania
Indiana, Pennsylvania 15705

Iona College
New Rochelle, New York 10801

◆ **Iowa, University of**
Iowa City, Iowa 52242

◆ **Iowa State University of Science & Technology**
Ames, Iowa 50011

Ithaca College
Ithaca, New York 14850

J **Jacksonville State University**
Jacksonville, Alabama 36265

Jacksonville University
Jacksonville, Florida 32211

James Madison University
Harrisonburg, Virginia 22807

John Carroll University
Cleveland, Ohio 44118

◆ **Johns Hopkins University**
Baltimore, Maryland 21218

Johnson C. Smith University
Charlotte, North Carolina 28216

Judson College
Marion, Alabama 36756

Juilliard School
New York, New York 10023

Juniata College
Huntingdon, Pennsylvania 16652

K ◆ **Kalamazoo College**
Kalamazoo, Michigan 49007

Kansas Newman College
Wichita, Kansas 67213

◆ **Kansas, University of**
Lawrence, Kansas 66045

◆ **Kansas State University**
Manhattan, Kansas 66506

Keene State College
Keene, New Hampshire 03431

Kennesaw State College
Marietta, Georgia 30061

◆ **Kent State University**
Kent, Ohio 44242

◆ **Kentucky, University of**
Lexington, Kentucky 40506

Kentucky Wesleyan College
Owensboro, Kentucky 42301

◆ **Kenyon College**
Gambier, Ohio 43022

King College
Bristol, Tennessee 37620

King's College
Wilkes-Barre, Pennsylvania 18711

◆ Phi Beta Kappa Schools   ■ Predominantly African-American Institution

◆ **Knox College**
Galesburg, Illinois 61401

Kutztown University
Kutztown, Pennsylvania 19530

L ◆ **Lafayette College**
Easton, Pennsylvania 18042

◆ **Lake Forest College**
Lake Forest, Illinois 60045

LaSalle University
Philadelphia, Pennsylvania 19141

La Verne, University of
La Verne, California 91750

◆ **Lawrence University**
Appleton, Wisconsin 54912

Lebanon Valley College
Annville, Pennsylvania 17003

◆ **Lehigh University**
Bethlehem, Pennsylvania 18015

LeMoyne College
Syracuse, New York 13214

Lenoir Rhyne College
Hickory, North Carolina 28603

Lesley College
Cambridge, Massachusetts 02138

Letourneau College
Longview, Texas 75607

Lewis & Clark College
Portland, Oregon 97219

Lindenwood College
St. Charles, Missouri 63301

Linfield College
McMinnville, Oregon 97128

Lock Haven University of Pennsylvania
Lock Haven, Pennsylvania 17745

Long Island University-Southampton College
Southampton, New York 11968

Longwood College
Farmville, Virginia 23909

Loras College
Dubuque, Iowa 52001

◆ **Louisiana State University**
Baton Rouge, Louisiana 70802

Louisville, University of
Louisville, Kentucky 40292

Lowell, University of
Lowell, Massachusetts 01854

◆ **Loyola College**
Baltimore, Maryland 21210

◆ **Loyola Marymount University**
Los Angeles, California 90045

◆ **Loyola University of Chicago**
Chicago, Illinois 60611

Loyola University
New Orleans, Louisiana 70118

◆ **Luther College**
Decorah, Iowa 52101

Lycoming College
Williamsport, Pennsylvania 17701

Lynchburg College
Lynchburg, Virginia 24501

Lyon College
Batesville, Arkansas 72501

M ◆ **Macalester College**
St. Paul, Minnesota 55105

MacMurray College
Jacksonville, Illinois 62650

Maine, University of
Farmington, Maine 04938

◆ **Maine, University of**
Orono, Maine 04469

Malone College
Canton, Ohio 44709

Manchester College
Manchester, Indiana 46962

◆ **Manhattan College**
Riverdale, New York 10471

Manhattan School of Music
New York, New York 10027

Manhattanville College
Purchase, New York 10577

Mansfield University of Pennsylvania
Mansfield, Pennsylvania 16933

◆ **Marietta College**
Marietta, Ohio 45750

Marist College
Poughkeepsie, NY 12601

◆ **Marquette University**
Milwaukee, Wisconsin 53233

Marshall University
Huntington, West Virginia 25755

◆ **Mary Baldwin College**
Staunton, Virginia 24401

Marycrest International University
Davenport, Iowa 52804

Marygrove College
Detroit, Michigan 48221

Maryland Institute-College of Art
Baltimore, Maryland 21217

Maryland, University of Baltimore County
Baltimore, Maryland 21228

◆ **Maryland, University of**
College Park, Maryland 20742

Maryville University-Saint Louis
St. Louis, Missouri 63141

◆ **Mary Washington College**
Fredericksburg, Virginia 22401

Massachusetts College of Art
Boston Massachusetts 02215

◆ **Massachusetts, University of**
Amherst, Massachusetts 01003

Massachusetts, University of
Boston, Massachusetts 02125

Massachusetts, University of
Lowell, Massachusetts 01854

Massachusetts, University of
North Dartmouth, Massachusetts 02747

◆ **Massachusetts Institute of Technology**
Cambridge, Massachusetts 02139

Massachusetts Maritime Academy
Buzzards Bay, Massachusetts 02532

Memphis, University of
Memphis, Tennessee 38152

Mercer University
Macon, Georgia 31207

Mercy College
Dobbs Ferry, New York 10522

Mercyhurst College
Erie, Pennsylvania 16546

Meredith College
Raleigh, North Carolina 27607

Merrimack College
No. Andover, Massachusetts 01845

Messiah College
Grantham, Pennsylvania 17027

◆ **Miami University**
Oxford, Ohio 45056

◆ **Miami, University of**
Coral Gables, Florida 33124

◆ **Michigan, University of**
Ann Arbor, Michigan 48109

Michigan, University of
Dearborn, Michigan 48128

◆ **Michigan State University**
East Lansing, Michigan 48824

Michigan Technological University
Houghton, Michigan 49931

◆ **Middlebury College**
Middlebury, Vermont 05753

Millersville University of Pennsylvania
Millersville, Pennsylvania 17551

Milligan College
Milligan College, Tennessee 37682

Millikin University
Decatur, Illinois 62522

◆ **Mills College**
Oakland, California 94613

◆ **Millsaps College**
Jackson, Mississippi 39210

Milwaukee School of Engineering
Milwaukee, Wisconsin 53201

◆ **Minnesota, University of**
Minneapolis, Minnesota 55455

Minnesota, University of
Morris, Minnesota 56267

Misericordia, College
Dallas, Pennsylvania 18612

Mississippi College
Clinton, Mississippi 39058

Mississippi State University
Mississippi State, Mississippi 39762

Mississippi, University of
University, Mississippi 38677

Mississippi University for Women
Columbus, Mississippi 39701

◆ **Missouri, University of**
Columbia, Missouri 65201

Missouri, University of
Kansas City, Missouri 64110

Missouri, University of
Rolla, Missouri 65401

Monmouth College
Monmouth, Illinois 61462

Monmouth University
West Long Branch, New Jersey 07764

**Montana College of
Mineral Science & Technology**
Butte, Montana 59701

Montana, University of
Missoula, Montana 59812

◆ Phi Beta Kappa Schools   ▮ Predominantly African-American Institution

Montana State University
Bozeman, Montana 59717

Montevallo, University of
Montevallo, Alabama 35115

Montclair State College
Upper Montclair, New Jersey 07043

Montreat College
Montreat, North Carolina 28757

Moore College of Art
Philadelphia, Pennsylvania 19103

Moravian College
Bethlehem, Pennsylvania 18018

◆ ■**Morehouse College**
Atlanta, Georgia 30314

Morningside College
Sioux City, Iowa 51106

◆ **Mount Holyoke College**
South Hadley, Massachusetts 01075

Mount Mercy College
Cedar Rapids, Iowa 52402

Mount St. Joseph
Cincinnati, Ohio 45233

Mount St. Mary's College
Emmitsburg, Maryland 21727

Mount St. Mary's College
Newburgh, New York, 12550

Mount St. Mary's College
Los Angeles, California 90049

Mount Union College
Alliance, Ohio 44601

◆ **Muhlenberg College**
Allentown, Pennsylvania 18104

Mundelein College
Chicago, Illinois 60660

Muskingum College
New Concord, Ohio 43762

N **Nazareth College of Rochester**
Rochester, New York 14610

◆ **Nebraska, University of**
Lincoln, Nebraska 68588

Nebraska Wesleyan University
Lincoln, Nebraska 68504

Nevada, University of, at
Las Vegas, Nevada 89154
Reno, Nevada 89557

New College of U.S.F.
Sarasota, Florida 34243

New England Conservatory of Music
Boston, Massachusetts 02115

◆ **New Hampshire, University of**
Durham, New Hampshire 03824

New Jersey, College of
Trenton, New Jersey 08650

New Jersey Institute of Technology
Newark, New Jersey 07102

New Mexico Institute of Mining and Technology
Socorro, New Mexico 87801

New Mexico State University
Las Cruces, New Mexico 88003

◆ **New Mexico, University of**
Albuquerque, New Mexico 87131

New Orleans, University of
New Orleans, Louisiana 70148

New York, City University of
◆ **Baruch College**, New York, NY 10010
◆ **Brooklyn College**, Brooklyn, NY 11210
◆ **City College**, New York, New York 10031
◆ **Herbert H. Lehman College**, Bronx, NY 10468
◆ **Hunter College**, New York, NY 10021
◆ **Queens College**, Flushing, NY 11367

New York, State University of, at
◆ **Albany**, New York 12222
◆ **Binghamton**, New York 13901
  Brockport, New York 14420
◆ **Buffalo**, New York 14214
  Fredonia, New York 14063
  Geneseo, New York 1445
  New Paltz, New York 12561
  Oneonta, New York 13820
  Oswego, New York 13126
  Plattsburgh, New York 12901
  Potsdam, New York 13676
  Purchase, New York 10577
◆ **Stony Brook**, New York 11794

◆ **New York University**
New York, New York 10011

Niagara University
Niagara Falls, New York, 14109

North Carolina School of the Arts
Winston-Salem, North Carolina 27117

North Carolina, University of, at
  Asheville, North Carolina 28804
◆ **Chapel Hill**, North Carolina 27514
  Charlotte, North Carolina 28223
◆ **Greensboro**, North Carolina 27412
  Wilmington, North Carolina 28403

◆ **North Carolina State University**
Raleigh, North Carolina 27650

North Central College
Naperville, Illinois 60566

North Dakota State University
Fargo, North Dakota 58105

◆ North Dakota, University of
Grand Forks, North Dakota 58201

North Florida, University of
Jacksonville, Florida 32216

North Georgia College
Dahlonega, Georgia 30597

North Texas, University of
Denton, Texas 76203

Northeastern University
Boston, Massachusetts 02115

Northern Arizona University
Flagstaff, Arizona 86011

Northern Colorado University
Greeley, Colorado 80639

Northern Illinois University
DeKalb, Illinois 60115

Northern Iowa, University of
Cedar Falls, Iowa 50614

Northern Michigan
Marquette, Michigan 49855

Northwestern College
Orange City, Iowa 51041

Northwestern College
St. Paul, Minnesota 55113

◆ Northwestern University
Evanston, Illinois 60201

Northwood University
Midland, Michigan 48640

◆ Notre Dame, University of
Notre Dame, Indiana 46556

Nova Southeastern University
Ft. Lauderdale, Florida 33314

O Oakland University
Rochester, Michigan 48309

◆ Oberlin College
Oberlin, Ohio 44074

◆ Occidental College
Los Angeles, California 90041

Oglethorpe University
Atlanta, Georgia 30319

◆ Ohio University
Athens, Ohio 45701

Ohio Northern University
Ada, Ohio 45810

◆ Ohio State University
Columbus, Ohio 43210

◆ Ohio Wesleyan University
Delaware, Ohio 43015

Oklahoma Baptist University
Shawnee, Oklahoma 74801

Oklahoma City University
Oklahoma City, Oklahoma 73106

◆ Oklahoma, University of
Norman, Oklahoma 73069

Oklahoma State University
Stillwater, Oklahoma 74078

Old Dominion University
Norfolk, Virginia 23529

◆ Oregon, University of
Eugene, Oregon 97403

Oregon State University
Corvallis, Oregon 97331

Otis Art Institute of Parsons School of Design
Los Angeles, California 90057

Otterbein College
Westerville, Ohio 43081

Ozarks, College of the
Point Lookout, Missouri 65726

P Pace University
New York, New York 10038

Pacific Lutheran University
Tacoma, Washington 98447

Pacific, U. of the
Stockton, California95211

Pacific University
Forest Grove, Oregon 97116

Palm Beach Atlantic College
West Palm Beach, Florida 33416

Parsons School of Design
New York, New York 10011

◆ Pennsylvania, University of
Philadelphia, Pennsylvania 19104

◆ Pennsylvania State University
University Park, Pennsylvania 16802

Pepperdine University
Malibu, California 90265

Philadelphia College of Pharmacy and Science
Philadelphia, Pennsylvania 19104

Philadelphia College of Textiles & Sciences
Philadelphia, Pennsylvania 19144

Pittsburgh, University of
Johnstown, Pennsylvania 15904

◆ Phi Beta Kappa Schools   ▌ Predominantly African-American Institution

Pittsburgh, University of
Bradford, Pennsylvania 16701

◆ **Pittsburgh, University of**
Pittsburgh, Pennsylvania 15260

Pitzer College
Claremont, California 91711

Point Loma Nazarene College
San Diego, California 92106

Point Park College
Pittsburgh, Pennsylvania 15222

Polytechnic Institute of New York
Brooklyn, New York 11201

◆ **Pomona College**
Claremont, California 91711

Portland, University of
Portland, Oregon 97203

Pratt Institute
Brooklyn, New York 11205

Presbyterian College
Clinton, South Carolina 29325

◆ **Princeton University**
Princeton, New Jersey 08544

Principia College
Elsah, Illinois 62028

Providence College
Providence, Rhode Island 02918

Puerto Rico, University of
CAYEY Puerto Rico 00633

Puerto Rico, University of
Rio Piedras, Puerto Rico 00931

◆ **Puget Sound, University of**
Tacoma, Washington 98416

◆ **Purdue University**
W. Lafayette, Indiana 47907

Q **Queens College**
Charlotte, North Carolina 28274

Quincy University
Quincy, Illinois 62301

Quinnipiac College
Hamden, Connecticut 06518

R **Radford University**
Radford, Virginia 24142

◆ **Randolph-Macon College**
Ashland, Virginia 23005

◆ **Randolph-Macon Woman's College**
Lynchburg, Virginia 24503

◆ **Redlands, University of**
Redlands, California 92373

◆ **Reed College**
Portland, Oregon 97202

Regis University
Denver, Colorado 80221

Rensselaer Polytechnic Institute
Troy, New York 12180

Rhode Island School of Design
Providence, Rhode Island 02903

◆ **Rhode Island, University of**
Kingston, Rhode Island 02881

◆ **Rhodes College**
Memphis, Tennessee 38112

◆ **Rice University**
Houston, Texas 77251

◆ **Richmond, University of**
Richmond, Virginia 23173

Rider College
Lawrenceville, New Jersey 08648

◆ **Ripon College**
Ripon, Wisconsin 54971

Roanoke College
Salem, Virginia 24153

◆ **Rochester, University of**
Rochester, New York 14627

Rochester Institute of Technology
Rochester, New York 14623

◆ **Rockford College**
Rockford, Illinois 61108

Rockhurst College
Kansas City, Missouri 64110

Roger Williams University
Bristol, Rhode Island 02809

Rollins College
Winter Park, Florida 32789

Roosevelt University
Chicago, Illinois 60605

Rosary College
River Forest, Illinois 60305

Rose-Hulman Institute of Technology
Terre Haute, Indiana 47803

Rosemont College
Rosemont, Pennsylvania 19010

Rowan University of New Jersey
Mahwah, New Jersey 08028

◆ **Rutgers University**
New Brunswick, New Jersey 08903

◆ Phi Beta Kappa Schools　　■ Predominantly African-American Institution

Rutgers University
Camden, New Jersey 08102

S **Sacred Heart University**
Fairfield, Connecticut 06432

Sage Colleges
Troy, New York 12180

St. Ambrose University
Davenport, Iowa 52803

St. Andrews Presbyterian College
Laurinburg, North Carolina 28352

St. Anselm College
Manchester, New Hampshire 03102

St. Bonaventure University
St. Bonaventure, New York 14778

◆ **St. Catherine, College of**
St. Paul, Minnesota 55105

St. Francis College
Brooklyn, New York 11201

St. John Fisher College
Rochester, New, York 14618

St. John's University
Jamaica, New York 11439

Saint John's University/College of Saint Benedict
Collegeville, Minnesota 56321

Saint Joseph's College
W. Hartford, Connecticut 06117

St. Joseph's College
Rensselaer, Indianna 47978

St. Joseph's College
Standish, Maine 04084

Saint Joseph's University
Philadelphia, Pennsylvania 19131

◆ **St. Lawrence University**
Canton, New York 13617

St. Louis College of Pharmacy
St. Louis, Missouri 63110

◆ **Saint Louis University**
St. Louis, Missouri 63103

Saint Mary's College
Notre Dame, Indiana 46556

Saint Mary's College of California
St. Mary's College, California 94575

St. Mary's College of Maryland
St. Mary's City, Maryland 20686

St. Mary's University of Minnesota
Winona, Minnesota 55987

St. Mary's University of San Antonio
San Antonio, Texas 78228

Saint Michael's College
Winooski Park, Colchester, Vermont 05439

St. Norbert College
DePere, Wisconsin 54115

◆ **St. Olaf College**
Northfield, Minnesota 55057

Saint Rose, College of
Albany, New York 12203

Saint Scholastica, College of
Duluth, Minnesota 55811

Saint Thomas, University of
St. Paul, Minnesota 55105

Saint Thomas, University of
Houston, Texas 77006

St. Vincent College
Latrobe, Pennsylvania 15650

Salem College
Winston-Salem, North Carolina 27108

Salem State College
Salem, Massachusetts 01970

Salisbury State University
Salisbury, Maryland 21801

Samford University
Birmingham, Alabama 35229

◆ **San Diego State University**
San Diego, California 92182

San Diego, University of
San Diego, California 92110

San Francisco Conservatory of Music
San Francisco, California 94122

San Francisco, University of
San Francisco, California 94117

◆ **San Francisco State University**
San Francisco, California 94132

San Jose State University
San Jose, California 95192

◆ **Santa Clara University**
Santa Clara, California 95053

Santa Fe, College of
Santa Fe, New Mexico 87501

Sarah Lawrence College
Bronxville, New York 10708

Schreiner College
Kerrville, Texas 78028

Scranton, University of
Scranton, Pennsylvania 18510

◆ Phi Beta Kappa Schools   ■ Predominantly African-American Institution

◆ **Scripps College**
Claremont, California 91711

Seattle University
Seattle, Washington 98122

Seattle Pacific University
Seattle, Washington 98119

Seton Hall University
South Orange, New Jersey 07079

Seton Hill College
Greensburg, Pennsylvania 15601

▌ **Shaw University**
Raleigh, North Carolina 27611

Shepherd College
Shepherdstown, West Virginia 25443

Shippensburg University
Shippensburg, Pennsylvania 17257

Siena College
Loudonville, New York 12211

Simmons College
Boston, Massachusetts 02115

Simpson College
Indianola, Iowa 50125

◆ **Skidmore College**
Saratoga Springs, New York 12866

◆ **Smith College**
Northampton, Massachusetts 01063

Sonoma State University
Rohnert Park, California 94928

◆ **South, University of The**
Sewanee, Tennessee 37375

◆ **South Carolina, University of**
Columbia, South Carolina 29208

◆ **South Dakota, University of**
Vermillion, South Dakota 57069

South Dakota School of Mines
Rapid City, South Dakota 57701

◆ **Southern California, University of**
Los Angeles, California 90007

Southern Illinois University
Carbondale, Illinois 62901

Southern Maine, University of
Portland, Maine 04103

◆ **Southern Methodist University**
Dallas, Texas 75275

Southern Oregon State College
Ashland, Oregon 97520

South Florida, University of
Tampa, Florida 33620

Southern Utah University
Cedar City, Utah 84720

Southwest Baptist University
Bolivar, Missouri 65613

Southwest Texas State University
San Marcos, Texas 78666

◆ **Southwestern University**
Georgetown, Texas 78626

▌ **Spelman College**
Atlanta, Georgia 30314

Spring Hill College
Mobile, Alabama 36608

◆ **Stanford University**
Stanford, California 94305

Stephen F. Austin State University
Nagogdoches, Texas 75962

◆ **Stetson University**
Deland, Florida 32720

Stevens Institute of Technology
Hoboken, New Jersey 07030

Stockton State
Pomona, New Jersey 08240

Stonehill College
North Easton, Massachusetts 02357

Susquehanna University
Selinsgrove, Pennsylvania 17870

◆ **Swarthmore College**
Swarthmore, Pennsylvania 19081

◆ **Sweet Briar College**
Sweet Briar, Virginia 24595

◆ **Syracuse University**
Syracuse, New York 13210

T **Tampa, University of**
Tampa, Florida 33606

Taylor University
Upland, Indiana 46989

◆ **Temple University**
Philadelphia, Pennsylvania 19122

◆ **Tennessee, University of**
Knoxville, Tennessee 37916

Texas, University of, at
Arlington, Texas 76019
◆ Austin, Texas 78712
San Antonio, Texas 78249

Texas A & M
College Station, Texas 77843

◆ Phi Beta Kappa Schools ▌ Predominantly African-American Institution

Texas A & M at Galveston
Galveston, Texas 77553

◆ **Texas Christian University**
Fort Worth, Texas 76129

Texas Tech University
Lubbock, Texas 79409

Thomas More College
Crestview Hills, Kentucky 41017

Toledo, University of
Toledo, Ohio 43606

Texas Wesleyan College
Fort Worth, Texas 76105

∎ **Tougaloo College**
Tougaloo, Mississippi 39174

Towson State University
Towson, Maryland 21204

Transylvania University
Lexington, Kentucky 40508

◆ **Trinity College**
Hartford, Connecticut 06106

◆ **Trinity College**
Washington, DC 20017

◆ **Trinity University**
San Antonio, Texas 78284

Truman State University
Kirksville, Missouri 63501

◆ **Tufts University**
Medford, Massachusetts 02155

◆ **Tulane University**
New Orleans, Louisiana 70118

∎ **Tuskegee University**
Tuskegee, Alabama 36088

◆ **Tulsa, University of**
Tulsa, Oklahoma 74104

U ◆ **Union College**
Schenectady, New York 12308

Union University
Jackson, Tennessee 38305

U.S. Air Force Academy
Colorado Springs, Colorado 80840

U.S. Coast Guard Academy
New London, Connecticut 06320

U.S. Military Academy
West Point, New York 10996

U.S. Naval Academy
Annapolis, Maryland 21402

◆ **Ursinus College**
Collegeville, Pennsylvania 19426

◆ **Utah, University of**
Salt Lake City, Utah 84112

Utah State University
Logan, Utah 84322

Utica College of Syracuse University
Utica, New York 13502

V **Valparaiso University**
Valparaiso, Indiana 46383

◆ **Vanderbilt University**
Nashville, Tennessee 37235

◆ **Vassar College**
Poughkeepsie, New York 12601

◆ **Vermont, University of**
Burlington, Vermont 05401

◆ **Villanova University**
Villanova, Pennsylvania 19085

◆ **Virginia, University of**
Charlottesville, Virginia 22903

Virginia Commonwealth University
Richmond, Virginia 23284

Virginia Military Institute
Lexington, Virginia 24450

◆ **Virginia Polytechnic Institute**
Blacksburg, Virginia 24061

Virginia Wesleyan College
Norfolk, Virginia 23502

W ◆ **Wabash College**
Crawfordsville, Indiana 47933

Wagner College
Staten Island, New York 10301

◆ **Wake Forest University**
Winston-Salem, North Carolina 27109

Wartburg College
Waverly, Iowa 50677

Warren Wilson College
Asheville, North Carolina 28815

Washington College
Chestertown, Maryland 21620

◆ **Washington & Jefferson College**
Washington, Pennsylvania 15301

◆ **Washington & Lee University**
Lexington, Virginia 24450

◆ **Washington University**
St. Louis, Missouri 63130

◆ **Washington, University of**
Seattle, Washington 98195

◆ Phi Beta Kappa Schools   ∎ Predominantly African-American Institution

◆ **Washington State University**
Pullman, Washington 99164

◆ **Wayne State University**
Detroit, Michigan 48202

Webster University
Lows, Missouri 63119

◆ **Wellesley College**
Wellesley, Massachusetts 02181

◆ **Wells College**
Aurora, New York 13026

Wesleyan College
Macon, Georgia 31297

◆ **Wesleyan University**
Middletown, Connecticut 06457

West Chester University
West Chester, Pennsylvania 19383

Western Connecticut State University
Danbury, Connecticut 06810

Western Kentucky University
Bowling Green, Kentucky 42101

◆ **Western Maryland College**
Westminster, Maryland 21157

Western Michigan University
Kalamazoo, Michigan 49008

Western New England College
Springfield, Massachusetts 01119

Western Washington University
Bellingham, Washington 98225

Westfield State College
Westfield, Massachusetts 01086

West Florida, University of
Pensacola, FL 32514

Westminster College
Fulton, Missouri 65251

Westminster College
Wilmington, Pennsylvania 16172

Westmont College
Santa Barbara, California 93108

◆ **West Virginia University**
Morgantown, West Virginia 26506

West Virginia Wesleyan
Buckhannon, West Virginia 26201

Wheaton College
Wheaton, Illinois 60187

◆ **Wheaton College**
Norton, Massachusetts 02766

Wheelock College
Boston, Massachusetts 02215

◆ **Whitman College**
Walla Walla, Washington 99362

Whittier College
Whittier, California 90608

Whitworth College
Spokane, Washington 99251

Widener University
Chester, Pennsylvania 19013

■ **Wilberforce University**
Wilberforce, Ohio 45384

William Jewell College
Liberty, Missouri 64068

◆ **William & Mary, College of**
Williamsburg, Virginia 23185

◆ **Williams College**
Williamstown, Massachusetts 01267

Willamette University
Salem, Oregon 97301

Wilmington College
Wilmington, Ohio 45177

◆ **Wilson College**
Chambersburg, Pennsylvania 17201

Winona State University
Winona, Minnesota 55987

◆ **Wisconsin, University of, at**
Green Bay, **Wisconsin 54311**
LaCrosse, Wisconsin 5460
◆ **Madison**, Wisconsin 53706
◆ **Milwaukee**, Wisconsin 53201
Platteville, Wisconsin 53818
Stevens Point, Wisconsin 54481

◆ **Wittenberg University**
Springfield, Ohio 45501

◆ **Wofford College**
Spartanburg, South Carolina 29301

Woodbury University
Burbank, California 91510

◆ **Wooster, College of**
Wooster, Ohio 44691

Worcester Polytechnic Institute
Worcester, Massachusetts 01609

◆ **Wyoming, University of**
Laramie, Wyoming 82071

X **Xavier University**
Cincinnati, Ohio 45207

■ **Xavier University of Louisiana**
New Orleans, Louisiana 70125

◆ Phi Beta Kappa Schools   ■ Predominantly African-American Institution

Y ◆ **Yale University**
New Haven, Connecticut 06520

✿ **Yeshiva University**
New York, New York 10033

York College of Pennsylvania
York, Pennsylvania 17403

◆ Phi Beta Kappa Schools
▌ Predominantly African-American Institution
✿ Predominantly Jewish Institution

APPENDIX B
The Miscellaneous Majors Colleges Used In This Study

Antioch College
Yellow Springs, OH 45387

Assumption College
Worcester, MA 01609

Atlantic, College of the
Bar Harbor, ME 04609

Aurora University
Aurora, Il 60506

Berklee College of Music
Boston, MA 02215

Bluefield College
Bluefield, VA 24605

Boise State University
Boise, ID 83725

Brooks Institute of Photography
Santa Barbara, CA 93108

California Institute of the Arts
Valencia, CA 91355

California Polytechnic State University
Pomona, CA 91768

California State University
Bakersfield, CA 93311
Fresno, CA 93740
Los Angeles, CA 90032
Northridge, CA 91330
Sacramento, CA 95819
(Sonoma) Rohnert Park, CA 94928
(Stanislaus) Turlock, CA 95380

California University of Pennsylvania
California, PA 15419

Castleton State College
Castleton, VT 05735

Centenary College
Hackettstown, NJ 07840

Cheyney University of Pennsylvania
Cheyney, PA 19319

Cleveland State University
Cleveland, OH 44115

Cornish College of the Arts
Seattle, WA 98102

Cortland State College
Cortland, NY 13045

Curry College
Milton, MA 02186

Daemen College
Amherst, NY 14226

Deep Springs College
Deep Springs Via Dyer, NV 89010

East Carolina University
Greenville, NC 27858

Eastern Kentucky University
Richmond, KY 40475

Eastern Montana College
Billings, MT 59101

Eugene Lang College (New School Social Research)
New York, NY 11743

Fashion Institute of Technology
New York, NY 10001

Findlay, University of
Findlay, OH 45840

Fitchburg State College
Fitchburg, MA 01420

Georgia State University
Atlanta, GA 30303

Hampshire College
Amherst, MA 01002

Kansas City Art Institute
Kansas City, MO 64111

Kean University of New Jersey
Union, NJ 07083

Kendall College of Art and Design
Grand Rapids, MI 49503

Lake Erie College
Painesville, OH 44077

Landmark College
Putney, VT 05346

Lesley College
Cambridge, MA 02138

Long Island University
Southampton Center, NY 11968

Lyndon State College
Lyndonville, VT 05851

Madonna University
Livonia, MI 48150

Marist College
Poughkeepsie, NY 12601

New School for Social Research
New York, NY 11743

North Carolina Wesleyan College
Rocky Mount, NC 27804

North Dakota State University
Fargo, ND 58105

Northeastern Louisiana University
Monroe, LA 71209

Parks College of St. Louis University
Cahokia, IL 62206

Pfeiffer College
Misenheimer, NC 28109

Portland State University
Portland, OR 97207

Ramapo College of New Jersey
Mahwah, NJ 07430

Rhode Island College
Providence, RI 02908

Ringling School of Art & Design
Sarasota, FL 34234

Robert Morris College
Coraopolis, PA 15108

Rowan College of New Jersey
Glassboro, NJ, 08028

St. Edward's University
Austin, TX 78704

Saint John's College
Annapolis, MD 21404

Saint Leo College
Saint Leo, FL 33574

Saint Thomas University
Miami, FL 33054

Salve Regina-The Newport College
Newport, RI 02840

San Jose State University
San Jose, CA 95152

Shenandoah University
Winchester, VA 22601

Simon's Rock College of Bard
Great Barrington, MA 01230

Slippery Rock University
Slippery Rock, PA 16057

Spring Arbor College
Spring Arbor, MI 49283

Springfield College
Springfield, MA 01109

Stephens College
Columbia, MO 65215

Texas Woman's University
Denton, TX 76204

United States Merchant Marine Academy
Kings Point, NY 11024

Webb Institute
Glen Cove, NY 11542

William Woods University
Fulton, MO 65251

Wingate College
Wingate, NC 28174

Wisconsin, University of
Oshkosh, WI 54901

Wisconsin, (Stout) University of
Menomonie, WI 54751

Worcester State College
Worcester, MA 01602

Wright State University
Dayton, OH 45435

Youngstown State University
Youngstown, OH 44555

APPENDIX C
Single Sex Colleges Included In This Study

WOMEN'S COLLEGES

Agnes Scott College (GA)
Bennett College (NC)
Bryn Mawr College (PA)
Cedar Crest College (PA)
Chatham College (PA)
Chestnut Hill (PA)
Converse College(SC)
Hollins College (VA)
Hood College (MD)
Judson College (AL)
Lesley (MA)
Mary Baldwin College (VA)
Meredith College (NC)

Mills College (CA)
Mount Holyoke College (MA)
Randolph-Macon Woman's Coll. (VA)
Rosemont College (PA)
St. Catherine, College of (MN)
Saint Joseph's (CT)
Saint Mary's College (IN)
Salem College (NC)
Scripps College (CA)
Seton Hill (PA)
Simmons College (MA)
Smith College (MA)
Spelman College (GA)

Sweet Briar College (VA)
Texas Woman's College
Trinity College (DC)
Wellesley College (MA)
Wesleyan College (GA)
Wheelock (MA)
Wilson College (PA)

MEN'S COLLEGES

Hampden-Sydney College (VA)
Morehouse College (GA)
Wabash College (IN)

APPENDIX D

Anyone who has been touched by the problem of alcohol or substance abuse, or who has worked with those struggling in recovery, knows that higher education will increasingly have to meet the needs of these persons. The colleges listed below are trying to address the needs of these students. The Wellness Institute at Ball State has published this list of wellness dorms. I cannot vouch personally for the level or quality of services here. I can only state that they do exist and that parents requiring such services would do well to contact colleges on their selection lists to determine the availability of such accommodations. More may indeed exist.

Respectfully submitted,
Joseph W. Streit
Secondary School Counselor in New Jersey

INSTITUTIONS OFFERING WELLNESS RESIDENCE HALLS

ALABAMA

University of Alabama/Tuscaloosa	Yoland Reese, Health Educator	205/348-3878
University of Montevallo	Freida Shivers, Director or Housing	205/665-2988

ARIZONA

Arizona State University	Tamra Summers, Asst. Director, Student Services	602/965-8900

ARKANSAS

John Brown University	G. Robert Burns, Chair, Health Promotion	501/524-2000
University of Arkansas	Jim Conneeley, Director, Residence Life	501/575-5000

CALIFORNIA

California Poly State Univ./Pomona	Ali Mossares-Rahmani, Director of Housing	909/869-3306
University of California/Irvine	E. Ellen Thomas, Director, Health Education	714/824-5806
University of California/Los Angeles	Alan Hanson, Director, Residence Life	310/825-3066
University of California/Santa Barbara	Wilfred Brown, Director of Housing	805/893-4155

COLORADO

Fort Lewis College	Bill Bolden, Director, Residence Life	970/247-7503
Regis University	Diane Cooper, Asst. Director, Residence Life	303/458-3505
University of Northern Colorado	Andy Blank, Director of Housing	970/351-2721

CONNECTICUT

Wesleyan University	Patricia Houmiel, Director, Residential Life	860/865-2222

DELAWARE

University of Delaware	Dave Buttler, Executive Director, Housing	302/831-6573

FLORIDA

Florida State University	Dr. Rita Moser, Director, University Housing	904/644-2860
Stetson University	Michelle Espinosa, Director, Residence Life	904/822-7201
University of Miami	Loreto Jackson, Director of Wellness	305/284-3253
University of North Florida	Doreen Perez, Director, Student Health	904/646-2900
University of Tampa	Monnie Huston, Director, Residence Life	813/253-6239

GEORGIA
Georgia Institute of Technology   Terry Sichta, Director of Housing   404/894-2486

ILLINOIS
Illinois State University   Linda Sorrells, Director, Wellness Program   309/438-7003
Northern Illinois University   Chika Nnamani, Exec. Director, Student Housing   815/753-9607
Northwestern University   Bill Tempelmeyer, Director, University Housing   708/491-7564
University of Illinois/Urbana-Champaign   Rosanne Proite, Assoc. Director of Housing   217/333-0770

INDIANA
Ball State University   Neil Schmottlach, Director, Fisher Institute   765/285-8259
Indiana University   Bruce Jacobs, Director, Residence Life   812/855-1764
Manchester College   Charlie Mackey, Director, Residence Life   219/982-5000
Purdue University   Tom Paczolt, Manager, Shreve Hall   317/494-2569
Valparaiso University   Christopher Rasmussen, Asst. Dean of Students   219/464-5413

IOWA
Iowa State University   Charles Frederiksen, Director, Residence Life   515/294-5636
University of Northern Iowa   Bob Hartman, Director, Dept. of Residence   319/273-2333

KENTUCKY
Centre College   Sherry Raitiere, Nurse, Wellness Center   606/238-5330
Northern Kentucky University   Patty Hayden, Director, Residence Life   606/572-5448
University of Kentucky   Melanie Tyner-Wilson, Director, Residence Life   606/257-4783

MAINE
University of Maine/Machias   Peter Schmidt, Coordinator, Residential Life   207/255-3313

MARYLAND
Coppin State College   Linda Dark, Director, Health Promotion   410/383-5859
Loyola College   Kathy Clark-Petersen, Director, Student Life   410/617-2488

MASSACHUSETTS
Boston University   Celine McNelis-Kline, Director, Wellness Center   617/353-3698
Framingham State College   Joe Onofrietto, Director, Residence Life   508/626-4632

MICHIGAN
Oakland University   Eleanor Reynolds, Director, Residence Halls   810/370-3570
Northern Michigan University   Mary McDonald, RD, Director, Residence Life   906/227-2396
Western Michigan University   Julie Gerard, Director, Residence Hall Life   616/387-4460

MINNESOTA
Augsburg College   Denise Anderson-Diffenbach, Hall Director   612/330-1109
Bemidji State University   Dale Ladig, Director, Residence Life   218/755-3750
Macalester College   Ann Bolger, Director, Residence Life   612/696-6215
University of Minnesota   David Golden, Director, Health Education   612/626-6738

MISSOURI
Central Missouri State University   Lisa Schulte, Director of Housing   816/543-4515, 4164

University of Missouri	Janet Snook, Coordinator for Fitwell	314/882-2066
Webster University	Sandra Henkes, Director, Residence Life	314/968-7030

MONTANA

Montana State University/Billings	Gina Swartz, Director of Housing	406/657-2376

NEW HAMPSHIRE

Plymouth State College	Time Keefe, Director, Residential Life	603/535-2260

NEW JERSEY

Rutgers University	Roselle Wilson, Vice President, Student Affairs	908/932-7255

NEW YORK

Binghamton University	Jeanne Mathias, Wellness Coordinator	607/777-2594
SUNY/Coll. of Tech./Delhi	John Leddy, Director, Residence Life	607/746-4632
SUNY/Cortland	Michael Holland, Director, Residential Services	607/753-2095
SUNY/Oswego	Marie Driscoll, Assistant Director, Housing	315/341-3039
SUNY/Potsdam	John Horan, Director, Residence Halls	315/267-2305
SUNY/Stony Brook	Andre Serrano, Residence Hall Director	516/632-2910

NORTH CAROLINA

Elon College	Alice Ledford, Director, Residential Life	910/584-2218
Univ. of North Carolina/Chapel Hill	Wayne T. Kunel, Director of Housing	919/962-5405

OHIO

Capital University	Ronald Bell, Director, Residence Life	614/236-6811
Miami University	Kim Rovansek, Director, Student Housing	513/529-5000

PENNSYLVANIA

Bucknell University	Kari Conrad, Director, Residence Life	717/524-1195
Dickinson College	Tom Matoua, Director of Housing	717/245-1555
Duquesne University	Sharon Goedert, Director, Residence Life	412/396-5028
Muhlenberg College	Scott Salsberry, Director, Residence Life	610/821-3167
Pennsylvania State University	Gail Hurley, Director, Residence Life	814/863-1710
Susquehanna University	Donald Hamum, Athletic Director	717/372-4271
University of Scranton	Fr. Reusseau, Assistant Director, Residence Life	717/941-6226

RHODE ISLAND

Bryant College	Doris Helmich, Health Educator	401/232-6703
Roger Williams University	Richard Stegman, Director, Student Life	401/254-3161
University of Rhode Island	Lester Yuesan, Director, Residential Life	401/874-5374

TENNESSEE

David Lipscomb University	Donna White, Director of Housing	615/269-1000 X2218

TEXAS

St. Mary's University	Lisa McDouglas, Director, Residence Life	210/436-3714
Southern Methodist University	Dr. Michael Lawrence, Director of Housing	214/768-2422
West Texas A&M University	John Davis, Director, Residence Life	806/656-3000

UTAH

Brigham Young University   David Hunt, Housing Services Director   801/378-2611

VERMONT

Lyndon State College   Lorraine Matteis, Director, Health Services   802/626-6440

WASHINGTON

The Evergreen State College   Mike Segawa, Housing Director   360/866-6000 X6132
Washington State University   Health and Wellness Services   509/335-3528
Western Washington University   Kay Rich, Director, University Residence   360/650-2960

WISCONSIN

Cardinal Stritch College   Janet Callender, Director, Residence Life   414/352-5400 X471
University of Wisconsin/Oshkosh   Jim Chitwood, Director, Residence Life   414/424-3212
University of Wisconsin/Stevens Point   John Munson, Assoc. Dean, Professional Studies   719/346-4614

CANADA

University of Calgary   Kelly Weltanffee, Director of Housing   403/220-5312

INSTITUTIONS REQUIRING UNDERGRADUATE WELLNESS COURSES

Albertson College   Dennis Freeburn, Dean of Student Affairs   208/459-5508
The **American** University   Stephanie F. Franchi, President   202/885-6282
Anderson University   Rebecca A. Hull, Department Chair   317/649-9071
Ball State University   Dr. Neil Schmottlach, Director   765/285-8259
Bellin College Nursing   Vicki A. Moss, Associate Professor   414/433-3409
Black Hills State University   Dr. Rob L. Schurrer, Assistant Professor   605/642-6169
Brigham Young University   Dr. Larry A. Tucker, Director of Health   801/378-4927
Bucks County Community College   Dr. Barry Sysler, Professor   215/968-8455
California State University   Sam J. Gitchel, Health Educator   209/278-2734
California State University   Nancy E. Shanfeld, Health Promotion Coordinator   818/885-3693
Capital University   Barbara A. Nash, Co-Director   614/236-6114
University of **Central Arkansas**   Dr. Arvil Burks, Department Chair   501/450-3191
Coastal Carolina College   Dr. Marshall E. Parker, Assistant Dean   803/349-2810
University of **Dayton**   Dr. Lloyd. L. Laubach, Wellness Program Director   513/229-4205
University of **Delaware**   Joyce L. Walter, Coordinator   302/457-8992
Delgado Community College   Jimmie R. Singeton, Director of Fitness Center   504/483-4255
Delta College   Sandy L. Wright, Health Service Director   504/483-4255
Dickinson College   Dr. Judith M. Vorio, Director, Truly Living Program   717/245-1525
East Los Angeles College   Dr. Sharon Deny, WPE Department Chair   213/265-8917
Eastern Montana College   Kamette C. Butterfield, Program Technician   406/657-2214
Elon College   Robert D. Pelley, Assistant Dean of Student Affairs   919/584-2218
Emporia State University   Dr. Darrell A. Lang, Director, Health Promotion   316/343-5929
Essex Community College   Thomas D. Kemp, Director, Health Fitness Lab   301/522-1415
Fayetteville State University   Dr. Nosa O'Bannor, Assistant Professor   919/486-1524, 1115
Fort Valley State College   Gwendolyn D. Reeves, Wellness Coordinator   912/825-9207
Gateway Community College   Sue Butler, Fitness Coordinator   Phoenix, AZ 85034
Georgia Insitute of Technology   Jami L. Fraze, Director, Wellness Center   404/853-0074
Georgia Southern University   Dr. Jerry E. Lafferty, Dean, Health & Prof, Stu.   912/681-5322

University of **Georgia**	Dr. Harry P. Duval, Associate Professor	404/542-4395
Gordon College	Dr. Peter W. Iltis, Associate Professor	508/927-2300, 4324
Goshen College	Willard S. Krabill, Director of Student Health	219/535-7474
Goucher College	Sally J. Baum, Assoc. Dir., Phys. Ed. Wellness Co.	301/337-6383
Hanover College	William D. Tereshko, Department Chairman	812/866-7375
Henderson University	Dr. Tom E. Ward, Associate Professor	501/246-5511, 3552
Hope College	Donna S. Eaton, Director, Health Dynamics	616/394-7693
Jacksonville State University	Dr. John B. Hammett, Coordinator, Wellness Center	205/782-5114
James Madison University	Nancy O. Grembi, Assistant Director	703/568-6177
Kalamazoo Valley Community College	Allan R. Thompson, Department Chair	616/372-5392
Kennesaw State College	Susan O. Bulter, Wellness Coordinator	401/423-6394
Lake Michigan College	Donald E. Alsbro, Instructor	616/927-3571, X330
Lane Community College	Sandra L. Ing, Director, Special Student Services	503/747-4501, 2666
University of **Maine**	Donna L. Duley, P.E. Lecturer and Women's Coach	207/255-3313, X352
Memphis State University	Dr. David J. Anspaugh, Professor, Division Head	901/678-2323
Millersville University	Dr. William V. Kahler, Chairperson	717/872-3674
Missouri Southern State College	Charles M. Conklin, Faculty Wellness Coordinator	417/625-9713
Montana State University	Dr. Gary F. Evans, Director of Employee Wellness	406/994-4001
University of **Montevallo**	Dr. J. W. Tishler, Professor of Health & P. E.	205/665-6587
Montgomery College	Karen M. Thomas, Assistant Professor	301/251-7582
Muhlenberg College	Connie R. Kunda, Wellness Director	215/821-3393
Murray State University	Dr. Pamela L Rice, Associate Professor	502/762-6826
Northeast Louisiana University	Dr. Luke E. Thomas, Professor	318/342-1310
University of **Northern Iowa**	Kathy M. Gulick, Director, Wellness Promo. Prog.	319/273-6921
Northern Kentucky University	Wiley T. Piazza, Wellness Coordinator	606/572-5684
Northern Michigan University	Dr. Harvey A. Wallace, CHES, Coor. HL Ed.	906/227-1135
Northwestern College	Ev Otten, Director of Health Services	712/737-4821, X251
University of **Richmond**	Carol Johnson, Director of Wellness	804/289-8404
Rockford College	Cecil Bristol, Director of Health	815/226-4118
Ursuline College	Denise Keary, Program Coordinator	216/646-8315
Western New Mexico University	Dr. Mary Cowan, Department Chair	505/538-6216
University of **Wisconsin**/Superior	Dr. Barbara P. Hamann, Program Coord., Health	715/394-8273
University of **Wyoming**	Annette K. Tommerdahl, Director, Cardiac Rehab	307/766-5423

APPENDIX E
A Simplified Timetable and Checklist for Seniors Planning on College

SEPTEMBER - OCTOBER	Write for college catalogs, applications, financial aid information and pick up a financial aid booklet.
SEPTEMBER - OCTOBER	Inquire at your high school Guidance Office about upcoming college nights.
SEPTEMBER - NOVEMBER	Continue campus visits as senior year academic commitments permit.
LATE SEPTEMBER	Deadline for mailing in the late October or early November National College Exam Forms.
OCTOBER	Think about which two teachers you will ask to write college recommendations for you.
LATE OCTOBER	Deadline for mailing in the December National College Exam Forms.
NOVEMBER	Prepare a final list of colleges.
NOVEMBER 1-15	Many early applications due.
NOVEMBER OR DECEMBER	Attend, with your parents, a local financial aid night given by an area high school.
NOVEMBER - DECEMBER	Apply to colleges.
EARLY DECEMBER	Last call for mailing in the National College Exam Forms (SAT/ACT).
DECEMBER 15	Profile of Financial Aid Form (Step 1) due to College Scholarship Service (CSS).
JANUARY	Fill out the Financial Aid Form (FAF/FAFSA/PROFILE) or Family Financial Statement. Your counselor has it. This form will probably help you get a good deal of your total scholarships, jobs, and loans. It is the big one.
JANUARY - FEBRUARY	Send mid-year reports to colleges.
FEBRUARY 1	Profile application (Step 2) to College Scholarship Service (CSS).
MARCH	Local scholarship forms available in the guidance office.
EARLY APRIL	All colleges will notify you by this time if they will accept you or not. The more competitive colleges usually deliberate longer and many of these top schools wait until April 5th to notify you.
MID-APRIL	If unhappy with the financial aid package at any of the colleges where you have been accepted, call that office and discuss it.
LATE APRIL	Send deposit to selected college.
MAY 1	Inform all colleges which accepted you whether or not you plan to attend.
MAY 1	Notify Guidance Office of your choice of college.
MAY - JUNE	Apply for summer jobs so that you can meet summer earnings expectations. Don't forget to graduate from high school!
SUMMER	Attend college orientation.

NOTE: Before your senior year, prepare preliminary list of colleges you're interested in and those you would like to visit.

APPENDIX F
The Get-Going Form

A simple, useful form to use with the college-bound to get them started applying to colleges.
The student and/or counselor and/or parent should fill in four colleges below,
complete with address and zip codes.

Dear Student:

Within the next two weeks, please write to the Director of Admissions at the schools listed below, requesting information. A sample letter is included at the bottom of the page.

1. _____
   _____
   _____

2. _____
   _____
   _____

3. _____
   _____
   _____

4. _____
   _____
   _____

SAMPLE LETTER

Date

Director of Admissions
Name of College
Address of College and Zip Code

Dear Director:

   I am a student of Easthampton High School in Easthampton, Massachusetts and expect to graduate in June, 1999.

   I am interested in your school and would appreciate your sending me an application for admission and information concerning your financial aid program, and your _____ program of studies. Thank you.

   Very truly yours,

                              Your signature
                              Your Name
                              Your Address and Zip Code

COUNSELOR'S NOTES

COUNSELOR'S NOTES

COUNSELOR'S NOTES

ABOUT THE AUTHOR

Frederick E. Rugg

Frederick E. Rugg is a nationally known expert on college admissions. He is the author of the prestigious *Rugg's Recommendations on the Colleges*, an annual guide to quality colleges. Unlike virtually all other college guidebook authors, Rugg is one of the true professionals, having directed secondary college counseling programs for 20 years in all types of communities. A 1967 Applied Math graduate from Brown, Rugg is the holder of advanced degrees and has written extensively in professional journals. He worked his way through Ivy League Brown, and was the only member of his class to enter public school teaching. Offering dozens of workshops yearly from coast to coast, Fred is an animated and humorous speaker, and has become well-known for giving the most practical college seminars around. In addition, he is a consultant to several private and public secondary schools, and has probably sent off more guidance professionals on their great careers than anyone else. He has lived and worked just about everywhere in America, has two daughters in their mid-twenties, has been married for 30 years, and, for over a decade, was a college basketball referee around the country.

FROM RUGG'S RECOMMENDATIONS...

INFORMATION THAT IS TO THE POINT, THAT YOU CAN USE IMMEDIATELY

Saving the college counselor enormous time with lists and answers found nowhere else—presented from the secondary school point of view!

FROM RUGG, YOU ALWAYS GET A NEW SLANT ON THE COLLEGES

---

1. THE NEW BOOK: *RUGG'S RECOMMENDATIONS ON THE COLLEGES 15h Ed.*
Locating Quality Undergraduate Colleges For Counselors, Parents & Students.
ISBN #1-883062-22-5 • LC89-062896 • $19.95 • © 1998 by Frederick E. Rugg

★ Over 1000 Entry Changes in the New BLUE Book ★

Rugg's Recommendations on the Colleges has been recommended by dozens of publications, including *The Washington Post, The College Choice Report, The New Jersey Monthly, The Cleveland Plain Dealer, College Bound, The Boston Globe, The Dallas News-Times,* and *The American Library Association's Booklist.* Rugg's 15th edition is available listing 5,750 quality departments at 780 quality colleges. The guidebook has been designated nationally as "a revered staple, the book parents and students must start with" in the search for a college to attend. The 15th edition is the accumulation of 26 years of work in the undergraduate college admissions process, and as always, Rugg's is independent of the colleges. There are over 1000 entry changes since the 14th edition, 80 majors, 106 recommended departments per major.

"A Revered Staple."
—West Coast Library Reviewer

"Your book is the foundation for my college counseling practice"
—George Gibbs, Gibbs & Wall Educational Consultants, Allentown, PA

"A gem."
—College Bound, Evanston, Illinois

"A treasure trove of input."
—Diane C. Donovan, The MidWest Book Review

---

2. THE SPECIAL REPORT: *TWENTY MORE TIPS ON THE COLLEGES, Revised*
Twenty new behind the scenes tips. Ideal for counselors, parents, and students. 3rd Edition.
ISBN #1-883062-23-3 • $8.95 • © 1998

Brutally honest information about colleges and the application process. This Special Report, *Twenty More Tips on the Colleges,* offers insights into assessing a college or university from the first "hello." Author Rugg succinctly presents 20 key tips to assist counselors, parents and students in selecting the best college for a student. Rugg honestly assesses the value of several college rating and reference books. Tips include colleges with high success rates for medical school acceptance, and what to consider before deciding to attend a military school. Overlooked state institutions, as well as other important and helpful comments, are included. The college search and selection process is incomplete without reading the valuable information contained within this Special Report.

"Brutally honest."
—The College Choice Report

"I can talk to some students and parents until I'm blue in the face, and they don't seem to listen. But if it's written by Fred Rugg, they accept it. And that's only one reason why I buy his special reports."
—Guidance Counselor, State College, PA

"I have used your information for years. It is a wonderful resource."
—Harriet Gershman, Academic Counseling Services, Evanston, IL

---

3. *FORTY TIPS ON THE COLLEGES* : THE REVISED SPECIAL REPORT *4th edition*
For all college bound students, parents, and their counselors. 17 pages. Over 35 college entry changes for 1998.
ISBN # 1-883062-24-1 • $9.95 (money back guarantee) • Revised 1998

Get the "insider's" advice on college admissions. In *Forty Tips on the Colleges,* author Rugg shares with the reader 40 key tips on the college admissions process. Rugg spent in excess of 1500 hours visiting with over 3500 secondary school counselors in 40 states, to compile the information contained in this transcript. These insightful suggestions provide the reader with some of the unwritten dos and don'ts in the college admissions process. Rugg presents his 40 tips, accompanied by his personal observations of the campuses, with honesty and a sense of humor. *Forty Tips on the Colleges* offers straight talk about selecting a college and gaining admission. The transcript contains helpful advice for the student, parent and school counselor alike. Topics include previously unpublished tips on which colleges really care about their students; colleges with good learning disabilities programs; and how to choose a college where the student "fits in." The tips also contain helpful information concerning financial aid, college applications and SAT/ACT scores. Throughout this transcript, Rugg cites several helpful reference books. This *must read* is our most popular transcript.

"After attending Fred's workshop in Bar Harbor, Maine, I was very eager to buy his special report, 40 Tips on the Colleges. This report is as 'on-target' as his workshop. I've used the report in English classes with juniors, in parent meetings, and in faculty meetings. Each time the response has been overwhelmingly positive. 'Finally, someone is telling it as it is!' is a common response. No glossy advertising or slick words, just honest, accurate information".
—Beulah J. Grant, Dean of Students, George Stevens Academy, Blue Hill, ME

"Our parents and students have really enjoyed and learned from your reports...keep up the great work—sure makes our job easier."
—Ned Nemacheck, College Counselor, Homestead (WI) H.S.

---

4. THE SPECIAL REPORT: *THIRTY QUESTIONS ON THE COLLEGES, Revised 4th Edition*
For all college bound students, parents and their counselors. 23 pages.
ISBN # 1-883062-25-X • $9.95 • Revised 1998 • Over 35 college entry changes

Thirty frequently asked questions with some answers even Deans of Admissions can't give you. This Special Report includes: The state university all others should visit and copy • 100 recommended colleges where black youngsters will maximize their education • What makes individuals happy at college? • Community college graduates – how do top colleges really view them at transfer time? • The best of the best journalism schools • Understanding student body make-up • Engineering schools – how to choose them and the best bets around the USA. And 22 other topics based on over 100 counselor meetings across the country. Counselors and parents find this transcript form extremely useful (yes, it's O.K. to copy it with appropriate acknowledgement).

""When I attended the college admissions institute this past summer, all of the private H.S. counselors and Ivy School directors of admission said that Rugg's work was the best."
—Colorado Public Secondary School Counselor

5. SPECIAL REPORT: *FINANCIAL AID IN LESS THAN 2000 WORDS, REVISED*
ISBN #1-883062-26-8 • $6.95 • Completely Revised 1998

From his 30 years studying the college admissions process, Rugg has boiled down the financial aid game in this special 5-page report. Find out why several U.S. publishers offered big money to buy this transcript outright. Takes the counselor and parent step-by-step through the aid process, with authentic examples of awards and family situations of present college frosh. This special report closes with 10 revised tips on financial aid for counselors, parents, and students that Rugg has put together from hundreds of meetings with counselors and parents around the country.

Especially for parents and counselors—gets Financial Aid off the Counselor's back.

"Rugg is the only critic who has been in the trenches, worked the cities, lived all over, and has the network and the contacts in place."
—Vern Vargas, College Counselor, Moreau H.S., Hayward, CA.

6. THE NEW VIDEO: *More Insights on the Colleges* (22 minutes)
ISBN #1-883062-21-7• $25 • August 1998 • 22 minutes
For staff meetings, parent's college night, library loan to parents and students.

Back by popular demand, another national Rugg video. Start your Parent's College Night with this 22-minute performance before a California live audience of parents and students, and their questions to Mr. Rugg. Twenty-five topics covered, including why only a few should attend Brown, MIT and the military academies. Generous doses of humor and inspiration. Guaranteed to generate many questions from the audience. VHS video cassette.

7. THE AUDIO: *Rugg on the Radio #2 : Colleges*
ISBN #1-883062-16-0 • $10 • 26 minutes
Behind-the-scenes info for parents, students, counselors

Rugg runs around the country recommending underrated colleges in this radio broacast with call-in. Behind-the-scenes information that will have parents, students and counselors listening again and again. The best edit of Rugg's many hours on the radio.

8. THE COLLEGE SEMINAR SUBSTITUTE (Now includes two new audios)
For Secondary School Counselors, public and private • $70 (lists updated monthly)

Can't make it to a college seminar? Do the next best thing: Order this special package. *The College Seminar Substitute* **provides you with** 98% of the 60 items covered in our seminar agenda. In this package you receive Rugg's four Special Reports, *Twenty More Tips on the Colleges, Forty Tips on the Colleges, Thirty Questions and Answers, Financial Aid In Less Than 2000 Words*, plus the *new video*, the *audio* and 20 seminar handouts. These handouts contain over 900 entries—a wealth of information. Topics covered include: a listing of safe campuses, college guidebook ratings, up-and-coming colleges; overrated colleges; prestigious school rankings; underrated schools, the top 100 schools for the learning disabled, the most generous schools, new information on financial aid; advice on school recommendations; a listing of intense (rigorous) schools; big colleges that play small; rated Catholic colleges; and four minority lists. This package gives the counselor a foundation in understanding and navigating the admission game. See why over 3500 secondary school counselors have attended Rugg's College Admission Seminars.

"It is the best single source of information that we have. It answers the questions most frequently asked by parents. Your college materials help both the beginning and experienced counselor. The various ratings and lists inspire both students and their parents to further research the college scene. When parents and students are clueless your information provides direction and humor in beginning the college selection process."
—Ira Lipton, Counselor, East Hampton (NY) High School

9. TWENTY SEMINAR SHEETS $20

Our most popular lists are now available separately. Includes all of the rankings in #8 above, plus colleges where the following youngsters maximize their education: Jewish (107), Hispanic (73), Asian (56), and Black (127). *Call us for a sample—5 sheets for $5.*

"I use Rugg's material and wit all over the place."
—Dr. John Dromgoole, College Search, Concord, MA

10. SPECIAL! *SEND IT ALL!* $90

Includes 1 book, 4 special reports, 2 audios, 20 seminar sheets—all our products.

11. SEMINAR SHEET SAMPLER! $5 for 5 Sheets

L.D., Jewish list, Turnaround a Shaky Kid list, Underrated and Rugg's 100 favorite colleges!

""What a wonderful surprise to get the mail today and find your most valuable update. Believe me, I study them and treasure them."
—Fran Fisher, Educational Consultant, Muskegon, MI

➡ **ORDER FORM ON REVERSE**

THE 1998 RUGG COLLEGE ADMISSION SEMINAR SCHEDULE (Most seminars are on Fridays)	**San Diego, CA** January 9, 1998	**San Francisco, CA** March 6, 1998	**Boston, MA** May 15, 1998
	Santa Barbara, CA February 6, 1998	**Washington, DC/ Baltimore** April 27, 1998	**New York (Rye), NY** July 2, 1998

For more information: Call or write for a brochure; e-mail us at frugg@thegrid.net; or visit our Website at http://www.thegrid.net/frugg

1998 PRODUCT ORDER FORM

ITEM #	TITLE OR DESCRIPTION	PRICE	QTY	AMOUNT
1	*Rugg's Recommendations on the Colleges:* The Book (15th ed.)	$19.95		
2	*20 More Tips on the Colleges:* Revised Special Report (3rd ed.)	$ 8.95		
3	*Forty Tips on the Colleges:* Revised Special Report (4th ed.)	$ 9.95		
4	*Thirty Questions & Answers:* Revised Special Report (4th ed.)	$ 9.95		
5	*Financial Aid in Less Than 2000 Words:* Revised Special Report (4th ed.)	$ 6.95		
6	*More Insights on the Colleges:* The NEW 22-minute Video	$25.00		
7	*Rugg on the Radio #2:* The Audio	$10.00		
8	*College Seminar Substitute:* Includes 2 thru 7 plus 20 sheets	$75.00		
9	*Twenty Seminar Sheets: Colleges*	$20.00		
10	SEND IT ALL!!! Send one of each	$90.00		
11	*Seminar Sheet SAMPLER:* 5 Sheets (L.D., Jewish list, Turnaround a Shaky Kid list, Underrated and Rugg's 100 Favorite Colleges.)	$ 5.00		

Order 5 or more books: Only $18.00 each! Discount price available *only* on the *book.*
Prepaid Orders over $89: Subtract $4 from total.
International Orders: Shipping and handling cost: Actual Cost.
California Residents: Please add 7.25% sales tax.
SHIPPING CHARGES: (all orders mailed first class)
$ 0-15 Postage $2
$16-35 Postage $4
$36+ Postage $5

SUBTOTAL
Less $4 for prepaid orders over $89
Sales Tax (CA only) 7.25%
Shipping
TOTAL ENCLOSED

Name

Address

City _____ State _____ Zip

Send to:
RUGG'S RECOMMENDATIONS
7120 Serena Court • Atascadero, CA 93422

For information on our 1998 COLLEGE ADMISSIONS SEMINARS, call us at 805/462-2503 or 805/462-9019 OR visit our Website at http://www.thegrid.net/frugg